Headlines from the Heartland

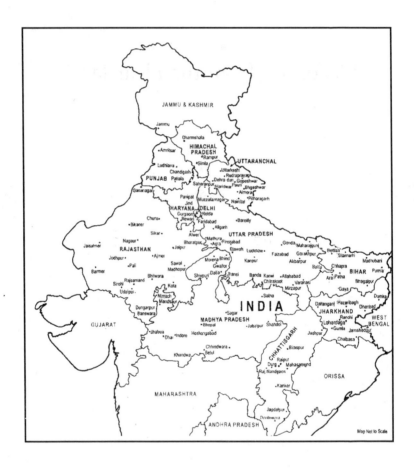

Praise for
Headlines from the Heartland

Sevanti Ninan's remarkable book draws readers deep into the media revolution that is changing India. Ninan's sweeping research project, which takes her from small-town print shops across north India to the share-markets of Mumbai, describes how Hindi-language newspapers are carrying politics and consumption into towns and villages. Ninan mourns three things: the collapse of small, 'printing-shop' newspapers, obliterated by capitalist rivals; the demise of independent, 'intellectual' editors, replaced by marketing managers and pushy young members of the owners' families; and the loss of wider regional identities as burgeoning newspapers become obsessed with village-well news. Yet rural people are drawn into political participation and world awareness unknown to their parents. Ninan strives to connect her richly woven stories into the larger pattern of media and newspaper development throughout the world in the past 200 years. This is a book for everyone interested in modern India, and in how print and capitalism shape societies.

— Robin Jeffrey, Australian National University

This is a fascinating and richly textured study of the rise to influence and power of the Hindi press across northern India. Basing herself on a huge amount of original research, yet wearing her learning lightly, Sevanti Ninan deftly links the world of the journal (and journalist) to wider trends in politics and economics. The developments that she narrates, with such verve and skill, have had a transformative impact on modern India. Therefore, no student of Indian society, politics or history can afford to be without this book.

— Ramachandra Guha, author and columnist

Sevanti's book braids together painstakingly gathered journalistic information with the history of post-Independence India. She argues her case with clarity and skill as she uncovers how Hindi journalism has constantly mutated and grown in India.

— Mrinal Pande, Editor, *Hindustan*

Headlines from the Heartland
Reinventing the Hindi Public Sphere

SEVANTI NINAN

SAGE Publications
Los Angeles • London • New Delhi • Singapore

First published in 2007 by

 Sage Publications India Pvt Ltd
B1/I1, Mohan Cooperative Industrial Area
Mathura Road
New Delhi 110 044
www.sagepub.in

Sage Publications Inc
2455 Teller Road
Thousand Oaks, California 91320

Sage Publications Ltd
1 Oliver's Yard, 55 City Road
London EC1Y 1SP

Sage Publications Asia-Pacific Pte Ltd
33 Pekin Street
#02-01 Far East Square
Singapore 048763

Published by Vivek Mehra for Sage Publications India Pvt Ltd, typeset in 10/12.5 Sabon by Star Compugraphics Private Limited, Delhi, and printed at Chaman Enterprises, New Delhi.

Library of Congress Cataloging-in-Publication Data

Ninan, Sevanti.
    Headlines from the heartland: reinventing the Hindi public sphere/
Sevanti Ninan.
        p. cm.
    Includes bibliographical references and index.
    1. Journalism—India—History—20th century. 2. Press—India—
History—20th century. 3. Hindi newspapers—India—History—
20th century. I. Title.

PN5374.N56   079.54—dc22   2007   2007003026

ISBN: 978-0-7619-3580-3 (PB)   978-81-7829-741-5 (India-PB)

The Sage Team: Ashok R. Chandran, Gayatri E. Koshy and
                              Rajib Chatterjee

In memory of my parents,
Anil and Kanon De,

And for Ninan

Contents

List of Tables   8
List of Illustrations   9
Acknowledgements   11

1. Overview: Reinventing the Public Sphere   13
2. The Evolution and Growth of Hindi Journalism   33
3. A Rural Newspaper Revolution   65
4. Creating New Media Hubs   91
5. Local News Gatherers   113
6. The Universe of Local News   143
7. Media and Commerce   185
8. Journalists and Politicians   204
9. Caste and Communalism   216
10. The Development Discourse   230
11. Reconfiguring the Public Sphere   246
12. Change and Attrition   260

Epilogue—Habermas Revisited   290
References   298
Index   301
About the Author   309

List of Tables

1.1 Top five dailies—rural and urban readership 16

3.1 Increase in rural readership between NRS 2002 66
     and NRS 2005
3.2 Readers per copy 68
3.3 Change in literacy rate, 1991–2001 69
3.4 Media intensity: UP vs India 83

4.1 Expansion—the top two 93

12.1 Resurgence in Rajasthan 286

List of Illustrations

1.1 *Hindustan*'s lifestyle supplement, *Metro Remix*,   19
    captures the transformation that came over Hindi
    newspapers in post-liberalisation India
1.2 Mastheads of local pull-outs catering to districts   21
    in Haryana, Madhya Pradesh and Chhattisgarh

2.1 A stamp issued in 1966 to commemorate the   40
    contribution to the freedom struggle of Acharya
    Mahabir Prasad Dwivedi, editor of *Saraswati*
2.2 A stamp issued in 1988 by the Indian Government   48
    to commemorate the contribution to the freedom
    struggle of Shivprasad Gupta, founder of *Aj*
2.3 An etching of Baburao Vishnu Paradkar, the father   49
    of Hindi journalism
2.4 A stamp issued in 1962 to commemorate the role   54
    of Ganesh Shankar Vidyarthi in the freedom struggle
2.5 Purnachand Gupta, founder of *Dainik Jagran*   55

3.1 *Rozgar aur Nirman* and *Panchayika*: panchayat-level 85
    publications in Madhya Pradesh

4.1 *Dainik Jagran*'s 23 March 2004 issue declaring that 100
    it had become No. 1 in readership in the country
4.2 Kesargarh, *Rajasthan Patrika*'s office in Jaipur—   102
    a newspaper in a fortress

6.1 *Khabar Lahariya* from Uttar Pradesh and *Ujala Jhadi* 146
    from Rajasthan, the uncommodified press, focused on
    village news
6.2 Religious news: *Nayi Duniya*'s Diwali special issue and 152
    Punjab Kesari's weekly supplement, *Dharm Sanskriti*
6.3 Serena Williams and Ally McBeal adorn the masthead   160
    of the Champaran edition of *Hindustan* in Bihar

6.4 *Dainik Bhaskar* Indore's Monday Mega Story on   177
rural indebtedness, 14 February 2005

7.1 An advertising supplement in the Indore *Dainik*   194
Bhaskar on 14 February 2005 intersperses
advertisements from local outlets with
Valentine's Day messages

7.2 Weekly supplements with English titles: *Dainik*   198
Jagran's *Property*; *Hindustan*'s *FEST*, the same
paper's classified advertisement section *Search*
Engine, and its *Metro Remix*; *Dainik Jagran*'s
Jagran City; *Navbharat Times*' *Hello Delhi*
and *Amar Ujala*'s *Career*

10.1 *Vikas* (development), is the title of *Prabhat Khabar*'s   232
84-page special edition on Bihar, 11 July 2005—
an exhaustive survey over seven sections of
Bihar's backwardness and the development
issues confronting the state

10.2 *Nava Bharat*'s special issue on the first anniversary   239
of the creation of Chhattisgarh, 1 November 2001

12.1 *Dainik Bhaskar*'s monthly *Aha Zindagi* presents its   272
Prem Ankh, its special issue on love, in
February 2005

12.2 Mastheads of newspapers in Rajasthan, UP,   280
Jharkhand and Chhattisgarh whose viability was
imperilled by the multi-edition localisers

Acknowledgements

This book is a based on a study of newspaper localisation funded by the National Foundation for India (NFI) in Delhi. The interviews for it were done between 2002 and 2006. All designations of persons interviewed related to the date on which they were interviewed. Many individuals have helped to make this study possible. Nandita Roy and Ajay Mehta at NFI who believed in the possibilities of this research, Indrajit Roy, Sushmita Malaviya and Vasavi who provided wonderful interviews for me to draw on, and Megha whose painstaking tabulation made the research data on content accessible. Manjula Lal did interviews in Uttaranchal, Devsagar Singh in Lucknow and Sunita Bhadauria, Aditi Vyas and Dhiraj Sinha provided the translations.

Mrinal Pande and her colleagues at *Hindustan*, particularly Naveen Joshi, Shekhar Tripathi and Vijay Bhaskar facilitated my research in many ways. Many individuals helped me in many cities: Ajay Kumat and Augustine in Patna, Pradip Maitra in Raipur, Ashok Kumat in Indore, Davinder Uppal in Bhopal, Chandrakant Naidu, Narayan Bareth and Sukhmani Singh in Jaipur, Neelima Khetan and her Seva Mandir colleagues in Udaipur, and Bizeth Bannerjee in Dehradun. In Lucknow, Vinod Shukla was very generous with his time, and Elizabeth and David Charles with their hospitality. Lalit Surjan of Raipur provided insights to be followed up on, and Harivansh gave generously of his time both in Ranchi and Delhi. In Chitrakoot, the women of *Khabar Lahariya* were an inspiration— may our small towns and villages produce more journalists like them. I am indebted to Shalini at Nirantar for making the visit to *Khabar Lahariya* possible.

Robin Jeffrey's sharp comments on a clumsy first draft forced me to restructure and refocus the manuscript. Mrinal Pande, Ajay Upadhyay and Aloke Thakore have each been generous with time and ideas, making my project their own. I am particularly indebted to Ajay Upadhyay and Aloke Thakore for pitching in with material for the second draft. I owe a debt of gratitude to Professor Imtiaz Ahmed for readily agreeing to read the manuscript of someone he did not know, and providing a magically simple solution to problems of structure. And Nupur and Shrabani Basu came up with the main title for this book. The photographs were taken by Jagdish Yadav, and I am indebted to Aditi Dey and Shakti Sharma for their photo-editing.

At Sage Tejeshwar Singh has been a brick—supportive, involved and sometimes long-suffering. I am also grateful to my editor Anamika Mukharji for the hand-holding she did. And in Ashok R. Chandran I had an editor whose enthusiasm extended to taking photographs while on holiday for the book he was currently handling. The cover picture is his.

Families always bear the brunt of research and book writing, and mine will doubtless be relieved that it is finally over.

Sevanti Ninan
January 2007

1

Overview: Reinventing the Public Sphere

'When you launch a Newspaper you have to purchase the readership.'

The decade and a half from 1991 to 2006 in India belonged to television and the Internet. This was the period when satellite television took birth and took off. Shrewd media moguls like Rupert Murdoch and Sumner Redstone hastened to get a toehold in an emerging economy that promised to become a burgeoning media market with its fair share of domestic enterpreneurs. The policy of economic liberalisation launched in 1991 was delivering, by the mid-1990s, a growing volume of international advertising. In 1995 commercial Internet came to India, and took hold rapidly enough to enable a dot-com boom by the late 1990s. Both cable and satellite TV, and the Internet, captured the attention of a growing urban middle class eager for more media choice. All this changed media habits, transformed connectivity and created a new public discourse as television news channels, Websites and blogs blossomed.

Over the same period, a less visible media juggernaut was rolling across a less visible part of the country. When literacy expanded in India's Hindi heartland in the last decade of the 20th century, Hindi newspapers followed, picking up readers in places where there had been none. The changes wrought by this newspaper revolution are the subject of this book. Journalism flowered in unexpected and unorthodox ways, and media marketing unfurled across villages from Bihar to Rajasthan. Newspapers brought increased awareness, a growing consumerism, and civic participation in their wake, and no one was left untouched. Readers, civil society, politicians, panchayats all experienced a media saturation that was as rapid as it was new.

It brought the world outside to readers' doorsteps in the mornings, and put them all on the news map by expanding the local news universe. Local gentry, local corruption and the parlous state of the local infrastructure found space in the big newspapers circulating in the Hindi heartland even as they added local pages to woo the new readership. Many small towns in the states of Uttar Pradesh (UP), Uttaranchal, Madhya Pradesh (MP), Chhattisgarh, Bihar, Jharkhand, Rajasthan and Haryana already had newspapers which mirrored the local public sphere in India's districts. They carried national and statewide news, as well as reports from the region where they were published. Some, like *Nai Duniya* in Indore, strove to bring a holistic news universe to their readers, and did it so well that they acquired a national reputation. Others, like the weekly single-sheet *Ka* ('k' in the Devanagari script), published from Ballia in eastern Uttar Pradesh for over three decades, reflected local events.

The localisation that the Hindi-speaking belt saw from the decade of the 1990s, was what Prabash Joshi, founder-editor of *Jansatta*, described as outsider-localisation.[1] Established newspapers in the region such as *Dainik Jagran*, *Dainik Bhaskar* and *Hindustan* went into new territories in neighbouring states and began a multi-edition expansion that would localise their coverage to an unprecedented degree. The objective was to expand overall readership numbers to offer advertisers, both national and local. The stand-alone newspapers in the states which they entered, were squeezed. They could not invest as much in production or distribution as the competition. They could not compete effectively for advertising without pan-Indian numbers to offer. Some died, others put up a fight, still others became a pale shadow of their former selves. That has been one of the abiding ironies of the local newspaper revolution.

A Decade of Change

The decade of the 1990s saw the convergence of many changes in the country and in the Hindi belt which transformed the print media landscape. Literacy, which had been low in the region, grew rapidly, as reflected in the dramatic increase recorded by the 2001 Census.

Rajasthan recorded a decadal increase in literacy of 22.45 percentage points against an all-India increase of 13.17 percentage points. Madhya Pradesh and Chhattisgarh between them accounted for almost a fifth of the total decadal decline in illiteracy in India in 1991–2001, while accounting for less than a tenth of the population. Rising farm incomes and a growing service sector in the rural areas pointed to the emergence of a rural middle class whose purchasing power had made newspapers affordable. It was targeted by marketers who underwrote the expansion of newspapers in these parts. The market in small town and rural India was expanding. The rise of television and its penetration into the rural hinterland created a hunger for news. Across the Hindi belt, newspaper proprietors, circulation agents and hawkers alike assert that TV proved to be good for the newspaper business because it fuelled a curiosity that made the viewer turn to the next day's newspaper.

The advent of the modem, which made the Internet possible, also made possible the transmission of entire newspaper pages composed at different district centres. Expanding telecommunications, including the spread of broad-band telecom, made multi-edition newspapers more viable and affordable.

Hindi newspapers, harbingers of nationalism at the turn of the 20th century, had become harbingers of more material change by the turn of the 21st. They were now bursting with colour supplements and marketing coupons even as they brought politics, sports and news-you-can-use to rural and urban homes in village and small-town India. They brought a Hindi heartland, lagging in literacy till barely a decade earlier, onto the readership map and then rapidly to the top of the readership charts.

Newspaper circulation climbed, one of the few places in the world to still see this happen. The National Readership Survey (NRS) of 2005[2] put India's total readership at 200 million. This was up from 131 million in NRS 1999 and 155 million in NRS 2002.[3] Of this, 98 million, or almost 50 per cent, was from rural India. NRS 1999 had put rural readership at 29 per cent.[4] Two hundred million readers for dailies and magazines meant that the print media was now available to one out of five people in the country. As a result of the increased literacy, improved communications and rising rural incomes, as well as aggressive marketing strategies adopted by publishers, newspaper penetration in the Hindi belt increased. In Uttar Pradesh for instance, in 1997 there were 22 readers per copy, which came down in the divided state to 16 readers per copy in UP and 8.4 per copy in Uttaranchal. By 2006 however a rival readership survey had begun to suggest that the growth had begun to peak. The Indian Readership Survey (IRS) 2006 showed that urban press reach had dropped by roughly one percentage point between 2004 and 2006 but rural reach had remained unchanged.

The older stalwarts of the Indian regional media, such as the *Malayala Manorama* in Kerala, *Eenadu* in Andhra Pradesh (AP) and *Anandabazar Patrika* in West Bengal slipped in the 'Top 10' readership listings. *The Times of India*, claiming to be the world's largest circulated broadsheet in the English language, ranked at No. 11 in NRS 2006. Hindi newspapers occupied three of the top five positions in the all-India readership figures put out by the National Readership Survey in mid-2006, and five of the top ten. Just three years back, NRS 2003 had shown the southern stalwarts *Daily Thanthi*, *Eenadu* and *Manorama* occupying third, fourth and fifth positions in the top five. And in NRS 1999 only one Hindi newspaper, *Dainik Jagran* had figured in the top five in terms of readership (Table 1.1). The IRS of early 2006, meanwhile, was showing Hindi newspapers as occupying four out of five top positions in newspaper readership in the country.

TABLE 1.1 Top five dailies—rural and urban readership

NRS 1999	NRS 2003	NRS 2006
Daily Thanthi	Dainik Bhaskar	Dainik Jagran
Dainik Jagran	Dainik Jagran	Dainik Bhaskar
Malayala Manorama	Daily Thanthi	Eenadu
Eenadu	Eenadu	Lokmat
Mathrubhumi	Manorama	Amar Ujala

The Audit Bureau of Circulation figures which were released in September 2006 showed that the Hindi language had the highest number of newspapers (15) in the country with circulations of over 100,000. The second highest were English language newspapers which had 11 publications with circulation figures higher than 100,000. If editions of the bigger newspapers were to be taken separately the figure would be higher in both categories.

The backdrop to the Hindi newspaper revolution was a social and political churning which saw the consolidation of the conservative, middle and upper-class Hindu vote through the political ascendance of the Bharatiya Janata Party (BJP), which espoused *Hindutva*, as well as the simultaneous emergence of backward classes and Dalits as independent political forces, particularly in Bihar and Uttar Pradesh. The caste-based political mobilisation that followed the adoption of the Mandal Commission's report in 1990, created a new political scenario in the states of this region and saw the media being called to account by a new crop of backward-caste and Dalit politicians.

The latter political elite was sometimes at odds with the journalistic tribe, mostly drawn throughout this region from the upper castes. Lalu Prasad Yadav in Bihar would tell his backward-caste voters not to believe what the upper-caste newspapers were saying which, according to journalists themselves, contributed to the emasculation of the mainstream media in Bihar. Mayawati railed against the *manuwadi* (casteist) journalists in Uttar Pradesh. At the same time these politicians were sons and daughters of the soil who could communicate more effectively with and through the Hindi language press than with the more city-centric, English language publications.

As their commercial interests grew, Hindi newspapers ceased to be adversarial and learned to coexist with a backward-caste or Dalit chief minister in Uttar Pradesh or Bihar, much as they did with those from the Bharatiya Janata Party who went in and out of power in Madhya Pradesh. By 2006, the upper-caste chairman of the *Dainik Jagran* group, Mahendra Mohan Gupta, was gratified to accept a Rajya Sabha nomination from the ruling Samajwadi (Socialist) Party in Uttar Pradesh, headed by the backward-caste Chief Minister Mulayam Singh Yadav. *Jagran* had from its inception been associated with the right-wing, pro-*Hindutva* ideology. The chairman's older brother Narendra Mohan in his time had been a Rajya Sabha MP nominated by the BJP. Apart from belonging to an opposing political ideology, Mulayam Singh Yadav was an old foe for the *Jagran* group—in 1994 he had incited his followers to attack this and another newspaper, *Amar Ujala*, in an incident known as *Halla Bol* (literally, attack). But the need to consolidate and hold on to its leadership in the market had made the group pragmatic. It was at that point not only Uttar Pradesh's leading newspaper in terms of circulation and readership, but also the paper with the highest circulation and readership in the country.

In addition to the political transition of Uttar Pradesh from a Congress-ruled state to a state ruled alternately by political formations of Backwards and Dalits, a different kind of political transformation was also taking place. In most of this region the entry of print at the rural level had been preceded by the passing of the 73rd and 74th Amendments to the Indian Constitution in 1992. This enabled revival of panchayats, the third tier of local self-government in the rural areas, and the reservation of 33 per cent of seats in these bodies for women. The revitalisation of panchayati raj (the new tier of local self-government) began in Madhya Pradesh in 1994. When close to half a million people's representatives are chosen in a single state, it spells a considerable degree of grassroots political participation, creating awareness and a hunger for news. Moreover, the state financed the supply of a newspaper to every panchayat office, which was often the first copy of a newspaper to reach that area. As they grew into their roles, *sarpanch*es began to subscribe to newspapers at home, to keep themselves abreast of state, national and local news. Together with rising literacy and a growth in purchasing power both urban and rural, panchayats helped to create a basis for growth in newspaper circulation.

From all this flowed a discourse which was more broad-based than ever before. The press was moving from being an elite to a mass medium. And the Indian newspaper was evolving from being a politics-driven product for the serious-minded reader into one that was fashioning itself for the upwardly mobile, as well as for the reader who had barely begun to read, and was looking for news of his immediate universe. In these parts of the heartland, print was a post-television phenomenon. Television connected to cable and satellite via small local entrepreneurs had already brought consumer aspirations into rural and semi-urban homes, and print had to cater to these. It met aspirational demands with supplements on careers, property, lifestyle, society and education (Figure 1.1). In mid-2006, *Hindustan* was already giving one career supplement a week in Uttar Pradesh, and was getting ready to introduce a second one.

FIGURE 1.1 *Hindustan*'s lifestyle supplement, *Metro Remix*, captures the transformation that came over Hindi newspapers in post-liberalisation India

At the turn of the century, then, both television and newspaper audiences in India were evolving into cheerful amalgams of modernity and tradition. Language and English newspapers alike sprouted cutouts of Indian and Western celebrities, often half clad, on the masthead. Saucy pictures adorned colour supplements, satchets of consumer products began to arrive with the daily newspaper. But Indians wanted to hold on to tradition even as they embraced globalisation. The print equivalent was the feedback the editorial department of *Hindustan* in Delhi was getting from its marketing division. In 2006 the paper launched a daily column aimed at young Indians telling them what that day's religious observance was, for any religion, and how it should be observed.[5] With urbanisation and the break-up of joint families, a paper that catered to this need for guidance on year-round rituals would be able to endear itself to its readers.

Consequences of Expansion and Localisation

The expansion and localisation of the Hindi press began to accelerate from the early 1990s. In addition to the converging of the trends already described, this had to do with a new generation taking charge in the families that owned newspapers. As in *The Times of India* and *Hindustan Times,* where a new generation at the helm was identified with radical changes in newspaper marketing, the coming of the sons of Ramesh Agarwal into the management of the *Dainik Bhaskar* preceded an aggressive expansion drive from the mid-1990s. At *Rajasthan Patrika* a third generation cut its teeth at a time when the *Bhaskar* was storming the *Patrika*'s bastion. Apart from helping him craft a comeback strategy, Gulab Kothari's young sons took the conservative newspaper into new media businesses such as cable, Internet and FM Radio—all of which involved a strong marketing orientation. At *Dainik Jagran,* the second and third generation together plotted the paper's expansion and localisation strategy. The exception was *Hindustan.* It languished even as its third generation proprietor focused on the English *Hindustan Times,* until the management by its own admission woke up to its potential only in the year 2000.

This book explores the supposition that media expansion and localisation in the Hindi language—located at a juncture when the economic, political and social landscape of the Hindi heartland was changing—created its own set of social transformations. In addition to more traditional notions of public space in small town and village India where both public issues and private scandal were discussed, you now had a newsprint-enabled and advertising-supported civic square where local gentry, local governance and local crime competed for attention. Competition led to the creation of more than one such paper *choupal*[6] where crime was covered as never before and local politicians were delighted at the coverage they got, though sometimes there was a monetary price to be paid for it.

The local supplements and pages created a new genre of news which encompassed a much wider ambit of society than before, and a new tribe of news gatherer drawn from the community, but representative of only some sections of a stratified society (Figure 1.2). Inasmuch as they were open to all kinds of news being delivered to

FIGURE 1.2 Mastheads of local pull-outs catering to districts in Haryana, Madhya Pradesh and Chhattisgarh

them by those who wished to feature in the next morning's newspaper, media access was democratised. Religious news found ample and prominent space, and cheating in school exams became a seasonal news staple. Local news documented street-level civic problems and panchayat politics more copiously than ever before. Even though it seldom confronted authority, it created a demand for local level accountability.

Advertising and incentive-driven marketing began to make decentralised expansion possible, and more copies began to be subscribed to in large roadside villages. The commercial instinct which leads Maruti or Godrej to seek consumers in the Indian countryside makes possible a newspaper produced for the rural mass, underwritten by these companies' advertising. It also made viable the offering of newspaper subscriptions at a low price, sweetened with gifts and commercial discounts.

In February 2005 Mahesh Shrivastava, newly-appointed editor of the yet to be launched *Raj Express*, sat in an office overlooking a real estate development outside Bhopal city and declared succinctly, 'When you launch a newspaper you have to purchase the readership.' The owners of that estate were getting into the newspaper business, and their wooing of hawkers was the talk of the media in the city. Deepak Shourie, the chief executive who had launched *Outlook* magazine in 1995 with expensive gifts for subscribers, could have told him that 10 years before. But the culture came shortly after that to the fast-growing world of Hindi newspapers. A combination of price incentives, gifts and subscribers' schemes that involved publishing daily coupons over a couple of months, are put in place almost routinely now, when a new newspaper enters a market. Both readers and hawkers are enticed. A single plastic chair giveaway could achieve a 30 per cent circulation jump over a rival, albeit for a short period of three months—a lesson both for young marketers and young journalists.

But without such incentives the price-conscious Indian reader, particularly in rural India, would not have sampled newspapers in the numbers he did and print would not have expanded as rapidly as it did.

A media sphere catalysed by market dynamics was reflecting these dynamics in other ways as well. In January 2005, the panchayat elections which took place across Madhya Pradesh saw the advent of paid political advertising placed by aspirants. On the pages of local district supplements of the *Dainik Bhaskar* could be found not just small paid advertisments but also sponsored reporting which a pragmatic publisher was introducing into grassroots politics in this state. These were advertorials called Impact Features, introduced by *India Today* and used by politicians such as Chief Ministers Narendra Modi of Gujarat and Chandrababu Naidu of Andhra Pradesh.

The resident editor of the *Bhaskar* in Bhopal argued that there was nothing wrong: the distinction in display was there for all to see.[7] (It looked like a page of text but was used in the advertising columns.) A politician however counter-argued that village readers were not yet sophisticated enough to tell the difference. He was also asserting that you got distinctly less enthusiastic coverage from this publishing group if you did not take their advertising packages.[8] So in addition to a purchased readership, there was evidence of purchased coverage.

Local Editions and Democracy

But the flip side to this was that both in January 2005 in Madhya Pradesh, and in August the same year in Uttar Pradesh, news from thousands of villages carried in highly commercialised newspapers played an unprecedented role in creating interest in the panchayat elections. Their editions going down to the village level carried news every day of the preparations in the run-up to the elections, even as their pages were full of advertisements from panchayat candidates informing voters of their symbols. Thousands of election results were carried every day, from village constituencies where the margin of victory was sometimes a single vote. Elections are always big news in India. Now village-level elections were being exhaustively covered for the first time, because the same main paper was going to both urban and rural audiences.

Robin Jeffrey's case study of Kerala had led him to theorise that there were three stages of print in a society in which the media is growing and maturing. He defined these stages as 'rare', 'elite' and 'mass' medium and concluded that the impact of print lessened when it became a mass medium spewing trivia (Jeffrey 2004). It also became, according to him, more likely to appease the establishment, and therefore less likely to

> generate public action as it had done in its ideology-driven days as an *elite* medium .... In short, in the elite mode, print may serve evolving nationalisms; but in the mass mode it serves the interests of the state ideologies within whose boundaries vulnerable proprietors have their money invested.

While this last point is certainly borne out to some extent by the example of *Dainik Jagran* already quoted, there is some evidence that even the trivia-laden local pages that arrived in the Hindi heartland's villages created civic and political awareness in first-time rural newspaper consumers. They talked about financial allocations made for the village, they focused on the state of civic amenities, and highlighted lapses in governance. Social workers felt this new flow of information had succeeded in altering the tenor of popular participation in panchayat meetings. 'Awareness has increased and the village level dynamics has changed. This is reflected in the interaction in the Gram Sabha too, especially in the kind of questions that people have begun to ask'.[9]

What's more, with sometimes as many as four local pages to fill for an area where not that much was happening, the coverage could be exhaustive. At a round table in Udaipur those who worked with village communities felt that small news items, locally generated, served as a useful early warning system for drought, or crop failure, or impending economic distress.[10]

Some of the changes triggered by newspapers were not anticipated. As localisation grew, administrative and political repercussions surfaced. The mapping for segmentation of newspaper editions had to do with the presumed area of reader interest—a Betul (Madhya Pradesh) reader, for instance, would want news of adjoining regions as well—and the combining of contiguous areas which could make an edition viable, and make printing and delivery convenient. But the basis of demarcation of political constituencies has to do with population, and the creation of administrative blocks for the purposes of governance and law and order had to do, historically, with revenue collection. Because these mappings often varied, an administrator seeking news from areas under his jurisdiction found that this had to be gleaned from more than one local edition. A politician seeking news from his entire constituency (of up to a million voters), had the same problem. And when you had to take an advertisement in a local pull-out section before the local part-time reporter could be persuaded to cover your election campaign, it became an expensive problem.

A more significant consequence of multi-edition newspapers was that this was producing a newspaper which both united and divided communities. The localising big dailies created a national–local product that blurred an existing regional identity which people living in India's states, voting in state-level elections, had acquired. The first part of the newspaper brought the national universe into rural and semi-urban homes, the second part brought the immediately local universe that the reader would recognise. As a result, news of even neighbouring districts disappeared from local editions. With the pressure of advertising on pages, coverage of the state as a whole, shrank. The intermediate picture, the amalgamation of many local universes, got squeezed out.

Over time newspaper localisation, driven by reader interests, had its political fallout though it was scarcely noticeable. Many a politician and activist became better known in his backyard, thanks to the increased coverage, but his fame died a local death. Local news for the most part remained local, rarely making it to the edition which was published from the state capital. Politicians fretted that achieving state-level recognition was becoming more difficult. They were concerned that there would soon be no statewide debate on issues, only local exposure. Members of state legislatures worried that questions raised in the assembly by them were now used only in local editions of the area to which the question pertained. Social workers and activists complained that regional was being replaced by local; and while the news coming out of the districts was more voluminous than before, its impact on backwardness was minimal. Since local news rarely found its way to other editions, their efforts to mobilise support on issues across a state often came to naught. By 2005 the worries were echoing in some editorial boardrooms, and debates began on how to contain the negative social fallout of excessive localisation.

Evolving a Public Sphere

This book argues that localisation of coverage by the print media expanded the existing public sphere at the district level, and then reinvented it unconsciously through its segmentation of editions. This had consequences for the political class and for civil society. It reshaped the individual citizen's sense of belonging, it added a new dimension to his identity. At the same time in nurturing the local it made newspapers relevant to a much wider readership. And when these new readers began to subscribe to newspapers it widened their horizons by bringing the national and international universe into their homes, through the main section of the newspaper. Even as it gave them a new local consciousness, it widened their information horizon. Its commercialisation of the election process, its democratisation of access to its pages, and the resulting inclusiveness of the news universe, its revival of dialect and its self-conscious reassertion of tradition in order to win over the mass reader, were all processes within this reinvention. It may seem fanciful to attribute changes in social dynamics to the impact of the print media. But that is precisely what writings on the notion of a public sphere have tried to establish for the influence of print media in other parts of the world.

The public sphere has become, over the past decade and a half, a much explored and interpreted concept. When Jurgen Habermas, the German philosopher of the Frankfurt school, first enunciated a model of what he called the 'bourgeois public sphere', he generalised from developments in Britain, France and Germany in the late 18th and 19th centuries. He defined the early public sphere as consisting of organs of information and political debate such as newspapers and journals, as well as institutions of political discussion such as parliaments, political clubs, literary salons, public assemblies, pubs and coffee houses, meeting halls and other public spaces where socio-political discussion took place. According to Douglas Kellner,

> For the first time in history, individuals and groups could shape public opinion, giving direct expression to their needs and interests while influencing political practice. The bourgeois

public sphere made it possible to form a realm of public opinion that opposed state power and the powerful interests that were coming to shape bourgeois society.[11]

Habermas' treatise was written in German in 1962 but began to be debated and theorised about only after it was translated into English in 1989.

Inherent in the transition from elite to mass audiences for newspapers in India, from newspapers full of politics to those geared to giving the reader entertainment and news-they-could-use, was this concept of a public sphere that Habermas evolved. The early public sphere, which he conceptualised as an instrument for nurturing or transforming democracy, became in the Indian context in the early 20th century an instrument for waging a battle for freedom from colonial rule. The early years of newspaper growth in Uttar Pradesh conform to these theoretical assumptions. 'Just as in Europe, the Indian newspapers emerged as an arena between state and civil society where public opinion could be formed' (Stahlberg 2002: 53).

In the history of *Aj* in the pre-independence era, you had the emergence of a newspaper which was founded to act as a vehicle for nationalism in a country under colonial occupation. It was devoid of commercial intent. Between 1920 and the attainment of independence in 1947, in what was then the United Provinces, it was fairly pivotal to the struggle against British occupation. A chronicler of the paper's history described it as the vehicle for reporting revolutionary acts, for stirring up the populace and making it aware of what was going on in the national movement.[12] Its first editor was a revolutionary who had trained others in firing arms, and was asked— after he emerged from a spell in jail—by the paper's founder Shiv Prasad Gupta, to create what was described as a revolutionary newspaper. He went on to consciously evolve both a medium and a vocabulary for propagating the freedom movement.

From Habermas' own articulation of the structural transformation of the public sphere that took place from the 17th and 18th centuries to the present, and from the interpretations that others have done of his thesis of the emergence of a public sphere and its subsequent disintegration, emerge a theoretical framework that helps understand the changes that have been taking place in the Hindi heartland. Indeed, the parallels are fascinating. In his introduction to *Habermas and the Public Sphere*, Craig Calhoun (1993: 3) describes the transition:

> The early bourgeois public spheres were composed of narrow segments of the European population, mainly educated, propertied men and they conducted a discourse not only exclusive of others but prejudicial to the interests of those excluded. Yet the transformations of the public sphere that Habermas describes turn largely on its continual expansion to include more and more participants ....

The expansion on account of the transition from elite to mass press had to do with literacy and with affordability. Habermas describes the initial period when most people were still outside the public sphere created by print. In Great Britain at the start of the 18th century, he says, more than half the population lived on the margins of subsistence. 'The masses were not only largely illiterate but also so pauperised that they could not even pay for literature. They did not have at their disposal the buying power needed for even the most modest participation in the market of cultural goods' (Habermas 1989: 38). But with the emergence of the diffuse public formed in the course of the commercialisation of cultural production, he says, a new social category arose.

In England, the illiterate masses were transformed because of initiated state policy, and reforms such as Forster's Education Act of 1870 (Hill 1985: 208–9). State-promoted literacy in UK in the 19th century, as in India in the 20th, helped lay the basis for a growth in newspaper readership. Michael Schudson looking at the public sphere in America says that 19th century Americans were more educationally equipped for participation in a public sphere than their 18th century forbears because in the 19th century the intellectual resources of the population expanded. Literacy shifted from being intensive to extensive, schooling became much more accessible, and the secularisation of culture, along with the democratisation of religion, spread a wider range of ideas to more and more people (Schudson 1993: 151).

Not only should there be more participants, says Habermas, they should also be capable of participating in the political public sphere. What makes this possible in addition to literacy is affordability and a de-intellectualisation as reflected in the popularity of the penny press. Describing the advent of the American mass press he says it was based on the commercialisation of the participation in the public sphere. 'In the case of the early penny press it could already be observed how it paid for the maximisation of its sales with the depoliticisation of its content.' In the next para he adds, 'In relation to the expansion of the news-reading public, therefore, the press that submitted political issues to critical discussion in the long run lost its influence' (Habermas 1989: 169).

According to Calhoun, Habermas suggests that ultimately this inclusivity brought degeneration in the quality of discourse, but contends at the same time that both the requirements of democracy and the nature of contemporary large-scale social organisation meant that it is impossible to progress today by going back to an elitist public sphere. To this Schudson adds that the extent of participation was an essential dimension of publicness, a key criterion for evaluating a public sphere. Calhoun stresses that it has to be kept in mind that Habermas' two-sided constitution of the category of public sphere meant that it was simultaneously about the quality or form of rational–critical discourse and the quantity of or openness to popular participation.

The evolving public sphere in the Hindi speaking states at the close of the 20th century conformed to this notion of quality in the early part of the century, and quantity and popular participation by the end of the 20th century. But it occurred within the space of a single century. In the 20th century people went from mass illiteracy to growing literacy, and then the ability to read a newspaper. When they came into the readership net the public sphere here was becoming accessible, both in terms of commercial incentives to the first-time reader, as well as in terms of depoliticisation and the creation of a cultural product that people would want to consume: a colourful product in which local news, crime, magazine supplements, and religious and cultural news was displacing the emphasis on politics that newspapers in the earlier part of the 20th century had.

Contrary to Habermas' later belief that commercialisation only degrades the public sphere, commodification of news in this part of the world helped to turn more people into readers, thereby achieving his stated requirement that an effective public sphere should also have more and more participants. And while he did not attribute widespread political consciousness to the masses, in India you had a situation where even without literacy, political consciousness was increasing. This was because of the emergence of new political formations that had constituents drawn from Dalits and backward castes and served to broadbase political participation, and because of the emergence of village self-governance and the widespread popular participation that it triggered. By 2006, elected village councils or panchayats had become the bodies through which the central and state governments disbursed substantial development funds.

In the context of India's Hindi belt, the early public sphere was the site for nationalism and gathering resistance to British rule. When it was re-invented, in a manner of speaking, some 75 years later in the mid-1990s, it was consciously developed as a commercial vehicle. It did not, however, necessarily speak to its readers primarily as consumers. It spoke to them as consuming, upwardly mobile, politically and culturally aware citizens. Also, in its second avatar, the print public sphere strove to create a sense of local community among readers who were assumed to have already acquired a national and state identity.

When media theorists discuss government, citizenship, information and the public sphere, they also grapple with the question of access. 'If citizens are to participate, the level of interaction with the public sphere must be two way—both to retrieve information and to introduce and circulate it as part of the creation of technoculture' (Green 2001: 120). As later chapters of this book demonstrate, an essential feature of the way the localised print public sphere developed in the Hindi-speaking states was that it democratised access: it accepted what passed for news from all and sundry, even as it incentivised reading of local editions by offering gifts and circulation packages. In addition to the practice of accepting news handouts in very small towns and in rural areas, first *Dainik Jagran* and then *Hindustan* introduced the 'sms' (short message service on mobile telephones) mode of interactivity with readers. You could message for information, or give news ideas from your locality that you wanted the newspaper to investigate. You could also sms to complain about something that had appeared in the newspaper—a 21st century variation of a letter to the editor. But on both counts, this sort of democratisation of access was superficial. It served those classes that had the wherewithal to interact: the education, the confidence, the technology. Those still at the bottom of the economy (landless labour, migrants, poor Dalits and backwards, victims of hunger and indebtedness) could figure in this public sphere only if a conscientious reporter sought them out. They were not readers and not likely to feature on the circulation agent's radar. There was however one small fortnightly newspaper, *Khabar Lahariya*, which sought them out and presented a subaltern view of how people were faring in the villages of the region of Uttar Pradesh known as Bundelkhand. It was in the Bundeli dialect and was produced by a group of women, some of whom were Dalits.

Conclusion

To sum up, a decade and a half beginning from the early 1990s saw the expansion and reinvention of the public sphere in the Hindi belt, making it both inclusive and more commercially driven. Newspaper penetration increased, and marketers quickly followed. Print went from being an elite to a mass medium and very ordinary people living in very small towns (known as *kasbas*) and villages became both news consumers and newsmakers as newspapers localised.

This expanded public sphere was catalysed in significant ways by the explosion of local news. It carved up the states of the Indian Union which made up the Hindi belt, into mappings imposed by the way newspapers evolved their local pages and editions. This had implications for politicians, administrators and social workers, and activists working in villages and small towns on various issues. News of even neighbouring districts disappeared from local editions. With the pressure of advertising on pages, coverage of the state as a whole, shrank. The larger picture, the amalgamation of many local universes, got squeezed out. By 2005 the worries on this score were echoing in some editorial boardrooms. And debate began on how to contain the negative social fallout of excessive localisation.

This book locates the dynamics of 21st century Hindi journalism against the backdrop of its historical beginnings, as it evolved up to independence and thereafter. It traces the histories of some of the major newspaper-owning families, whåt led them to move across states in the Hindi belt, and the role played by the second and third generations in these families in expanding and diversifying the business. New modes of financing came in: the leading Hindi newspaper first divested its shareholding to a foreign partner, and then went to the stock market to raise further capital. It touches upon the influence on the media of political changes, predicated on caste, class and communal strategies. Out of all of this emerged a Hindi journalism in modern India that was pragmatic and market-oriented, and reader rather than editor-driven.

Notes

1. Prabhash Joshi, interviewed by author, Delhi, 18 May 2003.
2. http://www.indiantelevision.com/mam/headlines/y2k5/june/junemam47.htm, downloaded 29 July 2006.
3. Dionne Bunsha, 'The Rise of Print', 6 July 2002, *Frontline*.
4. Praveen Swami, 'Recording Media Trends', 25 September–8 October 1999, *Frontline*.
5. Mrinal Pande, interviewed by author, 24 June 2006.
6. The Hindi term for a traditional village meeting place.
7. Babulal Sharma, interviewed by author, Bhopal, 19 February 2005.
8. Suneelam, Samajwadi Party MLA, interviewed by author, Bhopal, 19 February 2005.
9. Amitabh Singh, Member Working Committee, Debate, interviewed by Sushmita Malaviya, Bhopal, 31 January 2004.
10. At Seva Mandir, Udaipur, 2 December 2004.
11. Douglas Kellner, *Habermas, the Public Sphere, and Democracy: A Critical Intervention*, http://www.gseis.ucla.edu/faculty/kellner/papers/habermas.htm, accessed December 2006.
12. Dhirendranath, interviewed by author, 18 March 2005.

2

The Evolution and Growth
of Hindi Journalism

'Our Hindi is no longer the Hindi of Pandits.'

Hindi journalism is young, some 50 years younger than English journalism in India which had late 18th century origins.* And while today it has the status of a national language in a huge, multi-lingual country, Hindi itself is a relatively recent construct, almost consciously developed as a vehicle for nationalist sentiment in the 19th and 20th centuries. Those who wrote in it strove to develop a political vocabulary, and a language that communicated with a wider audience than those acquainted with Persian or Urdu. These latter were the languages used for literature and discourse in the 19th century for a region which extended geographically from Rajputana in the west to Bihar in the east, from Punjab and Garhwal in the north to the Central Provinces and Berar in the south. The Mughals had ruled over this area, one legacy of which was a Persian-educated gentry. Press and publishing was in Urdu and Persian, Hindi was for the hoi polloi.

According to one chronicler of the emergence of spoken Khari Boli Hindi, the precursor of modern Hindi, it was the 'lingua franca of the bazaar over the whole of northern and central India, and the mother tongue of a relatively small area around Meerut in western Uttar Pradesh.' It was also the mother tongue of merchant castes like the Agarwals who used it for long distance trade communications. But not the language of poetry, which was more likely to be

*India's first newspaper, *Hicky's Bengal Gazette*, appeared in Calcutta on 29 January 1780.

Braj Bhasa, derived from Sanskrit (Orsini 2002: 3). Such theorising was too simplistic for a scholar of Hindi such as Amrit Rai who did not subscribe to neat divisions between Hindi, Persian and Urdu, and held that Hindi evolved over a much, much longer period assimilating many influences along the way. He challenged the logic that classified Urdu and Khari Boli Hindi as two separate languages, and listed basic words of Urdu which were identical to those of Hindi (Rai 1984: 4). Khari Boli literally means pure speech.

Hindi journalism at any rate is less than 200 years old, since the first known publication of a journal in Hindi was in 1826. It had its origins in Bengali-speaking Calcutta (now Kolkata), not in the region which today comprises the Hindi speaking states. Away from the heartland, Hindi in the 19th century evolved more rapidly as the language of publishing. The growing number of littérateurs who wrote in the weeklies and monthlies of this period were a sizeable expatriate community in Bengal. This has been attributed to the concentration of Marwari capital and Bengali publishing (Orsini 2002: 63). Calcutta was at that time both the commercial and political capital of India, Hindi-speaking people from all over northern India lived there, and were to some extent prospective patrons of journalistic ventures in that language. They were also most certainly influenced by the forces of Indian Renaissance which made its first impact on the Bengal Press (Kumar 1971).

Hindi publishing also got an impetus from the activities of the missionaries at the turn of the century. Hazariprasad Dwivedi credits them with helping to modernise the language. In 1799 the Danish Mission was founded in Serampore by William Carey and others, and undertook the propagation of the Bible in Indian languages. In striving to translate the Bible into Hindi, as well as into Bagheli, Chhattisgarhi, Kanauji and Bhojpuri the fonts for the script got developed (Dwivedi 1999: 200–201).

The early journalism coming out of Bengal in Hindi was literary—essays, verse and fiction sustained the earliest Hindi journals to be published, in the mid and late 19th century. Journalism as we know it evolved from these literary origins, hence the use of the term *sahityik patrakarita* (literary journalism) in the early 20th century for the genre used in newspapers like *Aj,* and journals such as *Saraswati. Sahityik* because of its emphasis on language, and because those who laid its foundations, were also literary figures, participating in Hindi *sahitya sammelan*s (literary gatherings) which periodically took place in the early decades of the 20th century. *Aj*, for one, was consciously used by its founder editor as a platform for debate on literary questions. He would reprint in its pages articles and speeches by leading figures of the Hindi *sahitya sammelan*.

In the 19th century there were two parallel tracks of development, in Bengal and in the provinces which later became the Hindi-speaking states of contemporary India. The primary development of the genre was in Bengal, while in the provinces Hindi journalism evolved as an appendage to Urdu journalism. But in both places experiments in simultaneous publishing in three or four languages took place.

First, Bengal. In 1826 the earliest known Hindi journal, a weekly called *Oodunta Martand* (Rising Sun) made its appearance on 30 May. Its owner and editor was Jugal Kishore Sookool (Shukla) a Kanpur lawyer practising in one of Calcutta's two courts, who obtained, on 16 February under the Press Act of 1823, a license to publish a Hindi weekly. The editor's statement in this weekly indicated that he knew of no other venture that may have preceded it. He wrote that while there were news publications in English, Parsi (Persian) and Bengali, and while these served those who could speak those languages, there was a need for '*satya samachar*' (truthful news) which Hindustani people could read for themselves. Its existence was brought to light by Brijendra Nath Banerjee, associate editor of *Modern Review*, when he wrote an article titled '*Hindi ka Pratham Samachar Patra*' which was published in February 1931 (Bhatnagar 2003: 48–50).

Before he graduated to being a lawyer there, Sookool had been a clerk in the Sadar Diwani Adalat, the court which conducted its business in Persian or Farsee. He brought knowledge of Sanskrit, Braj Bhasa, Khari Boli and Farsee to bear on his publication, which carried in its first issue *shloka*s (verses) in Sanskrit and couplets in Braj. The language used in *Oodunta Martand* was an early form of Hindi before it became standardised. However Jagdish Prasad Chaturvedi, writing a history of Hindi journalism, says he used two languages in this publication, Braj Bhasha as well as a form of Hindi from the Central Provinces, described as *Madhyadeshiya bhasha* (Chaturvedi 2004: 23). He gives a sample of Sookool's reporting as he described Lord Amherst's visit to Lucknow in December 1826, the pomp and colour of his procession, and the decking out of the shops and balconies which lined his route.

Oodunta Martand's monthly subscription was Rs 2 and it published 79 issues before ceasing publication on 15 December 1827. Though it carried commodity prices and information about the arrival and departure of steamers, among other news, it did not get enough support from Hindi-speaking traders to survive. When it closed down it carried a rather plaintive statement that the weekly had hoped that the British Government would have taken favourable notice and given it aid, but this had not come to pass. It collapsed when it ceased to be viable (Bhatnagar 2003: 50).

The second known Hindi newspaper to follow also emerged in Calcutta, and was *Bangdoot* (1829) published by Raja Ram Mohun Roy and others. One hallmark of Roy the reformer was his eagerness to propagate his thoughts in as many languages as he could. Metropolitan Calcutta in those days spoke English, Bengali, Hindi and Urdu, and Roy started newspapers in all these languages. *Bangdoot* was published in English, Bengali, Persian and Hindi. Also a weekly, it began publication on 10 May 1829, and was initially edited by Nilratna Haldar. It came out every Sunday morning, and cost Re 1 per month.

Five years later one finds an advertisement in the Bengali newspaper *Samachar Darpan* for a newspaper called *Projamitra*. It is announced as a new newspaper to be launched in English as well as Hindustani, to be published weekly and sold at Rs 2 a month, or Rs 20 a year. The advertisement was in Hindi, using the word '*atishigra*' (very soon) to indicate that its publication was imminent. However, Dr Ramratan Bhatnagar, who has chronicled Hindi journalism in its first 119 years, goes on to say that no issue of *Projamitra* was traced and it was difficult to tell whether it ever saw the light of day (ibid.: 51).

Lord William Bentinck was the governor-general at this time and allowed the press the freedom to flourish. More publications emerged in Calcutta including two described as penta lingual or published in five languages within the same issue. *The Indian Sun* which appeared on 11 June 1846 had five parallel columns in five different languages, including Hindi. So did *Martand* also published from Calcutta in 1846, in Hindi, Urdu, Persian, Bengali and English. In 1850, the dogged Pandit Jugal Kishore Sookool, undeterred by the closure of *Oodunta Martand* tried again with the publication of *Samyadand Martand*. It survived until April 1852.

In June 1854 Calcutta got its first Hindi daily, *Samachar Sudhavarshan*, published from Bara Bazar and edited by Shyam Sunder Sen. It was bilingual, while the news items and editorials were in Bengali, business news relating to merchandise, market reports, and ships was written in Hindi. It survived till 1868 (Kumar 1971).

In the provinces which later became the Hindi-speaking states of contemporary India the journalism in the early 1800s was in Persian, and when the court languages in these provinces changed to Urdu in 1837, a rapid rise of Urdu journalism followed Persian journalism. Hindi journalism did not take root here until the middle of the 19th century, beginning as an appendage to Urdu journalism. Bhatnagar records the publication in 1849 of the first Urdu–Hindi paper from Malwa, *Benares Akhbar*, which was in Urdu written in Devnagri script. However Vijaydutt Sridhar who has chronicled 150 years of journalism in Madhya Pradesh says *Benares Akhbar* was published from Benares in 1845, and it was *Malwa Akhbar* that began publication in 1849 from the press of the Holkar kingdom in Indore. *Malwa Akhbar* counts as Madhya Pradesh's first Hindi weekly newspaper with half the page taken up with Urdu and the other half with Hindi. Later it was also published in Marathi. In 1852 *Akhbar Gwalior* followed, simultaneously in Hindi and Urdu, a weekly published at the instance of the Gwalior Maharaja Jiyajirao Scindia at a press established in Gwalior for the purpose. A series of other weeklies and monthlies followed and in 1923 this region got its first Hindi daily (Sridhar 1999: 15).

The history of Hindi journalism in the 19th century and the early part of the 20th century has been classified into broad phases by chroniclers. Its origin and early phase was between 1826 and 1867 when papers were published out of a desire to give Hindi a foothold, and had stability of neither language nor form. Its rise and growth was in two phases. Between 1867 and 1883 the language was consolidated with the chief journalism of this period being literary. Bharatendu Babu Harishchandra launched *Kavi Vachan Sudha* from Kashi, a monthly magazine which published both ancient and modern literary work in book form. When it became a fortnightly it widened its canvas to include articles on political and social topics. Still later, it became a weekly.

He followed this up in 1873 with the publication of *Harischandra Magazine* which was named as *Harishchandra Chandrika* in 1874. The title page, entirely in English, called it *Harish Chandra's Magazine*. It published poetry in folk metre on contemporary social issues such as taxation, famine and societal change (Bhatnagar 2003: 97). A veritable rash of literary magazines and newspapers followed. Two influential publications and nine lesser known monthlies and weeklies were launched in a single year, 1877. *Bharat Mitra*, which would survive for 60 years, till 1937, began as a fortnightly from Calcutta, became a weekly and later a daily. It started a movement for the popularisation of Hindi and inspired the launch in 1900 of *Chattisgarh Mitra* from Raipur, edited by Pandit Ramrao Chincholkar and Pandit Madhavrao Sapre. Its first four and last four pages were printed on colour paper and it was intended to create an awakening in a backward region. The political monthly *Hindi Pradeep* launched by Pandit Balakrishna Bhatt survived till 1910.

Meanwhile, the people of Bihar were getting a Hindi voice. *Bihar Bandhu* was founded in 1872 in Calcutta by the same Balakrishna Bhatt and Keshavram Bhatt. It was edited by Munshi Hasan Ali. In 1874 the paper's press was moved to Patna from where it began to publish, it had a succession of editors who took it into the first decade and more of the next century. It had a feisty career. It campaigned successfully for the introduction of Hindi in law courts, and was served at one point with a notice from the Commissioner of Patna for attacking the character of European women. It ceased publication in 1915 after its assets were sold in an auction to pay for accumulated debts (Kumar 1971: 43–44).

Age of Press Propaganda

The second phase of the rise and growth of the Hindi press which occurred between 1883 and 1900 is labelled as the age of press propaganda by Dr Bhatnagar. The notion of the Hindi press as a vehicle for social and political messages grew in a period which saw

15 sessions of the Indian National Congress being held. Nationally the following papers were prominent during this period: *Kesari, Amrit Bazar Patrika, Bangbasi* and *The Hindu*. In 1883 *The Hindu* became a tri-weekly paper, and then in 1889 a daily. The same year *Amrit Bazar Patrika* published a confidential foreign office document concerning Kashmir and invited the Official Secrets Act which came into force that year. The Indian press grew in assertiveness and in numbers. Also in 1883 *Hindusthan* began to be published from London in English, Hindi and Urdu. It would shut shop in 1885.

In the last 17 years of the century well over a 150 Hindi publications appeared, many of them short lived. A number of them such as *Kayastha Samachar, Kayastha Patrika, Gaur Kayastha* and *Kayastha Conference Samachar* were devoted to the interest of the Kayasth community. Others were devoted to propagating the tenets of the Arya Samaj. The age of press propaganda did not denote merely political propagation:

> ... the Hindi press was dominated by one primary motive—the propagation of some definite notion about religion, social reform, or the language to be adopted universally by the people of Hindi Pradesh. The most important stimulus was the Arya Samaj. Social reforms of the period were chiefly associated with this religious movement. (Bhatnagar 2003: xiii)

As for publications with political content, there were those which supported the Congress, and those that opposed it. *Arya Darpan, Bharat Varsha, Brahman, Hindusthan* and *Hindusthani* (Hindi–Urdu) were among those which supported it. Those that opposed its politics have been dismissed as insignificant and not been named. A paper called *Khichri Samachar* took on the government, and in 1891 the editor was sentenced to a fine of Rs 250 and three months imprisonment for libel. The editor of *Bharat Varsha* also suffered both fine and imprisonment as did three or four others.

The Hindi journalism of this period was chiefly in the form of essays, and for the most part non-political in outlook. Urdu journalism was much more in evidence. In the closing year of the century there were 73 publications in Urdu compared to 20 in Hindi. A few individuals of this period shaped Hindi as a language for purposeful prose. The tallest among them was Bharatendu Babu Harishchandra who in developing a language for his journals steered a middle course between drawing heavily on Urdu and Persian, as Raja Shiva Prasad did, and filling it with Sanskrit derivatives as Swami Dayanand did. He influenced two important prose writers, Pratapnarain Misra and Balakrishna Bhatt whose magazines *Hindi Pradeep* (1877) and *Brahman* (1883) were influential in different ways, catering to different segments of readers.

The next 20 years, 1900–1920 would see writing in Khari Boli Hindi develop further though still primarily through literary forms. Most of the journals of the period were weekly magazines, but a couple of dailies appeared before World War I, and half a dozen during it. Mahabir Prasad Dwivedi's (Figure 2.1) *Saraswati* was the best regarded magazine of the period, for the singular contribution it made to the standardisation of Hindi. He was appointed its editor in 1903,

FIGURE 2.1   A stamp issued in 1966 to commemorate the contribution to the freedom struggle of Acharya Mahabir Prasad Dwivedi, editor of *Saraswati*
Reprinted with permission from the Department of Post, Government of India.

and is credited with developing a grammar for the language (Singh 2003: 124). The journal developed Khari Boli for both prose and poetry, it brought Sanskrit literary fare to popular attention, it fostred the development of literary reviewing and criticism, and promoted the short story as a literary form. *Saraswati's* content was a miscellany, and for its pages authors and poets sent original contributions. It enabled new writing to emerge in the public domain. Its other significant contribution was a deliberate effort to include articles which would inculcate scientific knowledge in its readers. It popularised and perhaps even coined scientific terms, thoughtfully giving translations in brackets, alongside, in English!

This steady pace of creative literary output was galvanised by World War I into a more energetic phase in which weeklies metamorphosed into dailies. G.S. Vidyarthi's *Pratap* published from Kanpur began as a weekly in 1913, became a daily during the war, and continued as one after it (Orsini 2002: 63). A new daily, *Calcutta Samachar* was launched from Calcutta, and the weeklies *Abhudaya* (Prayag), *Shri Venkateshwar Samachar* (Mumbai), *Hindi Bihari* (Patna) and *Jayaji Pratap* (Gwalior) were converted into dailies. One observer noted that this signified that the ordinary Hindi reader had developed an appetite for news (Bhatnagar 2003: 191). But it was not ordinary news, it was war news. When the war ended some of the dailies reverted to their weekly status, while a few continued as dailies.

Orsini records that between 1910 and 1920 political weeklies flourished and grew into focuses of political activity as well as of factionalism, attracting activists and writers. The nationalist leader Madan Mohan Malaviya launched the weekly *Abhyuday* (1907) and a monthly called *Maryada* in 1910. The already launched *Pratap* of Ganesh Sankar Vidyarthi mentioned above would be the bridge to the next phase, when Hindi daily newspapers evolved journalism as a genre and defined for themselves broader audiences reaching into the countryside.

Newspapers such as *Aj* (1920) and *Pratap* epitomised a significant shift in the first quarter of the 20th century. The Hindi political press made the transition from being journals of ideas to journals of news, catering increasingly, to a wider public, and widening the Hindi public sphere in the process (Orsini 2002: 65). There was some articulation at this stage of how the Hindi readership was different from the English one. B.V. Paradkar, the founder editor of *Aj* dwelt on this in his speech at the Sampadak Sammelan in Brindavan:

> We (Hindi) editors completely ignore facts like what classes our readers belong to, how they live, how they earn their living, what are the difficulties they face in the battlefield of life, how they enjoy themselves, what are their interests, and what they want. If we found out about them and gave our readers the news they want, and if we turned ourselves into their helpers in the struggle for life, our newspapers would become popular in no time at all ... until we adopt the common folk and we turn our newspapers into a reflection of them, we shall not progress and serve the real nation. (Translated, Orsini 2002: 65–66)

The above articulation contained the germ of the commercial strategy that the fast expanding Hindi press would implement by the end of the 20th century: the common reader wanted, above all, a reflection of his life and problems in the newspaper. Therefore, localise, take your newspaper down to the grassroots. And use news gatherers drawn from that level. Long, long before the proprietors of *Swatantra Bharat, Dainik Bhaskar, Hindustan* or *Dainik Jagran* thought to use stringers (part-time reporters who are paid by the length of their reports, measured initially by a string), *Pratap* and *Aj* were creating networks of local stringers, rather than relying on English news agencies (ibid.: 65). The difference is, by the end of the century it was a clear-cut commercial strategy to expand to the villages. But in the second decade of the century a grassroots approach was advocated out of an idealistic vision of how the needs of ordinary people could set the agenda for an awakening of India.

Beyond Uttar Pradesh

Apart from Uttar Pradesh other parts of the Hindi belt were also acquiring their own dailies during this period. In June 1923 the first daily newspaper for the region which is now Madhya Pradesh (MP) began publication from Sagar. *Prakash* proclaimed through a couplet on its masthead that it was intended to awaken patriotism in its readers. It carried on its pages every single item of news it could find related to the freedom movement. Its editor was Baldev Prasad (Sridhar 1999: 75). *Nai Duniya, Nava Bharat* and *Dainik Bhaskar* would follow in later years and become the leading papers in the state. *Nai Duniya*, begun in 1947 in Jabalpur would become an Indore newspaper with a national reputation, *Nava Bharat* founded in 1950 would be the MP edition of a Nagpur-based newspaper, and *Bhaskar* (1958) would go on by 2002 to top the readership charts in the country for two years, before being displaced by another Hindi newspaper, *Dainik Jagran*.

In Bihar in the last decade of the 19th century several Hindi journals—weeklies and monthlies—were published from Patna, Arrah, Gaya, Bhagalpur, Saran and Champaran. During this period as well as in the first two decades of the 20th century a number of caste journals also appeared, of which the important ones were *Dwija Patrika, Kshatriyay Patrika, Kashatriya Samachar, Katri Hitaishi, Teli Samachar, Mhuri Mayanka, Bhumihar Bharman Patrika, Rauniar Hitaishi, Kayastha Kaumudi, Madhya Deshiya Vanik Patrika* and *Rauniyar Vaishya*. The dates of publication of most of these are not given. After 1912 when Bihar and Orissa became separate administrative units, nationalist journals in Hindi began to be established. *Desh* from the Searchlight Press began as a weekly Hindi supplement to *Searchlight* intended for publishing court notices and court sale proclamations in Hindi. When it was given a separate status the name of Babu Rajendra Prasad (who later became free India's first president) began to appear as editor, though he never did attend to its editorial work (Kumar 1971: 65–71).

The earliest known publications to emerge from the area that was later to become the state of Haryana were intended for the Jain community. *Jain Prakash*, a weekly, was published in 1884 from Farukhnagar in Gurgaon district in Urdu and Hindi, and a monthly called *Jain Prakash Hindustan*, in 1888, also from Gurgaon. In 1907 a weekly called *Gyanoday* began publication from Hissar, carrying articles on political, social and religious subjects. These included articles on lack of governance and corruption as also literary pieces (Vaidik 2002: 206–7).

After 1950 when Hindi journalism began to gain force, more than 30 publications, mostly monthlies, were launched from towns such as Gurgaon, Bhiwani, Rohtak, Ambala, Jhajjar, Narnaul, Rewari and so on. There was the odd daily but since papers published from Chandigarh, Jalandhar and Delhi such as *Nav Bharat Times, Hindustan, Vir Pratap, Hindi Milap, Punjab Kesari* and *Pradeep* were popular in Haryana, local dailies never did manage to establish themselves. Today the best known local daily is *Hari Bhoomi*, head-quartered in Rohtak.

The giants of today's Hindi newspaper world were therefore the relatively later entrants to the market, not the early birds who are supposed to get the worm. Among significant Hindi dailies born in the 1930s was *Hindustan*, published from Delhi, a sister publication of *Hindustan Times* which had been established in 1923. It was founded in 1936 and the entry for it in the Indian Press Yearbook reads, 'Policy: Nationalist'. In Bihar *Aryavarta* made its appearance from Patna in 1939, 'Policy: Independent Nationalist.' It was owned by the Maharaja of Darbhanga who also published the English daily, *Indian Nation*. *Nava Bharat*, listed as a paper belonging to Vindya Pradesh was established in Nagpur in 1934. *Mahakoshal* was established in 1935 at Raipur. In 1956 it was describing itself as the 'largest circulated Hindi daily and weekly of Madhya Pradesh and adjoining states' (Gates-Reed 1956).

In 1946 *Indore Samachar* was launched from Indore. Around the year that India gained independence a large number of newspapers made their appearance. Bennett, Coleman & Co. launched *Navbharat Times* in April 1947 with the stated mission of addressing independent India in a language of its own. By the mid-1980s it grew to acquire national status with editions in Delhi, Bombay, Patna, Jaipur and Lucknow. When Rajendra Mathur moved from editing *Nai Duniya* to editing *Navbharat Times*, it acquired an editorial reputation for quality, and grew rapidly in circulation. But trade union problems led the management to close down the Lucknow and Patna editions in 1990 after an eight month shut-down in Lucknow in 1989. In 1991–92 it took a policy decision to shut down all editions except Delhi and Bombay. That left the field open for *Dainik Jagran* to grow unhindered in this part of UP from 1990 onwards. Though

Navbharat Times would in 2005 claim leadership in the Hindi market in Delhi and Mumbai, it had long ceased to be a serious national contender for the Hindi newspaper market. *Amar Ujala* was launched on 18 April 1948 from Agra, as a four-page newspaper with a circulation of 2,576 copies. This too had a lofty stated aim: promoting social awakening and inculcating a sense of responsibility among the citizens of a recently independent India. By 1968 it had a stated circulation of 20,000 copies and was covering over 14 districts of western Uttar Pradesh. It then ventured into other neighbouring states and by 2005 the paper ranked fifth nationally in all languages in the National Readership Survey of that year, and was one of the leading newspapers in Chandigarh, Punjab, Haryana, Himachal Pradesh and Jammu & Kashmir, in addition to Uttar Pradesh.

Other Hindi newspapers launched in 1947 were *Pradeep* from Patna, *Navjivan* and *Swatantra Bharat* from Lucknow and *Nai Duniya* from Indore. The last began its publishing life as a four-page eveninger, and would go on to become a morning daily which despite not being published from a state capital, acquired a national reputation for journalistic excellence. It pioneered photo composing and offset printing in 1967, the first paper in the country to do so.

Rajasthan was to get its first daily only in 1951 with the publication of *Rashtradoot*. As his son tells it, Hazarilal Sharma was a pharmacy graduate from Benares Hindu University when he heard Pandit Nehru make a speech in Calcutta in 1947, complaining that there were too few newspapers and he had to suffer lectures from Ramakrishna Dalmia (a prominent businessman who had acquired control of Bennett, Coleman & Co., publishers of *The Times of India* and *Navbharat Times*). Sharma decided then that he would start a newspaper. He was advised to do so in his native Rajasthan. As a first step he decided to acquire a printing press which would also be used to print labels for his ayurvedic pharmacy. The British Information Service's press was moving and wanted to sell their printing machine which he acquired. But back in Rajasthan when he finally moved the cylinder press there were no people who could operate it so the compositors came from Bengal, Hindi-speaking Maithili Brahmins.[1]

The *Navjyoti* had begun publishing from Ajmer in 1936 but became a daily only after the launch of *Rashtradoot*. An employee of *Rashtradoot*, Kapoor Chand Kulish would later strike out to start his own newspaper, *Rajasthan Patrika*. In the account that he has written of how he came to launch the paper in 1956 and sustain it he says that he was motivated to do so by the fact that newspapers published from Jaipur and Ajmer were aligned to one or other political personality and he felt there was scope for a truly independent paper. He started the *Patrika* as an evening paper, and sustained it with local advertising. He describes how the district and local courts came forward to require litigants to get court summons published in the *Patrika* for which payments used to be made in cash (Kulish 1996). By 2005 *Rashtradoot*, Rajasthan's oldest daily was barely surviving, but the *Patrika*, infused with the dynamism of the third generation, was reigning in Rajasthan, despite formidable competition, publishing from four other states, and announcing an entry into Madhya Pradesh.

In 1958, *Dainik Bhaskar*, the newspaper from Madhya Pradesh which would become a 21st century stalwart, confident enough to take on the reigning English market leader in distant Mumbai, made its appearance from Bhopal and Ujjain. It was founded by Dwarka Prasad Agarwal, would grow after his son Ramesh Agarwal took over part of the publishing empire, and expand out of Madhya Pradesh after the latter's sons came into the business. In 1967 the paper started a Gwalior edition, in 1983 it mustered the courage to take on a well-established *Nai Duniya* in Indore, and it was only by 1992 that it became the leading newspaper in Madhya Pradesh, seeking fresh pastures to conquer, which took it to Rajasthan in late 1996.

In Punjab, Lala Devraj, the founder of the Kanya Mahavidhyalaya in Jalandhar, launched a publication called *Panchal Pandita*, which began to publish in Hindi from 1901, and had a fair sphere of influence. It campaigned for reform in the status of women. In 1929 the Lok Sevak Mandal, established by Lal Lajpat Rai, began to publish a weekly called *Punjab Kesari*. Its publisher was Purushottam Das Tandon, and its editor Bhim Sen Vidyalankar. Lala Lajpat Rai's autobiography was first serialised in it, and Pandit Nehru contributed articles to it in Hindi. During the Lahore Congress it began to publish as a daily. First hand accounts of what was happening to the

Congress used to appear in this paper which closed down thereafter. The title would be reincarnated by a publishing group in the 1960s (Vaidik 2002).

Until the late 1990s the largest circulated Hindi daily in northern India was *Punjab Kesari*, first published from Jalandhar in Punjab from 1965, and later from Ambala and Delhi as well. Its founder Lala Jagat Narain had fled to India from west Punjab at partition in 1947; he started an Urdu-language newspaper, *Hind Samachar*, in the town of Jalandhar in 1948. The Hindi paper came some 17 years later when the Hindi-reading public in Punjab was judged to be large enough to make it worthwhile (Jeffrey 2001) By 1986, publishing from three centres, *Punjab Kesari* sold 460,000 copies a day, the largest circulating Hindi daily in India (Jeffrey 1997: 77–83). By 2005 however, it had lost its pre-eminence, losing ground to newspapers such as *Dainik Jagran*, *Dainik Bhaskar*, *Hindustan* and *Amar Ujala* which were growing far more aggressively.

Aj, Pratap, *and the Shaping of Hindi Journalism*

Though the paper is still sold in UP and Bihar, *Aj* is now a pale shadow of the institution it once was. Much colourful pre-independence history is woven around it. It was founded by Shivprasad Gupta, described by his family as the ruler of Azmatgarh, a wealthy landlord who put much of his wealth at the service of the national movement (Figure 2.2). According to his great-grandson, apart from landed wealth the family owned mills and Gupta was a money lender who even lent money to the East India Company.[2] He generously bore the expenses of the Congress Party and when leaders like Mahatma Gandhi, Madan Mohan Malaviya and Lokmanya Bal Gangadhar Tilak felt the need for a vehicle to carry news of the national movement to the people, it was Gupta who came forward to underwrite the starting of a newspaper. He was already keen on the idea; in 1920 he had returned from what is described as a world tour, determined to start in Kashi (Benares), a newspaper in Hindi which would be as influential as the *Times* of London.

FIGURE 2.2   A stamp issued in 1988 by the Indian Government to
commemorate the contribution to the freedom struggle of
Shivprasad Gupta, founder of *Aj*
Reprinted with permission from the Department of Post,
Government of India.

He found someone who could be persuaded to pioneer this editorial venture. In the heart of Varanasi is a three-storey building called Paradkar Smriti Bhavan, built by the Uttar Pradesh Government in the memory of a man commonly described as the father of Hindi journalism. It houses the Kashi Patrakar Sangh, has an auditorium and library, and a guest room for visiting journalists on the terrace. It is named after Baburao Vishnu Paradkar, the founder-editor of *Aj*, a man credited with establishing the tenets of Hindi journalism in its most idealistic phase (Figure 2.3).

FIGURE 2.3   An etching of Baburao Vishnu Paradkar, the father of Hindi journalism
Courtesy of the Kashi Patrakarita Sangh.

In the early years of the 20th century, when the freedom struggle was gathering force, being associated with politics was a badge of honour for a journalist, though by the end of the century combining a career in journalism with one in politics was viewed as opportunism. In a book on his journalism[3] he was described as being noted for being a revolutionary leader of the struggle for independence, and a literary luminary in addition to being an illustrious journalist.

While he was still a student, an early meeting with his uncle Sakharam Ganesh Deoskar, the Bengal-based editor of the Bengali weekly *Hitvadi*, drew B.V. Paradkar to journalism as well as to revolutionary ideas. Deoskar introduced him to *Kesari*, the weekly edited by Lokmanya Tilak. He said later that he subscribed to it for a year, but scarcely read it because it was in Marathi, and he did not follow the language (Vyas 1960: 148). In 1905, volunteering at a session of the Benares Congress, he met Tilak and was profoundly influenced. He began his journalistic career in 1906 at *Hindi Bangvasi*, published from Calcutta, at Rs 25 a month. When the magazine he worked for poked fun at the Congress he quit the job and went on to work for *Hitvarti*, the Hindi edition of *Hitvadi*, and later, between 1910 and 1915, for the daily, *Bharat Mitra*.

Paradkar was also becoming drawn to revolutionary activities. In the period before Mahatma Gandhi evolved his doctrine of non-violence, the exemplar of patriotic conduct was going cheerfully to the gallows, a copy of the *Gita* in hand. Along with his magazine editing, Paradkar became involved with revolutionary groups including an underground society in Chandranagar. He spent close to four years in various jails and by 1920, when he was released as part of a general amnesty, he had acquired a heroic reputation as a journalist-revolutionary (ibid.).

Shivprasad Gupta heard of Paradkar's return to Kashi and asked him to join the circle discussing the idea of starting a newspaper. The philospher Dr Bhagwandas, his Congress politician-son Babu Sriprakas, Shivprasad Gupta, and Pararkar would meet and ideate. What should it be called? Bhagwandas suggested *Yugsandhi*. His son suggested, *Aj*. The word means 'today', and to Gupta it had the same connotation as *The Times*.

Paradkar was appointed editor and sent in May to confer with Tilak in Pune on how the paper should be conceived. When he returned, however, a new plan was drawn up to have a chief editor with some exposure to Europe and produce a paper using Reuters news, which would make it unnecessary for people to read an English paper. Babu Sriprakas was to be the chief editor. Paradkar wrote a resignation letter but was ultimately persuaded to accept the arrangement. There is an interesting exchange of letters at this point between all three on the subject of editorial non-interference and mutual respect. Sriprakas assures Paradkar that the situation is not of his making, and should there be any unintended offence on his part, Paradkar should not hesitate to take it up with him. Moreover, he was the journalist, not Sriprakas, and the latter would abide by his judgement. Gupta as the proprietor tells Paradkar that the chief editor has declined to take a salary much higher than Paradkar's, believing it to be not right.

There were three dummy editions produced, after which *Aj* was launched on 6 September 1920, shortly after the death of Tilak in August. It was initially an eight-page paper, and teething troubles led this to be reduced to six, but with the launch of the Civil Disobedience Movement the increased volume of news led to its becoming an eight-pager again. Paradkar did not adjust to the editorial arrangement. First he shifted to becoming a writer and columnist, then moved out of the paper. Sriprakas continued to plead with him to remain a part of *Aj*.

In 1924 when Sriprakas stepped down, Paradkar took charge of the paper and proceeded over the next 30 years to write some fine editorials that have been preserved, and to develop principles of whom journalism should be about, and to develop a language and craft for the profession. One version has it that he adapted the *New York Times* code of conduct for *Aj*.[4] He was a daily newspaper editor who was an exponent of the concept of *sahityik patrakarita*, where the language in which to practise the craft was still being evolved. The efforts which began in the 19th century to develop Hindi as a *rashtriya bhasha* (national language) were still being consolidated in the 20th. Paradkar used the pages of *Aj* to campaign for the cause. The paper has been described as the nursery of Hindi journalism. His biographer recalls sitting in on sessions where Paradkar would debate the fine points of grammar and usage. Which sentences could carry *ko* after a noun, and which could not (Vyas 1960: 48). His newspaper helped to further the debate on literary questions by reprinting in its pages articles and speeches by leading figures of the Hindi Sahitya Sammelan. *Aj* published many of Munshi Premchand's short stories, with Paradkar writing of the former's style that he had made Hindi literature accessible to the man in the street.

Paradkar and a subsequent editor, R.R. Khadilkar, developed the lexicon of Hindi journalism. Substitutes had to be found for many English words which were in currency. Paradkar cogitated over this and drew some of these from other Indian languages: more than 200 such words were incorporated into the evolving Hindi vocabulary. He came up, according to his biographer, with the term *Sri* to replace mister and the word *rashtrapati* for president. The bigger challenge was evolving a vocabulary for scientific terms and there was constant debate in the letters column of *Aj* over the newspaper's experimentation in this context. Should the translation for the word mine be *surang*, the paper's proprietor Shivprasad Gupta queried on one occasion, delineating the other connotations that the word *surang* has. Khadilkar also contributed scientific terms in Hindi. Then there were economic terms to be coined, like *mudrasmiti* for inflation. A trust called Gyan Mandal, set up by the same owners, financed both work on the vocabulary and on evolving Devanagari fonts. It had its own foundry to do this, and published books and a dictionary.[5]

Together with the discussions over language came the ideating over both the craft and the future of the profession. Several editorials written in *Aj* have been preserved, and the paper's very first editorial in 1920 sets the tone for agenda-setting journalism. Politics, it said, is not the only thing a nation in the making needs to debate. 'What educational, social, economic and religious policies should be pursued is a question begging to be answered.' It went on to say that debate on every aspect of the country's education policy would find space in the pages of the newspaper. It declared that social and religious reform in India could only be possible with independence. The editorial urged its readers to use the pages of *Aj* to debate social and religion-related issues.

In 1925 Paradkar presided over the first Editors' Conference at the 16th Hindi Sahitya Sammelan meeting in Brindavan, and in making the presidential speech foresaw the coming of commercialism to newspapers. Progress would from now on be through commercial means, he said. 'Now capitalists (invest) out of patriotism or indirect interest, later when success comes they will invest out of interest, and it will be a tough time for editors and for the independence of news' (Orsini 2002).

Qualitatively different from Paradkar's contribution to Hindi journalism was that of Ganesh Shankar Vidyarthi in Kanpur, the founder-editor of *Pratap*. Orsini describes him as broadening the Hindi public sphere in a popular direction with his own activism. In contrast to Paradkar's image as a literary scribe and erudite editor, Vidyarthi was a trade unionist, Congress worker and legislator who raised questions regarding peasants and labourers within the provincial Legislative Council. As mentioned earlier, Pratap was founded in 1913 as a weekly and later became a daily. Vidyarthi devised a colloquial language for his paper which reported on the agitations and demands of peasants and workers. His public and journalistic activism gave him enormous urban and rural influence. District surveyors would record *Pratap*'s influence on the political thinking of teachers. He played a literary role too, publishing a monthly journal *Prabha* which gave space to nationalist poetry, and publishing political literature and historical novels under the *Pratap* imprint. He was killed in 1930 during the Kanpur riots (Figure 2.4).[6]

Post-independence Expansion

Kanpur was also the birthplace of another publication with its roots in the freedom movement. Purnachand Gupta is described by his second son as a freedom fighter who developed a passion for the freedom movement as a young lad (Figure 2.5). He founded a group called Hindi Sampraday with his friends in 1926. They were initially supporters of revolutionaries, later of Mahatma Gandhi. Gupta joined the Congress to work for the independence movement. In 1937 he started a printing press in Kanpur with his brother. They printed leaflets for the movement as well took on job printing to earn their bread and butter. Jagdish Chandra Kulsia, who was then working with *Pratap*, was also a member of Hindi Sampraday. One fine morning, as Yogendra Mohan Gupta puts it, Kulsia suggested starting a

FIGURE 2.4   A stamp issued in 1962 to commomorate the role of Ganesh
Shankar Vidyarthi in the freedom struggle
Reprinted with permission from the Department of Post,
Government of India.

Hindi weekly to publish news of the movement. They started the
Swatantra (Free) weekly in 1939, with Kulsia as editor, and Gupta
as managing editor.[7]

Within a year the magazine attracted the unfavourable attention
of the British administration. The promoters decided to move it to
Jhansi, the centre of the British military, on the assumption that if
they indulged in such an activity under the very nose of the British
they might not notice. So they moved the press to Jhansi to a house

FIGURE 2.5   Purnachand Gupta, founder of *Dainik Jagran*
Courtesy of the *Dainik Jagran* Group.

on rent. In 1942 Purnachand felt confident enough to start a daily. He was travelling frequently to Bombay (now Mumbai), Madras (now Chennai) and Delhi in connection with his work in the freedom movement and also to get advertising for *Swatantra*. So *Dainik Jagran* began publishing as a daily from Jhansi. Shortly thereafter, Mahatma Gandhi gave a call for the swadeshi movement to stop publication of all papers. When the suspension was lifted, *Jagran* also resumed publication.

In 1946 Gupta thought he should start an edition from Lucknow, the capital of Yukth Pranth. So he selected a building, took it on rent, and despatched the machine to Lucknow. But Lucknow, unknown to him was about to get two more newspapers, for *National Herald* and *Pioneer* were starting their Hindi counterparts *Navjeevan* and *Swatantra Bharat*. *Aj* and *Pratap* were already available there. When he was informed of this by a friend, he took an almost instant decision to head to Kanpur instead. As his son Yogendra Mohan tells it, the truck was diverted to Kanpur, premises hired and *Jagran* started from Kanpur on 21 September 1947.[8]

Shortly after independence Gupta left the Congress party, disillusioned with the jostling within it and with the refusal of Congressmen to heed Mahatma Gandhi's call to resign from the party. He decided to focus on developing *Dainik Jagran*. Its financing was initially a source of worry: he borrowed from the family. But he learned quickly that you could run a Hindi newspaper fairly inexpensively as far as editorial costs were concerned: political players, educationists and social workers were always hungry to get their writings published, so free contributors and news syndicates charging nominal amounts for articles provided material for the paper. He also got the idea of appointing reporters on a part-time basis during his constant visits to the metropolitan cities.

The paper learned early to make a pitch for advertising. In the 1956 edition of *The Indian Press Year Book* there is an advertisement by the *Daily Jagran*. 'For effective coverage in UP, Vindhya Pradesh and adjoining areas, depend on *The Daily Jagran*. Published simultaneously from three centers. Net paid Circulation exceeds 21,000 copies daily. "A must media for its area."' He was a man plugged into the national newspaper industry despite being Kanpur-based. He joined an industry vetting organisation like the Audit Bureau of Circulation and the publishers' club, the Indian and Eastern Newspaper Society (IENS) and got his newspaper registered with the Registrar of Newspapers of India. By 1960 he was an executive member of IENS.

Jagran's ideology as a somewhat right-wing newspaper wedded to the idea of Hindu nationalism was a reflection of the beliefs of its founder. Purnachand Gupta is described by his son as a staunch Hindu and Arya Samaji, influenced by vedic rituals. He differed with the Congress brand of secularism and supported the cause of the refugees from Pakistan, covering their plight to the annoyance of the ruling party.

This newspaper proprietor's beginnings had been far humbler than those of the founder of *Aj*. 'Shivprasad was born with a golden spoon in his mouth. Whereas my father was eight years old when his father died, he was almost an orphan.'[9] Brought up by his mother and brother, he would later induct his own six sons into the newspaper, starting with the ones who were old enough to help out while still at school. The name of the newspaper came from a chance remark made by *Purnachand*'s mother after an all-night brainstorming in Jhansi to find a name for the daily they were launching. 'Mother brought a tray of tea and said all night you did *jagran* [literally, kept awake] and have you decided anything? So they said, that is a good name.'

When the paper had reached the limits of the circulation that was available to tap in Kanpur and was making money, the sons urged their father to take the newspaper to other cities.

We went to Gorakhpur, as there was no newspaper in that belt, *Aj* was covering it from Benares. *Jagran* had to move out, it was cash rich and capital rich. Not because of *Aj* coming to Kanpur, we went to Gorakhpur before *Aj* came to Kanpur. Every three or four years we started an edition.[10]

Dainik Jagran went to Gorakhpur in 1975. The response was instant. *Aj* began an edition in Kanpur the same year. Both papers were later to go to Lucknow. *Jagran*'s expansion trajectory, which 30 years down the line would make it the country's highest circulated and read newspaper, had begun.

However, Vinod Shukla, the man who took *Aj* to Kanpur, and would later be taken on by *Jagran* to become their battering ram in Lucknow as they fought trade unions and competition, tells it a little differently. He visited Kanpur in 1974 to attend a marriage, was forced to read the *Dainik Jagran* for six days and found it a very poor paper. 'I thought there would be a *tehelka* [commotion] if *Aj* came here.' In December a printing machine that had been ordered by the owners of *Aj* arrived from Germany and in April 1975 *Aj* went to Kanpur, just two months before the imposition of the Emergency and press censorship, with a special supplement distributed with its inaugural issue that, according to Shukla, raised Rs 300,000 in advertising. He did not apply to the Registrar of Newspapers of India to register the edition, but submitted a statement to the district magistrate. When Indira Gandhi imposed the Emergency on 26 June 1975 *Aj* printed a supplement, proclaiming, 'Sab Narain Jail Mein' (All the Narains are in Jail). The reference was to Jayaprakash Narayan whose movement in Bihar was partly a trigger for the Emergency, and socialist politician Raj Narain. The proprietors of *Jagran* were jailed for leaving their editorial column blank in protest, as papers in other parts of the country also did. As Shukla tells it, the Emergency helped to created a demand for *Aj* in Kanpur which he established with the help of young hands recruited locally.

As others tell it there was more to establishing *Aj* in *Jagran*'s territory than daredevil Emergency-period journalism. There were battles to be fought. 'He [Shukla] actually fought the battle in the streets when *Aj* came to Kanpur. He entered the territory of *Jagran*. It was a free for all to establish *Aj* in Kanpur, fought with *lathis*, *golis* and *tamanchas*'[11] [sticks and small ammunition]. Shukla glosses over that aspect. The hawkers' commission was fiercely negotiated by the competing papers until they joined hands to beat down the hawkers.[12]

Post-Emergency, government policy changed to facilitate the growth of the print media, and newspaper publishing expanded as an industry and increased its dependence on advertising. Other developments too laid the basis for the broad-basing of Hindi journalism, for the consciously developed vehicle of nationalism to make the leap to a market-friendly mass medium. In the nearly three decades following the lifting of the Emergency[13] in 1977, India's newspaper industry has changed considerably in its character, and in its dynamics. The national media sphere has begun to be transformed, and regional newspapers including the Hindi press find themselves in the vanguard of a rapidly changing industry.

It is unlikely that the founders of the *Dainik Jagran* would ever have thought of the market value of their newspapers. Yet by 2006 the quest for expansion by this group was taking it to the stock market and inviting public shareholding, thus making it the first Hindi newspaper to be listed.

Language

The language used by Hindi newspapers has followed a fascinating trajectory. At the beginning of the 20th century Hindi was the vehicle for nationalism. It was being moulded, partly in newspaper offices and partly in *sahitya sabha*s (literary congresses), as a language for daily news as well as literary use. Post-independence, however, it suffered a serious bout of Sanskritisation, partly following the labours of the Raghuvira Committee, set up to introduce the use of Hindi in parliamentary affairs. Hindi became Hindu-ised and Hindustani

> which emerged as a conscious decision towards openness with no fanatical commitment to rigidity in the use of expression, became a victim of both the separatist tendencies in the linguistic engineering of language patterns and the notion of a single national language during the freedom movement.[14]

It became a victim of partition. Alok Rai, the author of *Hindi Nationalism* writes that over a period of time, 'the discursive space of the people's vernacular Hindi . . . was progressively usurped by Sanskrit Hindi' (2000: 108). What remained common in this transformation is only the continuity in the name. The internal linguistic forms underwent radical change. 'Sanskritised Hindi came into existence.'[15]

One manifestation of this was the disinclination to use the dot (or *bindi*) which coverted a 'j' into a 'z'. In 1930 Madan Mohan Malaviya in his weekly nationalist newspaper—*Abhyudaya*—wrote an editorial called *Hindi Mein Bindi Kyon*, arguing why the bindi ought to be used in Hindi. But increasingly, newspapers made their own choice of language. In their comparison of the Hindi used by *Punjab Kesari* and that used by *Dainik Jagran*, Robin Jeffrey, Peter Friedlander and Sanjay Seth have analysed how the need to respond to readers accounted for the variation between the two. The Punjab-based newspaper used Hindi which had features characteristic of Punjabi Hindi, which included the use of the dot under 'j' to connote the 'z' sound, which was equated with Urdu. *Jagran* on the other hand never used the dot, and the Devanagari font it used in its Internet edition did not have the dot. 'This means it is not possible to represent sounds in Urdu loan-words correctly' (Jeffrey 2001). According to Jeffrey (2001) the matter of dots represented 'a profound, even ag-gressive, political statement' by Hindi purists.

> To eliminate the dots implies a devaluation of the contribution of the Persian/Arabic lexicon to language in north India. Thus in the most subtle ways—e.g., abandoning a single written signal (a dot!)—newspapers, and their proprietors' values, in-filtrate and influence the daily practices of millions.

While the authors concluded that to omit such a character would have been a conscious decision made for ideological not technical reasons, this theory is somewhat discounted in newsrooms in Bihar and Lucknow. Editors and sub-editors would say that it had more to do with Hindi keyboards for computers which did not have a key for a 'j' with a dot under it, and trying to create the 'z' in Hindi on the keyboard was simply too much trouble. This was a mundane explanation, far removed from the heavy intellectualising over the use or omission of the dot. Perhaps the truth lay somewhere in be-tween: had enough newspapers wanted to use words with Urdu sounds in them, keyboard makers might have responded to the demand. Alok Rai contends that whereas this issue would earlier have been one of Hinduising Hindi words, an ideological stand per-haps on the part of newspapers like *Jagran*, the attitude to 'j' and 'z' today was likely to be more a matter of ignorance than ideology.[16]

A shift in the use of Hindi came with the Jayaprakash Narayan (JP) movement originating in Bihar in 1974. A lot of colloquial words came into the language at this point, possibly for political reasons. Shekhar Tripathi of *Hindustan* in Varanasi cited the example of the word *lamband,* meaning collective approach, which came out of the movement. According to him, the JP *andolan* (movement) accom-modated everybody from Samajwadi and Sarvodayi to the Rashtriya Swayamsevak Sangh at one point. Between 1977 and 1982 the first distortions came about in the formal Hindi used until then.[17] Rai suggests that the journalists emerging out of this movement would have adopted colloquial Hindi to distance themselves from the Brahminised Hindi of the Hindi *walas* (Hindi purists). 'The JP movement may have given confidence to a whole class of people that Hindi could be different.'[18] Surendra Pratap Singh, one of the prominent journalists to make his name at this time, would later pioneer on television a spoken Hindi so colloquial as to be the antithesis of what was used on Doordarshan, the official broadcaster.

With the launch of *Jansatta* in 1982 there were more changes in the language of journalism. Phrases such as *do phard* were coined to describe the splitting of a political party. Prabhash Joshi, the founder editor of *Jansatta*, brought Marathi words into Hindi. *Jansatta* brought a racy vitality into the language of journalism. It coined Hindi terms for cricket such as *golandaz*, *phalandaz* and *gaindbaz*.

Localisation's singular contribution has been to incorporate dialects into the language of district editions, mostly with the intention of endearing the publication to the local people, and making them think that it spoke their language. In Bhagalpur in 2003 a new resident editor introduced a satirical column on Angika, a dialect spoken by 15 million people. An All India Radio man was found to write it. However, in Patna the resident editor would observe dryly that the incorporation of dialects into local newspapers in Bihar was leading to a decline in grammar. Also in Bihar, *Prabhat Khabar* experimented with running columns in Maithili. In Banswara in Rajasthan the resident editor of *Dainik Bhaskar* was giving headlines in Wagri.

But the most noticeable change that came over Hindi newspapers in the post-liberalisation era was the extensive use of English. It was an apt concomitant of the cosmopolitan images which came flooding into a press eager to globalise. Babulal Sharma, the resident editor in Bhopal for *Dainik Bhaskar* who later became state editor in Chandigarh, declared, 'Our Hindi is no longer the Hindi of pandits. It has become modern.' If English words were common in Hindi newspapers, it was because these were words in common use. The paper's proprietor Ramesh Chandra Agarwal pointed out that even rickshawallas used English words these days. '*Aadmi shahar nahin bolta, city bolta*. We use *bolne wala* [spoken] language. *Dipti* [for deputy] commissioner, the rickshawalla in Punjab will say, or DC.

Not *zilla adhyaksh*. We are trying to use *bol chaal ka bhasha*' [the language of everyday use].[19] To Mrinal Pande, the editor of *Hindustan*, it was a manifestation of linguistic walls breaking down.[20]

Conclusion

Though today it has the status of a national language Hindi itself is a relatively recent construct, almost consciously developed as a vehicle for nationalist sentiment in the 19th and 20th centuries. Hindi journalism is less than 200 years old, since the first known publication of a journal in Hindi was in 1826. Those who wrote in it strove to develop a political vocabulary, and a language that communicated with a wider audience than those acquainted with Persian or Urdu. The primary development of the genre was in Bengal, while in the provinces Hindi journalism evolved as an appendage to Urdu journalism. But in both places experiments in simultaneous publishing in three or four languages took place.

Newspapers such as *Aj* (1920) and *Pratap* epitomised a significant shift in the first quarter of the 20th century. The Hindi political press made the transition from being journals of ideas to journals of news, catering increasingly to a wider public, and widening the Hindi public sphere in the process. There was some articulation at this stage of how the Hindi readership was different from the English one and this contained the germ of the commercial strategy that the fast-expanding Hindi press would implement by the end of the 20th century: that the common reader wanted, above all, a reflection of his life and problems in the newspaper. *Dainik Jagran*, founded in the early 1940s began expanding to other parts of Uttar Pradesh even before independence, and had learned to make a pitch for advertising by the mid-1950s. Along with *Hindustan* founded in the 1930s it is the only pre-independence Hindi newspaper to remain a major print media player today.

The language of Hindi journalism has evolved from the early 20th century to the present. At the beginning of the 20th century Hindi was the vehicle for nationalism. It was being moulded, partly in newspaper offices and partly in *sahitya sabha*s as a language for daily news as well as literary use. Paradkar and a subsequent editor

R.R. Khadilkar developed the lexicon of Hindi journalism. Post-independence, however, Hindi journalism suffered a serious bout of Sanskritisation, partly following the labours of the Raghuvira Committee, set up to introduce the use of Hindi in parliamentary affairs. One manifestation of this was the disinclination to use the dot which coverted a 'j' into a 'z'. Later, in the 1970s, the Hindi used by newspapers was influenced by the Jayaprakash Narayan movement, with an induction of colloquial words.

Localisation's singular contribution has been to incorporate dialects into the language of district editions, mostly with the intention of endearing the publication to the local people, and making them think that it spoke their language. And commercialisation's contribution has been to swamp Hindi newspapers with English words.

Notes

1. Rakesh Sharma, editor-proprietor *Rashtradoot,* interviewed by author, Jaipur, 17 September 2005.
2. Shardul Vikram Gupta, interviewed by author, Varanasi, 16 March 2005.
3. Lakshmi Shankar Vyas, 'Pararkarji aur Patrkarita,' Bharatiya Gyanpeeth, Kashi, 1960.
4. Vinod Shukla, resident editor, *Jagran,* interviewed by author, Lucknow, 25, 29, 30 August 2005.
5. Ibid.
6. This paragraph on Vidyarthi is drawn from Orsini's description of his contribution to Hindi political journalism. She in turns draws on Bhargava's Ganesh Shankar Vidyarthi, pp. 93–96, and Renuka Khosla's *Urban Politics (with Special Reference to Kanpur),* New Delhi, S. Chand & Co., 1992
7. Yogendra Mohan Gupta, interviewed by author, Kanpur, 26 August 2005.
8. Ibid.
9. Ibid.
10. Mahendra Mohan Gupta and Sanjay Gupta, interviewed by author, Delhi, 2 September 2005.
11. Naveen Joshi, resident editor, *Hindustan,* interviewed by author, Lucknow, 1 June 2005.
12. Shukla, Resident Editor, *Jagran,* interviewed by author, Lucknow, 25, 29, 30 August 2005.

13. Imposed by Prime Minister Indira Gandhi in June 1975, following her unseating by a court.
14. Language in India, http://www.languageinindia.com/march2003/hindustani.html.
15. Ibid.
16. Alok Rai, interviewed by author, New Delhi, 28 January 2006.
17. Shashank Shekhar Tripathi, interviewed by author, Varanasi, 15 March 2006.
18. Alok Rai, interviewed by author, New Delhi, 28 January 2006.
19. Ramesh Agarwal, interviewed by author, Mumbai, 27 January 2005.
20. Mrinal Pande, interviewed by author, 24 June 2006.

3

A Rural Newspaper Revolution

'I can read, but my paper does not talk to me.'

In 1982, the Second Press Commission complained, in its majority report, about the urban bias of the newspaper industry. But it incorporated a dissenting note in which three members of the commission wrote, 'The fact of the matter is that papers are not being read in the villages because of illiteracy, lack of purchasing power and lack of communications.' Whenever this situation changed, they added, newspapers would blossom in the rural hinterland without any prodding from the government of the day. In other words, the market would be there to tap the rural readership (*Report of the Second Press Commission* 1982: 224).

And indeed, that is what has transpired. Northern India's local newspaper revolution which began to flower across the Hindi-speaking states from the mid-1980s, was catalysed by a number of factors, but the most important were three. Literacy expanded, purchasing power increased and better communications made it possible to print newspapers from a number of small towns and deliver them to semi-urban and rural areas in the morning. Underlying these were two other important factors: a more politically aware rural population in the Hindi belt which had a hunger for news, as well as an increase in aspiration levels and consumerism as the rural market began to be strategically targeted by consumer goods marketing firms.

While citing the same three reasons as necessary for the expansion of newspapers Robin Jeffrey in his countrywide study of India's newspaper revolution offers the hypothesis that in making people into newspaper readers 'literacy and political participation precede raw purchasing power and advanced printing technology'. The fastest growth rates in newspaper circulation, he says, were in states which showed the strongest growth rates of literacy, not of per capita economic growth. These were Orissa, Uttar Pradesh, Andhra Pradesh and Karnataka.

Then again he cites Kerala's experience to show that political involvement is also crucial to improving newspaper penetration. In India's most literate state newspaper penetration of Malayalam was more than 85 dailies to a 1,000 people by 1996, twice the all-India ratio, even though Kerala's per capita income stayed below the national average. Its politics meanwhile remained fiercely competitive with governments changing in all but one of 11 elections between 1957 and 1996 (Jeffrey 2000: 32).

The readership surveys were reflecting the increased rural penetration of the print media, particularly in the Hindi belt. Between the NRS (National Readership Survey) rounds of 2002 and 2005, the overall readership of language publications rose, especially in rural markets. NRS 2005 showed that the rural markets of Bihar, Jharkhand and Uttar Pradesh had achieved 'tremendous growth' in their readership of language publications. The number of readers in Bihar and Jharkhand (combined), and Uttar Pradesh increased by 8.4 million each. In Madhya Pradesh and Chhattisgarh (combined), the number increased by 5.4 million readers in these three years, while in West Bengal, Orissa and Assam, the numbers had grown by 3.7 million, 3 million and 1.7 million respectively[1] (Table 3.1).

TABLE 3.1   Increase in rural readership between NRS 2002 and NRS 2005

(in millions)

State	Increase
West Bengal	3.7
Orissa	3.0
Assam	1.7
Bihar and Jharkhand	8.4
Uttar Pradesh	8.4
Madhya Pradesh and Chhattisgarh	5.4

Source: National Readership Survey (NRS) 2002, 2005.

Given that politics in all these states was becoming more broad-based on account of the rise in political parties representing backward castes and Dalits and on account of the spread of local self-governance in villages and towns, Jeffrey's hypothesis could also hold for the northern part of the country. But as this chapter will argue, rise in rural incomes and consumer aspirations was also catalytic. Overall readership figures in 2005 were showing that there almost as many readers in rural as in urban India.

If one were to divide the population of a state by the combined daily newspaper circulation for the same state, a per copy picture emerges which is one indication of newspaper penetration. However the findings below are only indicative because of the non-foolproof method adopted by the Registrar of Newspapers in India (RNI) in gauging total daily circulation in a given state. It bases its circulation statistics on statements returned by publishers. The number of statements submitted is far fewer than the total number of publications registered in a particular state and the RNI does not check the accuracy of statements filed. Still, assuming that the level of inaccuracy does not change over time, the trends are clear enough to allow firm conclusions.

In *India's Newspaper Revolution*, Robin Jeffrey used the available statistics, including those from RNI, to postulate that between 1976 and 1996 the number of people clustered around each copy of a newspaper declined from one newspaper for 80 people to one newspaper for just over 20 people. I have attempted a similar exercise with RNI numbers for some of the Hindi-speaking states. It shows that between 1997 and 2002 the number of readers per copy across this region declined. In Bihar in 1997 there were 45 people per copy of a daily newspaper. By 2002 the figure for the divided state was 32 readers per copy in Bihar, and 30 in Jharkhand (figures have been rounded off). In Uttar Pradesh in 1997 there were 22 readers per copy, which came down in the divided state to 16 readers per copy in UP and 8.4 per copy in Uttaranchal. The latter was the Hindi-speaking state which recorded 72.28 per cent literacy in the 2001 Census.

Rajasthan's 20 readers per copy in 1997 declined to 12 by 2002. Himachal Pradesh had high literacy (77.13 per cent) but few newspapers, as a result of which there were 125 readers per copy in 1997, which declined to 66 persons per copy in 2001. Madhya Pradesh (MP) in 1997 had 21 readers per newspaper; this declined in the divided state to 13 in MP in 2002 and 16 per copy in Chhattisgarh (Table 3.2). Readership per copy decreases as circulation increases.

TABLE 3.2   Readers per copy

State	1997	2002	
Bihar	45	32	(Bihar)
		30	(Jharkhand)
Uttar Pradesh	22	16	(UP)
		8.4	(Uttaranchal)
Rajasthan	20	12	
Himachal Pradesh	125	66	
Madhya Pradesh	21	13	(MP)
		16	(Chhattisgarh)

Source: Based on *Census of India* 1991 and 2001, and annual reports of RNI, 1999 and 2004.
Note: Population divided by total circulation according to RNI.

Literacy, which spread in this part of the country later than it did in the southern states, recorded a dramatic increase as reflected in the 2001 Census. In four states of the Hindi heartland—Bihar, Madhya Pradesh, Rajasthan and Uttar Pradesh—literacy had remained between 37 and 45 per cent as reflected by the 1991 Census. As the other socio-econonic statistics were equally unflattering, these states were given the derisive acronym of Bimaru, which means ailing. But the 2001 Census showed that the growth in literacy was now faster in each of these states and the new states carved out of them (except Bihar and Jharkhand), than in India as a whole (Table 3.3). The numbers tell the story but so does the heartwarming scene any early morning visitor to the rural Hindi belt will encounter: endless groups of children going to school, a cloth or gunny bag slung on their backs, many of them barefoot. As a block functionary in Banda district in UP said with quiet satisfaction, 'Aaj ki peedi bilkul sakshar hoga' (The current generation will be totally literate).[2]

Kerala in the south, long eulogised for its impressive literacy numbers, was suddenly paling in comparison with Uttar Pradesh which, in absolute numbers, now had three times as many literates as Kerala. What's more, Kerala's 25.6 million literates were 80 per cent of its population, whereas UP's 77.7 million literates spelt only 47 per cent of its population, so there was an even bigger potential audience waiting to be tapped. Rajasthan, which recorded a decadal increase in literacy of 22.45 percentage points, against an all-India

TABLE 3.3 Change in literacy rate, 1991–2001

State	Literacy rate (2001 Census) (in %)			Literacy rate (1991 Census) (in %)	Change in literacy rate (1991–2001) (in %)
	Person	Male	Female		
INDIA 1	65.38	75.96	54.28	51.63	13.75
Andaman & Nicobar Islands	81.18	86.07	75.29	73.02	8.17
Andhra Pradesh	61.11	70.85	51.17	44.09	17.02
Arunachal Pradesh	54.74	64.07	44.24	41.59	13.15
Assam	64.28	71.93	56.03	52.89	11.52
Bihar	47.53	60.32	33.57	37.49	10.04
Chandigargh	81.76	85.65	76.65	77.81	3.94
Chhattisgarh	65.18	77.86	52.40	42.91	22.27
Dadra & Nagar Haveli	60.03	73.32	42.99	40.71	19.33
Daman & Diu	81.09	88.40	70.37	71.20	9.89
Delhi	81.82	87.37	75.00	75.29	6.53
Delhi	82.32	88.88	75.51	75.51	6.81
Goa	69.97	80.50	58.60	61.29	8.68
Gujarat	68.59	79.25	56.31	55.85	12.74
Haryana	77.13	86.02	68.08	63.86	13.27
Himachal Pradesh	54.46	65.75	41.82	NA	NA
Jammu & Kashmir	54.13	67.94	39.38	41.39	12.74
Jharkhand	67.04	76.29	57.45	56.04	11.00
Karnataka	90.92	94.20	87.86	89.81	1.11

(Table 3.3 continued)

(Table 3.3 continued)

State	Literacy rate (2001 Census) (in %)			Literacy rate (1991 Census) (in %)	Change in literacy rate (1991–2001) (in %)
	Person	Male	Female		
Lakshadweep	87.52	93.15	81.56	81.78	5.74
Madhya Pradesh	64.11	76.80	50.28	44.67	19.41
Maharashtra	77.27	86.27	67.51	64.87	12.39
Manipur	68.87	77.87	59.70	59.89	8.97
Meghalaya	63.31	66.14	60.41	49.10	14.21
Mizoram	88.49	90.69	86.13	82.27	6.22
Nagaland	67.11	71.77	61.92	61.65	5.45
Orissa	63.61	75.95	50.97	49.09	14.52
Pondicherry	81.49	88.89	74.13	74.74	6.74
Punjab	69.95	75.63	63.55	58.51	11.45
Rajasthan	61.03	76.46	44.34	38.55	22.48
Sikkim	69.68	76.73	61.46	56.94	12.61
Tamil Nadu	73.47	82.33	64.55	62.66	10.81
Tripura	73.66	81.47	65.41	60.44	13.22
Uttar Pradesh	57.36	70.23	42.98	40.71	16.65
Uttaranchal	72.28	84.01	60.26	57.75	14.53
West Bengal	69.22	77.58	60.22	57.70	11.52

Source: 'Provisional Population Totals: India', *Census of India*, 2001, Paper 1 of 2001.

increase of 13.17 percentage points, also saw dramatic changes in readership figures after the mid-1990s and very rapid expansion and localisation by *Dainik Bhaskar* and *Rajasthan Patrika*. Female literacy in the state doubled during 1991–2001—from 20.44 per cent to 44.34 per cent.[3]

Between 1991 and 2001 Madhya Pradesh recorded a 19.41 percentage rise in literacy as Table 3.3 shows. The state's *Third Human Development Report* recorded proudly that 'more than one person out of six persons removed from the category of non-literates in India in the decade of the 1990s is from Madhya Pradesh.' This one state alone, taken together with Chhattisgarh, accounted for 17.9 per cent of the total decadal decrease in illiteracy in India in the 1990s. As for female literacy, the report said, almost one out of every five women removed from the category of literates in India was from Madhya Pradesh (*Third Human Development Report* 2002: 35).

Rural literacy in undivided Bihar grew from 27.7 per cent in 1981 to 33.83 per cent in 1991 and then to 44.42 per cent in divided Bihar in 2001. Total literacy grew from 32.05 per cent in Bihar in 1981 to 38.48 per cent in 1991 (*National Human Development Report* 2002: 87). Between the 1991 and 2001 Censuses Bihar recorded a 10.4 per cent rise in overall literacy, and the part of the state which became Jharkhand in 2000 recorded a 12.74 per cent increase (see Table 3.3). The growth over the last decade in this region was therefore rapid. The very states that had even in the early 1990s ranked lowest in national development indices on account of low literacy, high population growth and low industrialisation, were slowly acquiring a readership potential which made them desirable markets for manufacturers and media houses alike.

But literacy is only the first requirement for creating a newspaper reader. It has to be supported by much else. By education that goes beyond literacy, by politicisation in its broadest sense which creates a hunger for news, by a desire to read what the newspaper is offering, by the capacity to buy a daily newspaper at a price higher than urban readers (who were beneficiaries of price wars) were paying, and by the ability of publishers to reach a freshly minted newspaper to a rural clientele at the start of the day. All of this was beginning to converge in the 1990s.

Literacy and Readership

Literacy movements in different parts of the Hindi belt have generated their own understanding of the link between literacy and newspaper reading. In Chhattisgarh, two different social action agencies use newspapers in their literacy centres and offer different surmises of what these do for new literates. To Rajendra Sail of the Indian National Social Action Forum, literacy has to be qualitative in order to enable a person to read. While there are three stages to literacy, moving from recognition of letters to making sentences, and then to reading and writing, the literacy campaign has not gone beyond the recognition of letters.

> The person who really learns to read and write through literacy campaigns, such a person wants to read newspapers. But a new literate cannot read a newspaper. To my knowledge, in the 75 villages that I have visited in Mahasamund zilla (district), literacy means knowing how to write your name. If you say to them read this, they cannot.[4]

Yet the literacy centres that his organisation runs have explored the usefulness of newspapers in imparting literacy. They benefit from newspaper localisation because political, social and women-related news gets documented. These items are read out at their *baithaks* (group sit-ins) and analysed for the benefit of those who cannot really read yet. This helps to trigger the social awareness that creates the desire to read. Others at the Bharat Gyan Vigyan Samiti, which has been working on literacy in Madhya Pradesh and Chhattisgarh since 1990, make the same point: literacy has given rise to the desire to read papers. And they differ with Sail in asserting that literacy campaigns have in fact given people the capacity to read and write, not just sign their names.[5]

How much of the increase in the circulation of newspapers is on account of increasing literacy remains a conjecture in the absence of hard research data that bears out the connection. First, there is the question of how much of an increase in the literacy rate recorded by the census data is on account of primary education, and how much because of adult education. Primary school-going children are unlikely to govern the decision to become a newspaper-subscribing

household; nor is a child in Grade 1, treated as literate for the purpose of census data, likely to be able to read newspapers. Then there
is the question of how accurate the census is when enumerators base
their estimate on information given by the head of a household. without conducting any tests to ascertain literacy.[6] However, in the case
of Rajasthan and Madhya Pradesh, whose literacy rates increased
by 22.48 per cent and 19.41 percentage points respectively between
1991 and 2001, the increase has been linked to the likely success of
specific programmes.

In Rajasthan, there have been some noteworthy initiatives
in education during the late eighties and nineties such as Lok
Jumbish and Shiksha Karmi projects, which have apparently
made visible impact. In Madhya Pradesh also, the Education
Guarantee Scheme, the District Primary Education Programme
and programmes like Mahila Samakhaya have apparently made
some impact.[7]

If this surmise is correct, exposure to literacy may have resulted in a
genuine ability to read, but it does not establish the relationship with
other relevant factors.

Opinions on the relationship between circulation and literacy
vary even within the newspaper establishment. In Delhi, Om Thanvi,
the editor of *Jansatta* which is read across the Hindi belt, says of
the rural newspaper revolution that literacy may have been one
reason for the growth in circulation, but it was not the major reason.
People had begun to purchase newspapers because they were now
more aware, politically, socially and had more purchasing power.[8]
In Chhattisgarh, *Nava Bharat* and *Deshbandhu* had diametrically opposing views on this. The resident editor of the former in Raipur was
categorical that newspapers do not grow because of literacy, and
that a slightly educated person can never read a newspaper. 'I have
never heard or seen such an assertion that because of literacy a newspaper's circulation increases. *Nava Bharat* is the oldest newspaper
and has its own credibility. This is the reason for the expansion of
its circulation.' His circulation manager Ramesh Tiwari would assert
that their circulation agents knew the field, and their experience
did not bear out this assertion. 'We target the educated segment for

our circulation, both rural and urban. Becoming literate means being able to sign your name, that does not give you the ability to read a newspaper.'[9]

But *Deshbandhu* in Raipur sees itself as a newspaper with a development mission and its attitude to the question of literacy and newspaper expansion is different. For its editor, Lalit Surjan, the literacy movement in the region has definitely been a factor in increasing circulation.[10] For his circulation manager too, adult literacy and newspaper circulation have a direct linkage.[11] As also for the circulation manager of *Dainik Bhaskar* in Raipur:

> The two are interlinked. In Rajasthan, literacy kendras are sent newspapers by the government. The Kendra pays for the paper. But in Chhattisgarh this does not happen yet. If newspapers approach the literacy centres, circulation goes up. Readership increases because of literacy and a newspaper's approach.[12]

In Madhya Pradesh, however, the *Deshbandhu* circulation manager did not concur with his Raipur counterpart. He took a dim view of the well-publicised literacy efforts that had been made by Digvijay Singh's government (1993–2003) in the state. He thought migration rather than an increase in the numbers of literate people had caused the increase in his newspaper's circulation. People came to work in Bhopal from all over Madhya Pradesh, as well as from the bordering states of Maharashtra and Uttar Pradesh, and were desperate for news from their native areas. Those who were from UP took *Jagran* in Madhya Pradesh, and those who were from Maharashtra were catered to by *Nava Bharat* which covered both states.[13]

For newspaper reading to take root in a society requires not just literacy but the desire to read a newspaper based on felt need. Both the proprietor of a publishing empire and a school teacher in an Adivasi village understood this and explained it equally succinctly. The Agarwals of *Dainik Bhaskar* are fond of stressing this to explain why they lay so much store by reader feedback. As Girish Agarwal of *Bhaskar* puts it:

> There are three filters. One is literacy, the second is who can read. And the third is, who is reading. The housewife is happy in her own world, she is not interested in what the paper has

to offer. In Bombay city, out of a population of 13.4 million, 5.8 million can read English, but 2 million are reading. Literacy is not a factor. I can read, but my paper does not talk to me.[14]

And for a paper to talk to a potential reader, he was quite certain, it should talk about what is of greatest relevance to the reader, namely local news.

Far away in his Jharkhand village, the school teacher Mohammad Manjoor Alam would emphasize that news about Adivasi traditions and culture does not appear in the newspaper; if they did, people would be able to relate to newspapers much more.[15] A voluntary agency worker in the same village, Sindho, thought that 'if the name of our village appears even once in a month, people will start taking interest in the newspaper'. And when Mangal Soren, an educated youth there, asserted that if they start publishing potato, onion and garlic rates in newspapers every farmer would be interested in reading them, he was underscoring Agarwal's point about local relevance.

Political Participation

But there is more to the spread of newspaper reading than just local curiosity and local relevance. In many parts of the Hindi belt, literacy and a growing political awareness have gone hand in hand. A hunger for news has been nurtured by the increased inroads television has made into the rural areas. It has brought 'breaking news' to the rural interior. But deepening democracy and political participation have also fed this hunger. The revitalisation of panchayati raj (local self-government), which began in Madhya Pradesh after the 73rd/74th Constitution Amendments, dates back to 1994. When Madhya Pradesh became the first state to hold panchayat elections after the 73rd Amendment, the sheer scale of participation in it indicates the extent of political activity that must have preceded it. Nearly half a million people's representatives were chosen in that election, including fair numbers of scheduled caste and scheduled tribe candidates, women, and Backward Class candidates (Mathew 1999). By 2005, panchayat-level political activity was more than a decade old.

Since Chhattisgarh was carved out of Madhya Pradesh only in 2000, it began life with the legacy of a rejuvenated panchayat system.

In both these states, as also in other parts of the Hindi belt, panchayats and panchayat-level politics have played a discernable role in the penetration of newspapers into villages. The first reason was the state government policy of picking up the tab for subscriptions to newspapers. This was also true of Madhya Pradesh, as the circulation manager of *Nava Bharat* confirmed.[16] Many development workers report that this is often the only copy that reaches villages that do not have a social elite with the purchasing capacity to buy a newspaper. People read the newspaper that comes to the panchayat office, and their acquaintance with newspaper reading grows (unless, of course, unpaid bills prompt the local circulation agent to stop delivering the paper—as happened in Kothda block in Rajasthan).

As panchayat politics began to strike root and newspapers became available, panchayat leaders began to subscribe to them at home. Hindi-speaking India now had a rural middle class which was both aspirational and politicially aware. Panchayat elections increasingly reflected political party affiliations, which meant party mobilisation was now going down to the village level. Together with the greater spread of education, this led to a market for news, a demand for political and administrative accountability, and for media which feeds upward mobility. Even the weaker sections in a village, while being oppressed, were developing their political consciousness and seeking more information relevant to their needs.

If in a Naxal-dominated area like Dantewada in Chhattisgarh people are reading *Jansatta* and *Deshbandhu,* it has to do with all of the above. Advertising from panchayats is increasing, and *sarpanch*es want their pictures used in the newspaper! Political workers now subscribe to newspapers, since they are delivered in the morning. Lalit Surjan makes the point that the panchayati-raj system has seen the emergence of 1,200 panchayats in Chhattisgarh. Newspapers are now going to these panchayats.[17]

Jeevrakhan Lal Banjari, *sachiv* (secretary) of a gram panchayat, lives in village Khaira in the Mahasamund division in Chhattisgarh. He has begun to take a newspaper at his home because the panchayat's work has made reading newspapers a necessity. The village is 1 km away from a *pucca* (paved) road. *Deshbandhu* carries news from this village sometimes so he subscribes to it and his copy is read by 10–20 people every day.[18]

In Madhya Pradesh too, village-level social activists have been reporting that local news, especially news about block politics, panchayat politics and panchayat leaders, is being read avidly.

There has been an increase in readership in the interior areas of the state. In comparison to what it was two years ago, now every panchayat or the teacher in the village has a newspaper coming to them. Many a time, they share their newspapers. This leads to dialogue. Not just information sharing but discussions, leading to debate![19]

In Hoshangabad the secretary of the Gramin Sevak Committee thinks that there has been a visible increase in the number of newspapers reaching rural areas, that they give the most space to politics, and that they have served to increase the advantage that the upper classes who can read them and afford them have.

From the newspapers, the politically empowered people are keen to know what the political trends are, which leader is doing well for himself, who is not doing well for himself, etc. They read the news and make their decisions. While they may read crime news, nearly 50 to 60 per cent of them take the paper to read about politics.[20]

This entire process was catalysed by the emergence of political formations in these states representing the Dalits and Backward Classes from the late 1980s onwards. This will be dealt with later in this book. Apart from democratic decentralisation, the regionalisation of politics in the post-Congress scenario in states such as Uttar Pradesh and Bihar has created a politics based on social cleavages of region, religion and caste. Both Hasan (1998) and Yadav (2004) point out how the states became the primary arena of political contestation. Within the states there was a democratic upsurge, with electoral politics witnessing

... higher participation and more intense politicisation of the hitherto marginalised groups, first OBCs and dalits and then women and adivasis. Then, around 1990, there was the 'sudden arrival of three "M"s (Mandal, Mandir and Market) on the centrestage of Indian politics [which] changed the political idiom and the nature of ideological contestation' (Yadav 2004).

All of this must certainly have contributed to a greater hunger for news.

Communications and Printing

By the turn of the 21st century, the communications infrastructure in states like Bihar, Madhya Pradesh, Uttar Pradesh, Rajasthan and Haryana was making the morning delivery of newspapers to villages a viable proposition. With the improvement of road and rail links, the paper was reaching on time.

> Earlier, we had to rely on the sole government bus going to remote places in the state. Over the last eight years, we are now in a position to ensure that the paper is in Jhabua at 6 A.M. because of the increased use of taxis.[21]

The circulation manager of *Deshbandhu* in Bhopal was underscoring the fact that earlier there was only one bus and if they missed it, the edition never reached people. 'Today we have several options, we can send the paper by road, bus or by train. Alternatively, voluntary agencies subscribe to the paper by post. For instance, Eklavya takes the paper in as remote an area as Khategoan in Dewas district.'[22]

Meanwhile, improved telecommunication links meant that facsimilie transmission was facilitating the gathering of very local news for separate district pages. Fax and modem centres were sprouting in Bihar, Madhya Pradesh, Rajasthan and Uttar Pradesh, and in Jharkhand, Chhattisgarh and Uttaranchal which had been hived off from them in 2000. The blossoming of better telecommunications meant that even in small regional newspapers, modem transfers on high speed lines became the norm once computerisation came in and telecom cables began to be laid. Computers also did away with the need for subeditors at many locations, and the need to typeset at each edition. Some proprietors were more inclined to attribute the local newspaper revolution to this than to increased literacy. 'What has made localisation possible is better communications. We can give the latest newspaper in each and every place in two hours maximum,' Sanjay Gupta of *Dainik Jagran* would say in 2005. His paper at that point had the highest readership in the country.[23]

In addition to the spread of communication links, there was a sprouting of print sites across India, not just in the Hindi belt, because of other reasons. After the Emergency of 1975–77, foreign exchange controls and restrictions on the import of newsprint eased.* The Emergency with its 21 months of press censorship had created a hunger for news; when it ended and the Janata Government came in, a process of easing controls began which became marked in the early 1980s after Indira Gandhi returned to power. The import of printing equipment and technology increased. Jeffrey notes that whereas a 1974 survey of more than 200 daily newspapers located only six web-offset presses in India, by 1985 there were a thousand (Jeffrey 2000: 40). At the same time printing machines began to be manufactured in India, lowering costs.

Overall, therefore, the cost of getting a new print site going, and launching a new edition, came down. Running costs dropped, the cost of communications collapsed. It became economical to go into smaller towns and give people a newspaper at their doorstep at dawn as the rise in literacy opened up the market. The big newspapers still import expensive high-speed machines for colour printing, but the increased advertising support as well as high valuations of newspaper stocks have made such investments viable.

An Emerging Rural Middle Class

Other changes have shaped a growing market for newspapers. Somewhere along the way rural India ceased to be an economic backwater

*Imposed by Prime Minister Indira Gandhi in June 1975 and lifted in February 1977.

and began to display a consumer potential that had many chroniclers. Cropping patterns were changing, increasing purchasing power and thus making daily newspapers affordable. Farmers were switching from food crops to cash crops, and increased irrigation in some areas also led to increased family incomes. Whether it was the Tawa Dam reservoir in Madhya Pradesh or the Mahi Dam in southern Rajasthan, irrigation had meant increased incomes for farmers in their catchments.

The service sector in the rural areas was growing too. As the chief managing director of a leading rural marketing company put it, rural India was not now 100 per cent dependent on an agrarian economy. Unlike in the past where the ratio between those involved in agriculture and in other business was 75:25, today the estimated ratio is 50:50, if not 60:40. He estimated that 50–60 per cent of the rural population is involved in other businesses.

> A lot of people belonging to the second generation are getting white-collar jobs in nearby towns. So, there is a growing middle class with a monthly income in rural India and it is a drastic change from the past where their income was totally dependent on the monsoon, cropping season, etc.[24]

The National Council of Applied Economic Research published data in 2005 which showed that in the previous 10 years, incomes in rural India had grown several-fold, more than keeping pace with the increase in urban incomes. From 55 to 58 per cent of the average urban income in 1994–95, average rural income went up to 63 or 64 per cent by 2001–02 and then touched almost 66 per cent in 2004–05. The rural middle class was growing annually by 12 per cent, against the 13 per cent growth of its urban counterpart. And rural India was projected to have a 22–23 per cent share of the upper income class—those with household incomes of over Rs 1 million per annum—and whose numbers would be 21 million by 2009–10.[25]

The English language media in India had begun to carry stories on how the local arms of international consumer marketing companies were targeting India's rural market. Whether it was Hindustan Lever or Coca-Cola, rural India was where the action was. Lever had started Project Shakti in late 2000 to extend the company's reach into 80,000 of India's 638,000 villages. It enlisted some 20,000 poor and mostly illiterate women to peddle soap and toothpaste in villages. A correspondent from the *Washington Post* profiled one of these women.[26] And Coca Cola doubled the number of its outlets in rural areas from 80,000 in 2001 to 160,000 in 2003, which increased market penetration from 13 per cent to 25 per cent. It also halved the average price of its products from Rs 10 to Rs 5, thereby bridging the gap between soft drinks and local options like tea, butter milk and lemon water. In 2003, the company reported that the rural market accounted for 80 per cent of new Coke drinkers and 30 per cent of total volumes.[27]

By 2002 it was already being estimated that a third of all premium luxury goods was sold in the rural market, and two-thirds of India's middle-income households were now rural. Fifty per cent of the total sales turnover of Hindustan Lever at that point was estimated to be in the rural market, valued at over Rs 50,000 million. Discussions at marketing forums were recording how colour television was replacing black and white in rural markets, and the sales of washing machines, refrigerators and bicycles were going up. Even talcum powder, believed to be an urban market product, found many users in the villages.[28]

Against this picture of upward mobility, the National Sample Survey Organisation's (NSSO's) data, released at the end of 2002, reported that while there were 148.1 million households in the rural areas, consumer durables penetration had just begun to reach these. Twenty-six per cent of rural households possessed a television set, 6.7 per cent had a moped or scooter and 0.6 per cent had a car or jeep. Tractor ownership was 1.7 per cent, while 5.3 per cent of rural households had fixed telephones and only 0.9 per cent had cellphones. Urban demand too was hardly satiated, according to the NSSO. There were 58 million urban households, 66 per cent of whom had a TV set. But only 28 per cent possessed a refrigerator, 23 per cent a moped or scooter and a little over 15 per cent an air cooler.

In 2004 the rural market was estimated at 742 million people, accounting for 80 per cent of sales for fast moving consumer goods and was seen as a lucrative market by a host of new sectors. More than 50 per cent of insurance policies were being sold in rural India, as were more than 50 per cent of landline telephone connections.

Farmers were taking to *kisan* (farmer) credit cards (which gave them a credit limit with banks) with alacrity. The eminences of corporate India would gather periodically to brainstorm on such topics as 'Rural Marketing in the 21st Century'.[29]

To reach this market, you needed a vehicle for advertising that would reach this population. From the point of view of consumer goods marketers, the socio-economic categories to reach were B and C if the market had to expand.* They lived in small towns, semi-urban settlements and large villages. That became the marketing logic for opening up local newspaper editions that would increase circulation by bringing district towns, *kasba*s or sub-division town and villages into the readership net. Robin Jeffrey articulated this logic:

Newspapers do not seek readers because of an innate human desire to foster the free exchange of ideas, provide useful information or create informed 'public opinion'. Rather, newspapers push out to new readers when those readers demonstrate they are consumers or potential consumers. Newspapers localise because advertisers see a commodity worth buying: rural and small town spending power. (Jeffrey 2000: 75)

White goods and consumer appliance makers were ready to change their advertising targets to reach consumers further down the retail chain, so advertising budgets earlier earmarked solely for the national press were now going to the regional press as well. Advertising was shifting from towns to sub-towns. That is why, through the 1990s and the first decade of the new century, the regional press in north India was expanding much faster than the national press.

The advertising potential for any media that could demonstrate that it was reaching this rural market was immense. Hindi newspapers were not blind to this, their marketing departments went into overdrive to gauge potential, and the nature of their expansion was designed to provide a vehicle for such advertising. If you had a certain number of very local editions, in all-India terms you became the

*Socio-Economic Classification (SEC) is a matrix of occupation and education used in research in India to reflect lifestyle, as opposed to mere income, A1 being the highest group and E the lowest.

preferred vehicle over some other newspaper. Hence the push for 'outsider localisation', which saw the biggest players in the Hindi market entering new states at the rate of one a year, and multiplying printing centres to establish as many local editions as possible. The reach of the print media in the rural market increased from 17.1 per cent to 19.1 per cent between NRS 2002 and 2005.

Hindi newspapers were conscious of the numbers they had to offer. A power point presentation devised by *Dainik Jagran*'s marketing department sought to aggressively posit the paper's home state, Uttar Pradesh, as the premium destination for any marketer looking for numbers. It pointed out that UP has more literates than the combined literates of Kerala and Tamil Nadu, more post graduates than the total in the four southern states of Kerala, Tamil Nadu, Andhra Pradesh and Karnataka put together, as many households with a minimum household income of Rs 15,000 as Tamil Nadu and Andhra Pradesh combined, and so on. Companies sold more white goods in this state than they did in two or three other states put together. 'UP alone consumes more Coca-Cola than AP, Karnataka and Kerala put together.' In other words, UP had the numbers to offer advertisers and *Dainik Jagran*, the leading paper in the state, was where the advertiser should put his money[30] (Table 3.4).

TABLE 3.4   Media intensity: UP vs India

- Every 7th print media reader in India is from UP
- Every 8th TV viewer in India is from UP
- Every 22nd C&S viewer in India is from UP
- Every 6th FM listener in India is from UP
- Every 15th cinema goer in India is from UP
- Every 15th Internet surfer in India is from UP

Source: 'Destination Uttar Pradesh' *Dainik Jagran* power point presentation for marketers (Media Reserch Users Council–IRS 2002).

If all of this established the presence of a market in rural India and its importance for the advertiser, what was the situation with regard to potential readers? The man in charge of both news gathering and circulation for *Nava Bharat* in the Madhya Pradesh town of Itarsi described the changes in his catchment area. Ten to 15 years ago, he said, only one copy of a newspaper was likely to go to a village. Now there was demand for nearly 20–25 copies per village.

He attributed this to the spread of education, and the awareness that the electronic media had created.

TV creates the atmosphere for people to demand more news. Apart from this, today, thanks to the Tawa Dam Reservoir which has taken 30 years in the making, farmers have been able to improve their lot. There are a lot of well-to-do farmers here. They are in a position to buy newspapers. Earlier, farmers were able to raise only one crop and had to live on one meal a day. Today, farmers are able to take care of 20 acres of land and they have tractors, fridges, TVs and they like to read newspapers because people in the cities read newspapers. It has become a status symbol of sorts.[31]

Increased irrigation could well have been a trigger for better purchasing power. The gross irrigated area in Madhya Pradesh recorded a 51.47 per cent increase in the decade from 1988–89 to 1998–99 (*Third Human Development Report* 2002: 401).

Aspiration was becoming a visible driver. The presence of Navodaya (premium government-run) schools in the rural areas had also led to better-educated children in rural families. The desire for further education led to the mushrooming of educational institutes which in turn became a major category of advertisers in local editions. In Varanasi, an executive at *Hindustan Times* testified that in the last four or five years educational advertising had emerged as the most fertile category of advertising in his edition, and that was the case for other newspapers in the city as well.[32]

Elsewhere too you find a fascinating window into the nature of small-town and rural aspiration. The Madhya Pradesh Government publishes a weekly magazine called *Rozgar aur Nirman* (Livelihood and Development), which goes out to panchayats as well as individual rural subscribers (Figure 3.1). Its most popular feature is a career advice column called *Hamse Puchiye* (Ask Us) written by Jayantilal Bhandari in Indore. Some 8,000 to 10,000 postcards come every month posing queries for this column. It epitomises the sort of 'news you can use' that young people are clamouring for, and the kind of aspirations inherent in the upward mobility of a new generation. A scheduled caste girl would write to ask how she could become an air hostess. A student in Class XI in Satna district wanted to know how

FIGURE 3.1 *Rozgar aur Nirman* and *Panchayika*: panchayat-level
publications in Madhya Pradesh

he could be a tennis player. Another youth wanted to manufacture footballs and volleyballs, two young women from Sehore and Rajgarh wanted to manufacture soft toys ....

Bhandari clubbed the names as well as the towns or villages of questioners together for each question he answered, an indication that the questions were representative of several young ambitions. How can I become a hospital manager? This from both young men and women in Shahdol, Badwani, Ujjain, Bhopal, Datia, Sehore, Dhamnod and Rajgarh-Vyavara. Others writing from Guna, Javra, Sarani in Betul and Shivpuri, Morena and Shahdol wanted to be conservationists and wanted to know the career options in this field, and places which would train them. The list of those aspiring to be software engineers was the longest (*Rozgar aur Nirman*, 27 January 2005). People from small town India were aspiring to careers in forensic science, information technology and aviation. Possibly some of those aspirations had come from exposure to the media.

But every now and then there would be a query from a pragmatic soul interested in setting up a small-scale industrial unit in his or her village: two unemployed village youth from Jabalpur and Satna wrote to ask how they could set up units to produce mosquito coils that drive away mosquitos, another wanted to know how to go about setting up a cattle-feed unit in his village in Sagar. Rural India had large numbers of educated rural youth seeking avenues of employment. These also formed part of the readership base for newspapers in villages. As did educated women who came into villages as brides. Radhika Vaishnav, a recent subscriber to newspapers in her married home in Khaira village would tell an interviewer that she read *Nava Bharat* because she was looking for a job and needed to see the vacancies columns, but also to improve her general knowledge so that she could prepare for the public service exam.[33]

The readership surveys were also reflecting this positive shift. The Indian Readership Survey, Round 9 of 2002, showed that readership for the two largest-circulated Hindi dailies was not only 2.1 times higher than that of the most circulated English daily but also 5.5 million higher than the largest circulated Telugu daily and 4.7 million higher than that of the largest selling Tamil daily. Dailies from Bengal, Gujarat and Karnataka lagged far behind. The numbers for these two mass-circulation dailies, *Dainik Bhaskar* and *Dainik Jagran*, were coming precisely from the Bimaru states. With dramatic increases in literacy figures matched by the localisation thrust of the leading Hindi newspapers, the national readership map was being reconfigured. Out of the backward, overpopulated Hindi belt, were emerging the media powerhouses of the future.

Changing Readers

The proprietor of *Amar Ujala*, interviewed after the release of the National Readership Survey 2003, touched on all these factors and underscored a significant change in the reading universe in this part of the country.

The focus of newspapers has changed a great deal from a time when they played a catalytic role in our freedom movement. Till even a decade and a half ago, newspapers were essentially the preserve of the intellectuals. But that is not the case any more. Newspapers today reach out to the common man, and therein lies a huge challenge.[34]

A Hindi daily, he explained, now had to simultaneously do several things. It had to augment the breaking news that both urban and rural readers got from television, but it also had to cater to their life-style needs and aspirations. If the Hindi newspaper looked different in 2003 and had a greater quotient of 'news-you-can use', it was because readers had information demands in addition to the day's news. 'There is now a demand for education-related information, which was not the case some years ago. Similarly, readers take keen interest in subjects like health, lifestyle, etc., and hence newspapers bring out the periodical supplements.' Perhaps the most striking comment on upward mobility was the fact that both his newspaper and the *Navbharat Times* in Delhi carried regular weekly columns on how Hindi speakers could improve their English.

The fact that newspapers now had to cater to lifestyle aspirations was something that other editors too were very conscious of. A resident editor of the *Hindustan* in Bhagalpur said he was catering to a mixed readership, a combination of 'masses and classes'. People like him had to redefine the Hindi reader. 'If you go to sub-division towns you find CDs and DVDs of the latest Holywood films are available for rental. In a puja-time mela they are also showing *Anaconda*.'[35] And his chief editor in Delhi would point to the fact that visits to villages now revealed the existence of beauty parlours offering bridal make-up and facials. If glossy weekend supplements in local Hindi papers carried recipes for Western cooking and home decoration tips, it was because people wanted to aspire to the lifestyles these represented. 'The poor', she declared, 'don't want to read about poverty'.[36]

Television facilitated this process. Its presence throughout the country, not just in the urban areas, was growing. The National Readership Survey of 1999 was reporting that some 69 million homes had access to television and 276 million adults watched broadcasts in a typical week. Television was rapidly becoming the principal source of information and entertainment in most Indian homes.[37] By NRS 2002 there was 12 per cent growth in the reach of television since 1999. And cable and satellite television penetration in the country recorded 31 per cent growth.[38] The Indian newspaper trade believes that television has been an important trigger for print penetration, contributing in no small measure to a hunger for news that increased newspaper sales. TV penetration increased considerably between 1995 and 2005. To Suresh Dubey, the *Nava Bharat*'s man in Itarsi in Madhya Pradesh, who doubled as bureau chief and circulation agent for the paper, the fact that nearby villages now took 20–25 newspapers each when they had taken less than one each 10 years ago, was partly because the electronic media was creating the atmosphere for people to demand more news.[39] Hawkers who supplied newspapers in this region, made the same point. When people watched a big cricket match on television, they wanted to read about it the next morning. In Jaipur, Nihar and Siddharth Kothari, young scions of the family which owns *Rajasthan Patrika*, confirmed and elaborated on this theory: with the coming of television to semi-urban and rural India, the news habit was growing.[40]

As the rural print revolution made rapid inroads into the countryside, it created in the process a newsprint-enabled public sphere which was unprecedented in its reach, and in which a stratum of citizenry not reported on before, began to make itself heard.

Notes

1. 'Readership per copy goes down; language publications move up', Prajjal Saha, 10 June 2005, Mumbai, agencyfaqs.com, http://www.agencyfaqs.com/news/stories/2005/06/10/11699.html, downloaded August 2006.
2. Pramod Dwivedi, GramVikas Adhikary, Mohua block, Banda district, interviewed, 12 July 2006.
3. 'A Spectacular March by Rajasthan', C.S. Mehta, 7 December 2001, *Frontline*.
4. Rajendra Sail, interviewed by Vasavi, Raipur, 18 February 2004.
5. Dr Lakhan Singh, Bharat Gyan Vigyan Samiti, interviewed by Vasavi, Raipur, 16 February 2004.
6. Arun C. Mehta, 'Impact of Primary Education on Literacy: An Analysis of Census 2001 Provisional Data', www.niepa.org/libdoc/docservices/article.html.
7. A.B.L. Srivastava, 2002, 'Some Significant Features of Literacy Data of the 2001 Census and Projection of Literacy Rate for the Population of age group 15+'. Seminar on Progress of Literacy in India: What the Census 2001 Reveals, NIEPA, New Delhi, 5 October 2002.
8. Om Thanvi, interviewed by author, Delhi, 5 March 2003.
9. Anal Shukla, resident editor, *Nava Bharat* and Ramesh Tiwari interviewed by Vasavi, Raipur, 16 February 2004.
10. Lalit Surjan, editor *Deshbandhu*, interviewed by Vasavi, 16 February 2004.
11. K.K. Varma, circulation manager, *Deshbandhu*, interviewed by Vasavi, 16 February 2004.
12. Pradeep Jha, circulation manager, *Dainik Bhaskar*, interviewed by Vasavi, 17 February 2004.
13. Ravi Kant Jain, circulation manager, *Deshbandhu*, Bhopal, interviewed by Sushmita Malaviya, 6 February 2004.
14. Girish Agarwal, director marketing, *Dainik Bhaskar*, interviewed by author, Mumbai, 27 January 2005.
15. Aloka Kajoor, 2002. 'What Do Newspapers Mean to a Village?' www.thehoot.org, http://www.thehoot.org/story.asp?storyid=w2khoot L1K0613022&pn=1.
16. Brijesh Sharma, circulation-in-charge, *Nava Bharat*, Bhopal, interviewed by Sushmita Malaviya, 8 March 2004.
17. Lalit Surjan, interviewed by Sushmita Malaviya, 8 March 2004.
18. Jeevrakhan Lal Banjari, village Khaira, Mahasamund division, interviewed by Vasavi, 18 February 2004.
19. Sachin Jain, consultant, Action Aid, Bhopal, interviewed by Sushmita Malaviya, 17 March 2004.

20. Suresh Diwan, secretary, Gramin Sevak Committee, Hoshangabad, interviewed by Sushmita Malaviya, 25 March 2004.
21. Minhajuddin and Ashok Shrivastava, circulation managers, *Dainik Jagran*, interviewed by Sushmita Malaviya, Bhopal, 10 March 2004.
22. Ravi Kant Jain, circulation manager, *Deshbandhu*, interviewed by Sushmita Malaviya, Bhopal, 2 February 2004.
23. Sanjay Gupta, editor, *Dainik Jagran*, interviewed by author, Noida, 2 September 2005.
24. *The Rediff Interview*, R.V. Rajan, managing director, Anugraha Madison, Shobha Warrior, 2005, http://www.rediff.com/money/2005/jun/02 inter.htm.
25. Rakesh Joshi, 'Discovery of India' http://www.ibef.org/download/ discovery_jan19.pdf.
26. 'Building Wealth by the Penny', John Lancaster, *Washington Post*, 15 March 2006.
27. 'Corporates turn to rural India for growth,' *Business Standard*, 22 August 2003.
28. Strategic Marketing Forum, 17 May 2002, Mumbai, http://www. etstrategicmarketing.com/smJune-July2/forum.htm.
29. FICCI Rural Marketing Summit, 5 October 2004.
30. *Dainik Jagran*, power point presentation, unpublished.
31. Suresh Dubey, bureau chief/circulation-in-charge, *Nava Bharat*, interviewed by Sushmita Malaviya, Itarsi, 25 March 2004.
32. Yadvesh Kumar, senior manager, *Hindustan Times*, interviewed by author, Varanasi, 15 March 2005.
33. Radhika Vaishnav, village Khaira, Mahasamund Prakhand, interviewed by Vasavi, 18 February 2004.
34. Atul Maheshwari interviewed by Rajiv Raghunath, 31 May 2004, exchange4media.com, http://www.exchange4media.com/Content/ content.asp?content_id=58.
35. Vijay Bhaskar, resident editor, *Hindustan*, Bhagalpur, interviewed by author, Bhagalpur, 5–6 June 2003.
36. Mrinal Pande, interviewed by author, New Delhi, 5 March 2005.
37. Praveen Swami, 'Recording media trends', *Frontline*, 25 September– 8 October 1999.
38. Dionne Bunsha, 'The Rise of Print', *Frontline*, 6 July 2002.
39. Suresh Dubey, interviewed by Sushmita Malaviya, Itarsi, 25 March 2004.
40. Nihar and Siddharth Kothari, interviewed by author, Jaipur, 17 March 2006.

4

Creating New Media Hubs

*'Is the editor going to decide how much
and what news people need?'*

As the social contours of the Hindi heartland changed, the media
landscape also began to be transformed. Rising literacy numbers,
growing purchasing power and the blossoming of rural communications laid the base for accelerated expansion and localisation of the
Hindi press. Between 2000 and 2005, there was overall growth in
newspaper readership of 28 per cent, while the growth figure for Hindi
publications during this period was as high as 67 per cent.[1] The key
to such rapid growth was the rapid proliferation of newspaper
editions at the district level. In the districts of Bihar, Uttar Pradesh,
Madhya Pradesh and Rajasthan and in the new states of Uttaranchal,
Chhattisgarh and Jharkhand, beginning from the mid-1990s a readership began to be created at a hitherto untapped local level.

As the chief executive of *Hindustan* in Patna put it, the rapid
localisation achieved by Hindi newspapers was a matter of evolution
rather than a revolution. It was driven by different needs in different
parts of the Hindi belt. These had to do with deployment of accumulated capital, the need to summon publishing clout to protect
industries owned by the publishing group, the need to find alternative
advertising to compensate for advertising lost by publications to
television, and the need to decentralise printing to overcome the in-
frastructural barriers to reaching a newspaper to all corners of a
state. Expansion came first as a strategy, and localisation became its
editorial twin.

Expansion

For the owners of *Dainik Jagran* in Uttar Pradesh, expansion became imperative in 1975 because the paper was, as the owners
put, 'cash rich and capital rich' and Kanpur had reached saturation
point.[2] They were covering four districts from there and Purnachand
Gupta's sons were urging expansion. 'I asked my father to start from
Gorakhpur. The marketing people were saying, you are a regional
newspaper in UP.'[3] They went to Gorakhpur because there was no
newspaper in that belt, *Aj* was covering it from Varanasi. And then
every three or four years a new edition was started, partly as a process
of consolidation.[4] Meanwhile, the branch of the family settled in
Madhya Pradesh, Purnachand Gupta's younger brother P.D. Gupta,
had started editions of *Jagran* from Rewa in 1953 and Bhopal in
1956.

Aj expanded in the same year, 1975, for much the same reason.
The paper was well off financially but after *Jagran* came to Gorakhpur,
which had been in its circulation area, it realised that in a state in
which there were already three players, including *Amar Ujala*, remaining a single-edition newspaper for long was not viable. Moreover
the third generation had come into the picture. 'In 1974, Father said
I will play bridge, you run it. In 1975 I started the Kanpur edition.'[5]
Vinod Shukla, who had been with *Aj* since 1965, cites editorial reasons for responding to competition, even as *Aj* had monetary sur-
pluses. He visited Kanpur in 1974 and found *Dainik Jagran* a very
poor paper editorially, one that *Aj* would be able to take on quite
easily. Though the older proprietor was not keen on the paper going
to Kanpur, it needed to invest in expansion rather than distribute its
profits. It was giving a 28 per cent bonus to workers in those days,
and benevolently paying for its Muslim workers to go on the Haj.
So, supported by the son who says he rode to Kanpur in a Mercedes,
Shukla began *Aj*'s Kanpur edition in April 1975 and used the opportunities provided by the Emergency to consolidate it.[6]

Thereafter fairly rapid expansion followed, for both newspapers.
Aj crossed the state boundary and went to Patna in 1979, Gorakhpur
in 1980 and Ranchi in 1984. *Jagran* went to Lucknow and Allahabad
in 1979, and shifted the latter edition to Varanasi in 1981. Thereafter it
moved into *Amar Ujala*'s territory and began to consolidate there:

Meerut in 1984, Agra in 1986 and Bareilly in 1989 (Table 4.1). In 1990 it went to Delhi because, as Yogendra Mohan Gupta puts it, he asked his executives what *Jagran* had to do to become national and they said, simple, start an edition in Delhi. 'What a definition!'[7] Both *Jagran* and *Aj* were primarily publishing enterprises, but for a newspaper owned by a large industrial house such as the Birlas the motivation for expansion could be something more:

> I was working in *Searchlight* in Patna in those days. It was kept alive for the sugar mills. Excise inspection, weight inspection,

TABLE 4.1 Expansion—the top two

Dainik Jagran	Dainik Bhaskar
2005 Dharmsala	2005 Mumbai, DNA (English)
2005 Jammu	2005 Rajkot, Divya Bhaskar (Gujarati)
2005 Muzaffarpur	2004 Vadodara, Divya Bhaskar (Gujarati)
2004 Nainital	2004 Bhilwara
2004 Ludhiana	2004 New Jersey (USA)
2003 Panipat	2004 Banswara
2003 Bhagalpur	2004 Surat, Divya Bhaskar (Gujarati)
2003 Jamshedpur	2003 Ahmedabad, Divya Bhaskar
2003 Ranchi	2002 Patiala
2001 Moradabad	2001 Faridabad
2000 Allahabad	2000 Hissar
2000 Patna	2000 Panipat
2000 Hissar	2000 Chandigarh
1999 Jalandhar	1999 Sriganganagar
1997 Dehradun	1999 Kota
1993 Aligarh	1998 Udaipur
1990 New Delhi	1997 Bikaner
1989 Bareilly	1997 Jodhpur
1986 Agra	1997 Ajmer
1984 Meerut	1996 Sikar
1979 Varanasi	1996 Alwar
1979 Lucknow	1996 Jaipur
1975 Gorakhpur	1993 Bilaspur
1956 Bhopal	1992 Raipur
1953 Rewa	1983 Indore
1947 Kanpur	1967 Gwalior
1942 Jhansi	

who will raid your factory and arrest your owners—then the special correspondent based in the district is expected to do his bit. Papers have to be multi-edition to take care of businesses in different districts.[8]

Meanwhile, in Madhya Pradesh, Rajasthan and Haryana, the central player in catalysing expansion and localisation between 1983 and 2000 was the *Dainik Bhaskar* (Table 4.1). When Ramesh Agarwal and his sons took over after a division of the family business in 1978, they re-launched the Bhopal edition, moved from slow sheet-fed printing to faster web offset, and overtook the existing competition, *Nava Bharat*. In 1983, they decided to launch the Indore edition, taking on *Nai Duniya* which was the market leader. It took seven years for them to galvanise themselves to launch two more editions, Raipur in 1990 and Bilaspur in 1992. The latter was the year they became No. 1 in Madhya Pradesh and began to look outward. [9] The localisation of their home state continued apace; by 2005 every district in Madhya Pradesh had its own pull-out, and there was no significant competition in sight, with *Nava Bharat* being a poor second. However by the end of 2005 *Rajasthan Patrika* announced that it was going to enter Madhya Pradesh[10] and in April 2006 *Dainik Jagran* had actually launched an edition in Indore.

When Rajasthan was settled upon for further conquest, the third generation of *Bhaskar*'s Agarwal family was raring for action and decided to use methods never used before in launching a newspaper: a house to house pre-launch market survey in the capital city of Jaipur, to ask people what they wanted from their newspaper. Asked where they got the idea from, Girish Agarwal, the second son, would later say that a lot of it came from *The Making of McPaper: The Inside Story of USA Today*, 'Sudhir, my elder brother and MD of our company, had read about it and he admired how the paper had everything planned, and even a launch date announced six months before the actual launch. We followed the same strategy.'[11]

That meant announcing a launch date for December in September and doing a house to house survey, and they ended up covering an unprecedented 200,000 households. The survey was to tell people about their paper, and there was a second round to book orders. When the orders crossed 150,000 they bought a third printing machine overnight at a premium. According to Agarwal, this strategy gave them a print order of 172,000 on the day they launched. The established newspaper in the city at that point, *Rajasthan Patrika*, was selling close to 200,000 copies. Commenting on the approach to expansion that they evolved Agarwal would say, 'The way we operate, we go all out, or we just don't.'

Local Markets

Serious commercial expansion was predicated on the perception of markets. Advertising began coming to the local media from national advertisers who were waking up to the fact that sales volumes were coming from the smaller towns. Robin Jeffrey quotes representatives of Hindustan Lever Limited as acknowledging that the company had begun to place more than half its print advertising budget since the 1980s in the local language press (Jeffrey 2000: 61). In 2002 it was being asserted that the money spent on local advertising and promotions for FMCG (fast-moving consumer goods) companies and consumer durables manufacturers had increased in the previous five years from 10 per cent to 40 per cent.[12] The increasing diversion of advertising to the language media was also encouraging regional players to increase their bouquets within a state. *Vijay Karnataka*, the Kannada newspaper that had taken just five years from launch to become the leading daily in both circulation and readership, launched in early March 2005 yet another daily, *Usha Kirana*, priced cheaper than the flagship publication, and aimed at both a different readership and different advertisers who were looking for a cheaper option with a smaller circulation.[13]

Localisation of news content was taking place in cities with the development of city and suburb-oriented supplements. Between 1997 and 2002, *The Times of India* went from none to seven a week in Mumbai. Others, including local players, had the same idea. By 2002 Thane, neighbouring Mumbai, had seven local papers catering to it. And once the vehicles were there, local advertisers began to crawl out of the woodwork. Local restaurants, grocery stores and automobile dealers, dentists and coaching classes, made their presence felt across media. Cable TV operators drew them into the local advertising net, and netted figures nobody could have dreamt of earlier at the local level. In 2002, *Satellite & Cable TV* magazine estimated that 37,000 cable operators in India were netting about Rs 5,000 million in advertising from local retailers. They were also advertising on the new FM radio stations: One media buyer was estimating that 40 per cent of the commercial time sold by these stations was bought by local advertisers. As for newspapers, the *Malayala Manorama* in 2002 was saying that local advertising contributed 50 per cent of its ad revenues. In 2001, a single sari shop retailer in Delhi spent Rs 2 million advertising in local supplements of *Hindustan Times*, *The Times of India* and *Dainik Jagran*.[14]

In Jaipur city, meanwhile, *Rajasthan Patrika* had separate pages for the east, west, north and south zones of the city to net advertising from nursery schools, shops, restaurants and local cinemas. In January 2002, the paper's chief executive R.K. Mohla was pointing out that trader advertising had grown in volume over the last one year. The more local a newspaper became, the more retail advertising it could mop up. Even within a city, the more you localised, the more small advertising you were able to garner.[15]

Hindi newspapers required that potential markets have the ability to read and the capacity to buy. Only then could they expect advertisers to underwrite their entry into new territories. In Bihar, the dominant newspaper, *Hindustan*, of the Delhi-based Hindustan Times group, came to Patna in 1986 but its push for local expansion began only in 2000. The Birla group which owns it has had a long presence in the state through two newspapers, *Searchlight* and *Pradeep*, that were native to Bihar but acquired by this group. It closed them down and started *Hindustan* and *Hindustan Times* in the same year. But it was only 14 years later, after localisation had become a trend among Hindi newspapers, that the management woke up to the potential of *Hindustan* as a major local revenue earner.[16]

Despite its image as India's most backward state, Bihar was a good investment for a newspaper. It had a population that was politically aware even if literacy was low, and because of money order remittances from its people working elsewhere in the country, as well as because of its agricultural wealth, there was a lot of money in the state waiting to be tapped. A poor law and order situation ensured that the wealth was not visible. As the *Hindustan's* resident editor put it, '*Har admi apna income chupata hai*' (Every man hides his income).[17]

The consumer goods market was only just discovering the potential for both consumer durables and non-durables in Bihar, and they needed a media vehicle for their advertising. Individual satchets of consumables such as shampoo were going to all markets in the state, so the more local the vehicle the better. In May 2003 the marketing department of Hindustan Times Ltd made a presentation to advertisers.[18] Using numbers from the Indian Readership Survey of 2002, Round 1, it said that the national average of households with a monthly income of more than Rs 6,000 was lower than in Bihar. In Bihar the figure was 8.6 per cent. The Bihari family then had higher purchasing power than the average Indian household. The state has considerable agricultural wealth, blessed as it is with enormous water resources. Public deposits in all scheduled commercial banks in this money order economy had been growing at 16 per cent or so over the previous three years.

There were two approaches to attracting advertising in a state like Bihar. One was to go into the hinterland and widen the scope of local advertising. This proved difficult; retailers who were terrified of being kidnapped were loath to draw attention to themselves by advertising in the local edition. As one local marketing manager explained, 'They tell us take money for an advertisement if we must, but do not carry it in the paper!'[19] The other was to concentrate on capturing the Delhi advertiser wanting to reach Bihar. *Hindustan* had a national team and a local team for advertising. The former booked all-India advertising on the basis of numbers gained from a large number of local editions.

In Jharkhand again the number of households with a monthly income of more than Rs 6,000 was fractionally higher than the Indian average. To the advertiser that indicated enough purchasing power potential for low-cost durables and non-durables.[20] The third variable that spelt promising potential was the low penetration of consumer goods and media, relative to the the capacity to absorb these. Like Bihar, only 18 per cent of the population of Jharkhand read or looked at the print media on weekdays! In comparison, the all-India figure stood at 31.4 per cent. The penetration of consumer goods was also poor. Just 21.7 per cent of the households owned a TV set, against the all-India average of 37.8 per cent. The figures dropped even further when it came to other durables. In Jharkhand, only 4 per cent owned refrigerators whereas the all-India average then was 10.5 per cent. In terms of washing machines, the state had a penetration of 0.9 per cent, less than a third of the 2.9 per cent all-India average.[21]

The *Hindustan Times* presentation quoted the branch manager of a television brand as saying that the white goods business in Bihar and Jharkhand was going to register the maximum growth in the country in 2003–04. It listed the sale of 21-inch colour TV sets as being higher in Bihar and Jharkhand than the national average, and the size of the cellular phone market here as being ahead of Haryana and Rajasthan. The potential was there for advertisers to exploit and it gave newspapers the impetus to fan out to reach those consumers.

In Uttar Pradesh, *Amar Ujala* was also a beneficiary of the growing perception among advertisers that the Hindi heartland was an un-tapped market, and saw 29 per cent growth in its advertising revenue in 2003–04. Its managing director Atul Maheshwari made the point that the paper was the market leader in western Uttar Pradesh and the new state of Uttaranchal, a region that had huge population density. This, he said, was something that would not have escaped the attention of advertisers, particularly in the FMCG and consumer durables segments. [22]

Printing Centres

Hindustan did its homework and realised that it had to localise to reach newspapers to people across the state in the morning. Com-munications were poor in Bihar, the roads were in poor shape, and a state criss-crossed by rivers did not have many bridges. More print-ing centres would be needed to get newspapers to people's homes earlier. The decision to start these was hastened by the impending arrival of *Dainik Jagran* seeking new territories to conquer.[23] By mid-2003 *Hindustan* had 24 local editions from three printing centres in Bihar (Patna, Bhagalpur and Muzaffarpur), with a total circulation in Bihar and Jharkhand of 410,000.

Dainik Jagran was getting ready to put additional printing centres in exactly the same locations even as it had 13 editions coming out of Patna. Its circulation in Bihar according to Audit Bureau of Circulation figures for March 2003 was 111,000 copies, achieved since its entry in 2001. Before 2003 ended it had started a Bhagalpur edition. The Muzaffarpur edition followed in April 2005. Competitors tended to choose the same printing locations in a state, worked out as they were from the point of view of geographic areas to be covered. The Patna edition with 13 subeditions was meant to cater to the entire central and west Bihar which is in the pan-Gangetic plains. The Bhagalpur edition was targeted at the north-east districts such as Purnea, Ara, Kishanganj, Saharsa, Madhepura and Khagaria, apart from the neighbouring areas of north Bengal such as Darjeeling, Jalpaiguri, Coochbehar, North Dinajpur and Murshidabad, and Sikkim. This edition also catered to some parts of Jharkhand (as did *Hindustan*'s Bhagalpur edition). The Muzaffarpur edition, it was announced, would start with an initial print run of 60,000 and cater to districts such as Darbhanga, Madhubani, Samastipur, East Champaran, West Champaran, Sitamarhi and Seohar. Before its launch Sunil Gupta, the paper's CEO, declared that it was expected to add 400,000 readers to the existing 1,985,000 readers (IRS 2005, Round 1) in Bihar (Figure 4.1).[24]

The paper entered the new state of Jharkhand in February 2003. This mineral-rich state which had been carved out of Bihar's southern region in 2000,began to be looked at with interest by advertisers. The state was smaller than Bihar but was more industrially developed. Its literacy rate was higher. To the media the fact that over 14 per cent of the population of 27 million had been educated to the secondary school level and above indicated that the state had a potential of at least 3 million readers.[25]

Wooing Readers

The Americans call it 'community spirit boosterism'.[26] Local media in that country often take it upon themselves to be exemplary citizens, funding the provision of local amenities, organising reporting around

FIGURE 4.1   *Dainik Jagran*'s 23 March 2004 issue declaring that it had
become No. 1 in readership in the country

civic campaigns, organising activities to promote a sense of community among local citizens. The payback hoped for is reader loyalty,
or simply an identification with the newspaper which could grow
into loyalty. As Hindi newspapers expanded across the states of the
country's heartland, they were eager to pander to local sentiments,
to shore up their readership and circulation numbers, and in the
process displayed several instances of such boosterism.

The inaugural editorial in the first issue of *Jagran*, when it entered
Jharkhand on 13 February 2003, was almost unctuous in its ex-
pressed desire to be all things Jharkhandi to the people of the state.
It invoked the cultural traditions of the region, the names of its
martyrs and visionaries, and declared that *Dainik Jagran* was dedicat-
ing itself to the progress of the state. To be able to express the feelings
of the people in the state, it said, it had undertaken a survey of
800,000 households in different parts of the state and given the newspaper a particular style on the basis of these findings. It headlined
its editorial, 'Pranam'. (The word is a respectful salutation, albeit a

Sanskritised one. The context here is its formal greeting of the people of Jharkhand in its first issue.) 'That is the difference between an outsider localiser and a paper from the region', Harivansh, the editor of its established competition in the state, *Prabhat Khabar*, would point out tartly. 'We say, *Johar* Jharkhand!'[27] (*Johar* is the tribal term of greeting, appropriate in a state with a large tribal population.)

Newspapers took it upon themselves to promote a unifying cultural identity when new states were carved out of old ones. *Prabhat Khabar*, based in the new state's capital of Ranchi, set a precedent that was anxiously copied by rivals when it came out with a 75-page special issue on the day Jharkhand was carved out of Bihar. It harked back to the new state's tribal heritage; historians, sociologists and politicians wrote in its pages; and an editor from the competing *Hindustan Times* group was moved to privately commend the newspaper for the vision it had displayed. This anniversary issue would become an annual ritual, with *Hindustan* and *Jagran* doing the same.

Elsewhere too, local newspapers were scrambling to please. In Bihar, *Dainik Jagran* mounted local interactive programmes with civic authorities and public utility departments to find a remedy on the spot, part of its effort to woo readers. Its team covered issues such as water, electricity, community health, education, solid waste material and administration. *Jagran* also launched a supplement called '*Kasauti*' (touchstone) for its Bihar editions to cater to what it described as the 'intellectual class of the state'. By 2005 it was able to cite audited circulation figures to show that it had doubled its figures in the state between 2000 and 2004.[28]

One of the more original examples of boosterism came from *Dainik Bhaskar* which, according to its managing editor Sudhir Agarwal, decided to use the money from advertisement revenue generated by obituary notices that people put into their editions (a category known as *shok*, meaning grief) to improve the crematoria in the cities where it had editions. The paper announced that from its collections in this category, Rs 100,000 a month would go to improving crematorium facilities.

We have donated Rs 7 million overall to crematoria in all centres: Rs 3.5 million in Ahmedabad, Rs 2.8 million in Jaipur. We put in Rs 2.8 million, the public put in the rest, so that the

total investment in Jaipur was Rs 10 million. We run a cremation centre in Bhopal, we pay the staff gardeners. It is now lush
green, the moment you enter, *Hey Ram ka dhun* is played, and
we put a chip in the walkway. When you put the body (on the
cremation platform), *Raghupati Raghava Raja Ram* is played.[29]

The *Rajasthan Patrika* was no mean contender either for the badge
of being a good citizen (Figure 4.2). It prided itself on its civic sense
and cultural contribution to the state, but it went further, associating
itself with what is most precious in a desert state: water. It launched
movements to clean up and rejuvenate water harvesting structures
in the state which are described in a later chapter. It organised camps
for issuing driving licences in collaboration with the local transport
directorate, and camps to get certificates for those with disability. It
set up *Patrika* junctions where people could come and deposit electricity bills. 'This is also communication,' said chief editor Gulab
Kothari. 'It is showing that we care.'[30] And for its golden jubilee,
Patrika lit up the city of Jaipur. The *Hindustan* in Patna meanwhile
invited smses from readers on story ideas for civic coverage, and
featured their mobile numbers in the stories it did.

FIGURE 4.2   Kesargarh, *Rajasthan Patrika*'s office in Jaipur—a newspaper
in a fortress
Courtesy of *Rajasthan Patrika*.

Boosterism also applies to commercial wooing—gifts, trade incentives, price discounts and other inducements to make readers subscribe. How readers were incentivised is a tale that we will return to in greater detail.

Editorial Localisation

Lateral expansion across the smaller towns in the Hindi belt was accompanied by editorial localisation which deepened the public sphere. Generating news stories from villages and *kasbas*, and from the by-lanes of smaller towns, led to readers becoming newsmakers, and a democratisation of news to the point where everyday events were deemed newsworthy. These processes will be discussed in subsequent chapters. But when did localisation of news begin, and become a driver of readership? By the late 1990s, it was visible in the kind of reporting being done by *Dainik Jagran* in Uttar Pradesh, the *Punjab Kesari* in Punjab and Haryana, and the *Dainik Bhaskar* in Rajasthan.

In their article 'Subliminal Charge: How Hindi-language Newspaper Expansion Affects India', Robin Jeffrey, Peter Friedlander and Sanjay Seth described the process of localisation and the kind of stories it generated. They noted that the drive for readers 'has propelled Hindi newspapers ever deeper into the towns of North India and has led them to localize their coverage, because local coverage appears to create newspaper readers'. As a result the research paper said, Hindi newspapers were reporting local events in far more detail than the English-language press and cited the 'local enormities' which became news: residents in a locality demanding the removal of a telephone pole which was half uprooted because it could fall down any moment, the death of nine women, belonging to one village, from digging in an excavation which collapsed, or the rape and murder of a Dalit woman by high caste men (Jeffrey 2001: 147–66).

How did the idea evolve in this part of the country? Did it just grow out of discovering the kind of news that readers were hankering for? Did it come from what *Eenadu* was doing in Andhra Pradesh? This newspaper began a new phase of expansion in 1989 when it introduced district editions to increase coverage of local events (Jeffrey 2000: 97). Word spread to the north about what such localisation had done to increase the paper's circulation. 'We in Bihar would get copies of *Eenadu* flown in from Hyderabad to understand how they were doing it,' an executive with *Hindustan* would say later.[31] After Harivansh took over *Prabhat Khabar* in Ranchi, he set out to learn from what regional newspapers were doing elsewhere in the country. He visited the *Malayala Manorama* in Kerala and *Eenadu* in Andhra Pradesh, among others, to study them and formulate what he called his success strategy.[32] That included making *Prabhat Khabar* a champion localiser in Ranchi.

Other champion localisers in the north talk of localising even before *Eenadu* showed its paces. Girish Agarwal of *Dainik Bhaskar* is quite firm that their ideas on localisation evolved from in-house brainstorming rather than from any inspiration from the south. And Y.C. Agarwal of *Hindustan* maintains that localisation in UP preceded that of the *Malayala Manorama* and *Eenadu*.

The *Eenadu* people came and spent days with us. I was with *Swatantra Bharat*, the Hindi counterpart of *The Pioneer* in Lucknow. We did localisation. It covered 14 districts. In 1973–74 I travelled extensively across UP with ad executives from Bombay. One of the things that came out then was hunger for news, especially politics. We were already printing the Sitapur and Sultanpur editions in the job press.

Vinod Shukla of *Jagran*, who was in Lucknow when the Babri Masjid issue in Ayodhya became volatile enough to draw journalists from all over the country, recalls comparing notes with an *Eenadu* correspondent who dropped in at *Dainik Jagran*'s Faizabad office, in 1990. He confirms that what *Eenadu* was doing then was already being done at *Jagran*. 'He said they were inserting a local page. We had one page of local news in the paper, printed in tabloid form. We already had local content. We were printing six or seven editions. The motivation was to get the numbers.' The proprietors of *Jagran* add that this began in the 1970s. 'Even in the 1970s we had many editions in Kanpur. One or two in the city, and then for nearby areas. We sent news between cities by teleprinter and by a packet system.'[33] For *Dainik Bhaskar* from sending young surveyors to homes with questionaries emerged the wisdom that what was missing from the reader's point of view, was enough news from around where he lived. People said they wanted more city news. When the paper launched in Rajasthan and began to give it to them in December 1996, the *Rajasthan Patrika* quickly copied the strategy. By early 2002 it had nine editions with 28 different local pullouts. The *Bhaskar* had 32 different sets of local pages inserted in 10 editions.[34] The *Dainik Bhaskar* rapidly followed up its Jaipur launch with those in Alwar and Sikar in the next three days, and in Ajmer, Jodhpur and Bikaner in 1997.[35] And it developed its local news strategy. '*Patrika* was giving one page of Alwar news. Alwar is a big city. You can give more. We started giving four pages. Is the editor going to decide how much and what news people need?'[36]

His father, the chief editor, Ramesh Agarwal, would add, 'Localisation means two things for any reader. First, everybody wants the news from where he lives. In mohalla, in town , in state, in country. Then he wants news from his profession. If you are a journalist, you will look for news from media.'[37] Over a period of five years most of Rajasthan acquired a local public sphere which had been confined earlier to those towns which had small local newspapers started by individual entrepreneurs.

In Chandigarh which became for the *Bhaskar* group a gateway to both Punjab and Haryana, a similar strategy of house to house surveys and more local news pages was followed. It was important to decentralise to the point of giving an edition for practically every district. In Haryana, *Bhaskar* launched with 14 district editions from day one, printed from two cities.[38] Localisation in Chhattisgarh followed when it was carved out as a separate state from Madhya Pradesh in 2000. And it continued in Rajasthan until 2005. Between 1996 and 2004, 11 editions were launched in Rajasthan. In the process, the market was widened. When they entered Rajasthan the advertising revenue garnered by *Rajasthan Patrika* was Rs 500 million a year from the whole state. By early 2005, the total Rajasthan market was worth Rs 2,000 million, in advertising revenue.[39] And readers were hooked on local news. Each of the leading newspapers was selling more copies throughout the state than the solitary market leader did back in 1996.

The localisation which evolved experimented with devising carefully calibrated subeditions targeted at readers in specific urban or rural clusters. These would simply incorporate a page or two meant for these areas, into an exisiting edition. Suddenly, in less than a decade, every major multi-edition newspaper was devising multiple subeditions which combined and packaged news from contiguous areas of relevance to specific audiences.

At *Hindustan,* which in June 2003 was delivering 24 different editions with varying combinations of local pages to different parts of Bihar, the vice president, Y.C. Agarwal, explained the process thus: 'Crime news they want of the whole state. They do not want local political news. Crime is on top of everybody's concern, crime has to be there.' The paper's management had made a list of 35 requirements that the reader had.[40] Feedback was constantly elicited, from hawkers, vendors, agents and through interactive columns. Costs were also carefully calibrated; within the same copy of *Hindustan* you could have two or three grades of newsprint, the cheapest of which would be a murky grey in colour.

At *Jagran* the editor called it customisation of localisation. 'We give readers custom-built newspapers. We have 4–5–6 pages changed in every edition.'[41] Communications links and an abundance of printing centres made it possible to offer as many as 68 subeditions of the newspaper in just one state of Uttar Pradesh in early 2005. Nine each from Varanasi and Meerut, 12 from Kanpur, eight from Lucknow, and so on. The boast was that none of these was printed before 11 at night, and all gave the latest news.

New Media Hubs

Once expansion became a driver, it was no longer limited to the Hindi belt. Reaching beyond it to Hindi readers wherever they might be meant that in the east, West Bengal was being targeted by ambitious, outward-reaching newspapers. *Rajasthan Patrika,* a newspaper from the extreme west of the country, was already in the eastern metropolis of Kolkata because of the Hindi-speaking business community from Rajasthan that dominated trade in the city, and was now reaching out to north Bengal, to Siliguri, with a split edition printed in Kolkata that had four pages dedicated to Siliguri news. Along came *Prabhat Khabar* from the neighbouring Jharkhand in March 2006 with its Siliguri edition. The reason, said its editor Harivansh, was that the north Bengal region comprising Darjeeling, Coochbehar, Jalpaiguri, north and south Dinajpur districts, had a huge Hindi-speaking population that was not being served by a local Hindi daily.[42]

In July 2006, both Hindi newspapers had more competition in Siliguri when *Jagran* launched its edition there two days after the opening of the Nathu La Pass in Sikkim, on the Sino-Indian border, on 6 July. Siliguri is a growing trade centre and a passage to Sikkim.

Another lucrative market was Punjab. Until 1999 this remained the virtual monopoly of *Punjab Kesari*, but in July that year *Amar Ujala* from its nearby base of western Uttar Pradesh reached out to the state with an edition in Chandigarh. It followed up with an edition in Jalandhar, and before long *Dainik Jagran* and *Dainik Bhaskar* were in the Punjab market as well. Punjab and Haryana were more affluent states than neighbouring Rajasthan and Uttar Pradesh, with among the highest per capita income levels in the country, and it made sense to be able to offer readers from there to the advertiser.[43] In 2004, *Dainik Jagran* launched an edition in the prosperous town of Ludhiana.

Competitive localisation created new media hubs. By any reckoning, Palamu in Jharkhand is a backward district[44] but today it is media-rich. In 2003, a researcher tracking the media network in Palamu for this study found that the *Dainik Jagran* there had opened a bureau with 13 correspondents, a photographer, a computer operator and a bureau chief.[45] Meanwhile, the *Ranchi Express* had 22 part-time reporters covering what it called the Palamu zone, and *Prabhat Khabar* had eight for the city. There was even an English newspaper representative, the correspondent for *Hindustan Times*, and his Hindi counterparts for the Palamu bureau of *Hindustan*. Then there was a newspaper native to Palamu, the *Rashtriya Navin Mail*.

When asked whether the district generated enough news to keep them all in business, the answer from these correspondents was an emphatic yes. 'Correspondent' is not an adequate description of what they were. They were citizen-journalists, almost all of them graduates, and every one of them dependent on other means of livelihood. Many had public telephone booths, some were part-time farmers. But zamindars did not work for newspapers. When a single newspaper has a bureau of 13 in one district and there are six papers reporting from there, both the actors in that public sphere as well as the foot soldiers of the press become vulnerable. The citizen–reporters kept a hawk's eye on local institutions and on one another. For all its drawbacks, localisation set in motion a process of democratisation of the media and a level of accountability for local governance institutions that is possibly unparalleled in its scope in a developing country. This will be discussed in detail in the next chapter.

By the close of 2005, the expansion drive had extended to Himachal Pradesh in the north, which was estimated to have some 3.6 million Hindi readers (NRS 2005). *Amar Ujala*, *Punjab Kesari* and *Dainik Jagran* all had editions in Dharamsala, with *Jagran* and *Amar Ujala* launching there within two months of each other. This town in the Kangra Valley was used as a base from which to reach Kangra, Chamba, Mandi, Kullu, Hamirpur and Bilaspur districts in the lower hills of the state.[46] Before this, *Amar Ujala* had a presence in the state alright, using a network of some 650 newspaper selling agencies in Himachal alone to reach the paper to readers, but this edition did not have local content.[47] The inevitable next step, therefore, was to launch an edition. Suddenly, Dharamsala too had become a new media hub, with the new entrants bringing competition to *Divya Himachal*, a local player.

What was happening in the newspaper industry then was not very different from the way growing markets had been invaded by bigger players in other industries. It was like Cola-Cola coming in and swallowing up local colas, or ITC's cigarette brands swamping those of smaller local producers. When markets become attractive they see brands from metro centres fan out and swallow up local markets that had been the unchallenged turf until then of local brands. Big newspapers were growing by gaining scale, the local players either lost out or carved out niches for themselves.

Expansion by developing new media hubs called for constant investment in communication links and printing machines and more expensive means of delivery into the interior. If you wanted to close a newspaper late and get delivery bundles to villages in the hinterland by the crack of dawn you had to deploy dedicated taxis, rather than use local trains and buses. The financial outlays needed drove many a truly local newspaper out of the competition. Whether it was a stalwart like *Nai Duniya* in Indore or a very small Beawar daily like *Nirantar*, or *Pratah Kal* in Udaipur or an aspiring localiser like *Dainik Nav Jyoti* in Ajmer, they could not match the resources of the 'outsider localisers', *Rajasthan Patrika*, *Dainik Bhaskar* and *Dainik Jagran*. The advent of market penetration and localisation of news and advertising as a strategy by the big boys of the Hindi belt was sounding the death knell of those who had been local to begin with, and the winners would soon become the big boys of the national scene too, ready to challenge the English-language giants of the Indian newspaper world.

The catalysts for the shrinking of an existing local public sphere and its reinvention were the second and third generations of the leading newspaper-owning families, and their appetite for taking on the challenge of the market. Had the son of *Nai Duniya*'s proprietor Abhay Chajlani chosen to enter the newspaper business, the future of a newspaper with a besieged present and a celebrated past might have been different.

Conclusion

In the districts of Bihar, Uttar Pradesh, Madhya Pradesh and Rajasthan and in the new states of Uttaranchal, Chhattisgarh and Jharkhand, beginning from the mid-1990s a readership began to be created at a hitherto untapped local level. Expansion became imperative to keep the competition at bay. Expansion by localisation created a new tier of vehicles for advertising, and once they were there, local advertisers began to crawl out of the woodwork. The catalysts for the shrinking of an existing local public sphere and its reinvention were the second and third generations in the leading newspaper owning families, and their appetite for grasping the challenge of the market.

Editorial localisation was preceded by readership surveys in the case of the *Dainik Bhaskar*. Newspapers experimented with devising carefully calibrated subeditions targeted at readers in specific urban or rural clusters. These were made possible by an abundance of printing centres. Once expansion became a driver, it was no longer limited to the Hindi belt. When towns like Siliguri in West Bengal or Dharamsala in Himachal Pradesh or Palamu in Jharkhand acquired a number of local editions each, new media hubs were being created. Like local papers in other parts of the world, the new entrants wooed readers by resorting to community spirit boosterism.

Notes

1. 'FICCI Frames 2006 Day Three: Print is still king, for now', Gokul Krishnamurthy, 25 March 2006, www.exchange4media.com.
2. Mahendra Mohan Gupta and Sanjay Gupta, interviewed by author, Noida, 2 September 2005.
3. Yogendra Mohan Gupta, interviewed by author, Kanpur, 26 August 2005.
4. Mahendra Mohan Gupta and Sanjay Gupta, interviewed by author, Nodia, 2 September 2005.
5. Shardul Vikram Gupta, interviewed by author, Varanasi, 16 March 2005.
6. Vinod Shukla, later resident editor of *Jagran* in Lucknow, interviewed by author, Lucknow, 25 August 2005.
7. Yogendra Mohan Gupta, interviewed by author, Kanpur, 26 August 2005.
8. A.S. Raghunath, interviewed by author, Noida, 31 March 2005.
9. Interview with Girish Agarwal, agencyfaqs.com, Iqbal Singh, 6 August 2001.
10. 'After Hindustan, Rajasthan Patrika also plans to join Madhya Pradesh media war', Asit Ranjan Mishra, 4, 5 November 2005, exchange4 media.
11. Interview with Girish Agarwal, agencyfaqs.com, Iqbal Singh, 6 August 2001.
12. Vanita Kohli, 'The Rise of the Locals', *Businessworld*, 20 May 2002.
13. 'Vijaya Karnataka to have sibling, *Usha Kirana*, from 4 March', Noor Warsia and Gokul Krishnamurthy, 1 March 2005, www.exchange4 media.com.
14. Vanita Kohli, 'The Rise of the Locals', *Businessworld*, 20 May 2002.

15. R.K. Mohla, interviewed by author, January 2002.

16. Y.C. Agarwal, Vice President, *Hindustan Times*, interviewed by author, Patna, 3 June 2003.

17. Naveen Joshi, resident editor, *Hindustan*, interviewed by author, Patna, 1 June 2003.

18. 'Bihar & Jharkhand, Opportunities Unlimited, media marketing Presentation—Bihar and Jharkhand, Patna 28 May 2003', Internal Company Document.

19. Bimal Kumar, marketing manager, *Hindustan*, interviewed by author, Bhagalpur, 5 June 2003.

20. 'Jharkhand—A land of promise for the marketers and print media?' exchange4media.com, 21 February 2003.

21. Ibid.

22. Atul Maheshwari interviewed for Content is King, exchange4media. com, 31 May 2004.

23. Naveen Joshi, interviewed by author, Patna, 1 June 2003.

24. '*Dainik Jagran* to add another edition in Bihar', Prajjal Saha, 11 March 2005. agencyfaqs.com.

25. 'Jharkhand—A land of promise for the marketers and print media', exchange4media.com, 21 February 2003.

26. http://www.thesportjournal.org/2005Journal/Vol8-No4/doobo1.asp, downloaded 23 June 2006.

27. Harivansh, editor *Prabhat Khabar*, interviewed by author, New Delhi, 27 October 2005.

28. *Jagran* claims highest growth in Bihar based on ABC figures. www. exchange4media.com, 8 March 2005.

29. Sudhir Agarwal, interviewed 27 January 2005, Mumbai.

30. Gulab Kothari, interviewed by author, Jaipur, 17 March 2006.

31. A.S. Raghunath, interviewed by author, Noida, 31 March 2005.

32. '*Prabhat Khabar*: Expanding in Reach and Relevance', thehoot.org, 9 February 2002. http://www.thehoot.org/story.asp?storyid= webhoothootL1K092022&pn=1&section=S1.

33. Mahendra Mohan Gupta and Sanjay Gupta, interviewed by author, Noida, 2 September 2005.

34. 'Patrika-Bhaskar competition leads to localisation, commercialisation in Rajasthan', Sevanti Ninan. www.thehoot.org, 7 May 2002.

35. Girish Agarwal, interviewed by author, Mumbai, 27 January 2005.

36. Ibid.

37. Ramesh Agarwal, interviewed by author, Mumbai, 27 January 2005.

38. Girish Agarwal, interviewed by author, Mumbai, 27 January 2005.

39. Ramesh Agarwal, interviewed by author, Mumbai, 27 January 2005.

40. Y.C. Agarwal, Vice President, *Hindustan Times*, interviewed by author, Patna, 3 June 2003.

112   HEADLINES FROM THE HEARTLAND

41. Sanjay Gupta, interviewed by author, Noida, 2 September 2005.
42. 'Prabhat Khabar to launch its Siliguri edition on March 10', Sumita Patra, 6 March 2006. exchange4media.com.
43. 'Eyeing the Punjabi Pie', Shuchi Bansal, 23 August 1999. *Business World*.
44. See indices for it in *Jharkhand Development Report 2006*, published by *Prabhat Khabar*.
45. Vasavi, 24 April 2003, Palamu.
46. 'Amar Ujala launches Dharamsala edition', Indo Asian News Service, 7 December 2005.
47. Atul Maheshwari interviewed for *Content is King*. exchange4media.com, 31 May 2004.

5

Local News Gatherers

'Anyone who is willing to get advertisements
can become a stringer.'

Newspaper expansion and the localisation which followed had many
colourful consequences for daily journalism in the Hindi heartland.
It created a genre of news which did not exist before in this region,
and a new breed of news gatherer. A local public sphere rich in possibilities began to evolve once local pages for districts, and sub-
divisions thereof, became the norm. With newspaper managements
deciding that the way to create new readers was to give them news
from where they belonged, a new genre of news emerged brought by
a new tribe of news gatherers. 'How local is local? From the region, the
town, the neighbourhood or the street?' (Franklin and Murphy 1998).
To that question was added another one: how much of the everyday
jumble of local occurances qualify as news?

   The logic of creating a local public sphere was irrefutable. That was
after all the level where governance touched the citizen, and communities acted out their cultural rituals and social concerns. As urban
and rural local self-governance took root in India, as local communities become more vocal and more conscious of their rights, as local
commercial interests came forward to make viable the publications
that could engender such a space, its emergence became inevitable.
Local politics, civic services, law and order all demand discussion and
accountability in a democracy, even as cultural practices seek media
space. And because human nature rather than idealism governs the
realm of local discourse, crime news assumes primacy in the pages
of the local press.

Rise of the Citizen Journalist

The rapid plunge into localisation led to a democratisation of news-gathering which encompassed the citizenry at large. It turned local lawyers, teachers, shopkeepers and busybodies into citizen journalists. They had no conventional journalism training but a clear understanding of local concerns: crime, corruption, poor quality services in government schools and hospitals, and in terms of maintenance of roads and sewage systems. They also had a clear sense of how local interests operated, and approached issues with an instinct for self-preservation. And because the newsmakers and news providers were drawn from the more vocal sections of the community, the local public sphere also became a reflection of the local power structure in terms of caste and class. Mediators in the local power structure, such as panchayat leaders, religious leaders and social activists became both actors in, and beneficiaries of, the local news universe.

Local editions were open to news being brought and given to them in the same way that much bigger newspapers in the cities had a mechanism to receive press releases. At the *mofussil* level the dependence on these 'handouts' for space filling was much greater, and no news was too small to be dignified with space on the local pages. As space for such coverage expanded, stringers as well as district level news bureaus were eager to receive small handwritten items of who had said or done what, and where. The craving for publicity that a local school, hospital or ladies club might have was abundantly gratified. Though gentry were favoured, local district pull-outs also turned very ordinary people into newsmakers as reporters hunted for stories and pictures to fill the day's pages.

As more people read newspapers for a reflection of what was going on in their neighbourhood there was also an increase in popular awareness. If the space created in local pull-outs promoted self-aggrandisement of those who governed, it also demanded accountability. And if it served commercial intent, it also strengthened cultural bonds. Central to the shaping of this public sphere were the armies of local news gatherers who came into existence as newspapers calibrated their costs and benefits in publishing district-level pull-outs or additional pages within an edition for different areas.

Beginning with the mid-1980s in the Hindi-speaking states there was an exponential growth in the development of the rural and semi-urban news machine. Many cogs were put in place to create this news gathering and delivering operation, which expanded as the radius of the rural newspaper revolution grew. It began to take in roadside villages which could never have dreamt that they would figure on a news map. The newspaper industry cast its readership net wider and began to reach out to hitherto untapped readers because there was now commercial interest in the rural Indian. He was a potential consumer.

The parallel impetus for localisation came from the fact that television had come in from the early 1990s and begun to corner much of the advertising pie. By the 1990s regional newspapers were looking elsewhere, at local markets, for the potential they had to offer. The decade of 2000 began with an advertising recession and newspapers such as *Rajasthan Patrika* worked harder to create alternate sources of advertising by leveraging the paper's increasing small town and rural reach. The advertising was there then, waiting to be tapped, but you had to find news to fill the pages on which people could advertise. By then the *Patrika* was claiming to reach 300 panchayats and *tehsils* (development blocks). *Dainik Bhaskar* was claiming that 50 per cent of each edition's circulation was in the rural areas. So what news would you give these rural areas, and who would produce it?

District editions also demanded delivery networks that facilitated greater localisation. These originated with trains and then switched to taxis and buses, because train routes had limitations, you could only drop papers at five or six stations. With road transport you could drop smaller bundles in more places. But when your paper began to reach smaller places, your news network also had to encompass these places, to deliver incident-based, problem-based reporting that would draw readers.[1] How would a newspaper make a vast news gathering operation, that goes down to villages, viable? One solution was to do so by making it a participative effort where local people were encouraged to send news items about the community. As news-papers in Hindi-speaking states expanded their circulation base they invited circulation agents to send news about their areas so that the thrill of seeing their village and people figure in the daily pages would become an incentive for would-be subscribers to take the newspaper.

As the amount of space given to local news grew, the local news network also grew beyond the circulation agent to the advertising agent, as well as other interested individuals in the community. It was understood that this was a sort of altruistic unpaid activity, what was paid was a commission on the subscriptions or advertising brought in by the person who was also filing stories. In return many newspapers conferred a visiting card on the news filing individual, which gave him the status of a representative of the newspaper. When the paper involved was a large and influential one, a household name all over the state, the visiting card conferred status upon the local stringer. He became the local gentry's passport to figuring in the newspaper.

A significant agent of localisation was thus emerging. Together with a determined local marketing thrust which saw a culture of incentives to subscribe develop in rural, semi-rural and small town markets, these citizen-journalists (to use a term which had gained currency worldwide by 2005) spearheaded the penetration of news-papers into the rural hinterland. In more common parlance they were known as stringers (from an old international practice of paying part-time reporters by the column inch for the text that they pro-duced, and the fact that the length was measured by a piece of string).

As local news pages expanded with the growth of printing centres and the multiplicity of editions, the dependence on this local stringer led newspapers to induct more of them, and pay them small amounts of money that would not by any reckoning qualify as a respectable journalistic salary. Some of them were reimbursed for the cost of faxing the news. What the newspapers were investing in setting up printing centres was saved in a unique approach to creating the edi-torial product. Without exception every localisation drive in India's Hindi heartland was riding on the willing backs of a host of largely unpaid stringers, filing quantities of miscellaneous news from their immediate neighbourhood. A large publication such as *Dainik Jagran* or *Hindustan* may have anywhere from 200 to 1,000 stringers in a state, depending on how many editions it publishes. They were re-sponsible for transmitting news from *kasba*s and *mohalla*s (neigh-bourhoods) and for placing many villages and block headquarters irrevocably on India's news map.[2]

The southern part of the country had set the trend earlier. In the early 1990s *Eenadu* already claimed to have a stringer in every *mandal* (a unit of local government) in Andhra Pradesh. They were paid expenses and one rupee for every column centimetre of their copy that got into the newspaper. Other Telugu dailies also maintained hundreds of stringers to whom they paid rates varying from 75 paise a column centimetre at *Udayam* to Rs 1.25 at *Andhra Prabha* (Jeffrey 2000: 145).

Shortly after *Dainik Bhaskar* came to Rajasthan in December 1996 it decided to push ahead with district-level expansion and by 2002 both this newspaper and *Rajasthan Patrika* had built up networks of stringers though neither claimed that such information providers ('informants', as Rajeev Harsh, the resident editor of *Patrika* in Udaipur would later describe them)[3] were journalists. Babulal Sharma, the *Bhaskar's* Jaipur editor at that point would say expansively that the *Punjab Kesari* may appoint shopkeepers, but their own stringers were more like to be a lawyer, teacher or social worker. 'If an MA or PhD comes to me and wants to help, we let him become our correspondent.' He would add in the same breath that they also let their circulation agents send news.[4] 'Anyone who is willing to take on an agency of circulating 50 copies can become a correspondent/stringer. Anyone who is willing to get advertisements can become a stringer. Thus, circulation and advertisements together determine who becomes a reporter.' This, from the bureau chief of *Dainik Jagran* in Nautanhwa, Gorakhpur district.[5]

In the early stages stringers helped to attain a newspaper's circulation objectives without expanding its area of editorial influence. Increasingly, some newspapers used them to collect advertising or publicise advertising rates. The news too was collected rather than written, when a circulation agent doubled as a stringer.

Abolishing Gatekeepers

In the Kanker and Bastar districts of Chhattisgarh, the road which connects Raipur to Jagdalpur is dotted with small commercial establishments which announce a dealership for one or other of the region's newspapers. Most of these dealers or agents also sent news. If insurgents attacked a village nearby, or an outbreak of an epidemic occurred, or the member of parliament or legislature from the area did something newsworthy, the shopkeeper cum circulation and advertising agent cum correspondent, would handwrite a little despatch, and hand it to the driver of a transport bus going to Jagdalpur where the local pages for the Bastar edition are made. One evening newspaper called *Highway Channel* in Jagdalpur even had a mailbox at the local bus stand, where such news despatches could be deposited.

Rural sales varied from 15 to 20 copies in a modest village to 50 or 100 in a *kasba*, Many roles get collapsed into one at this local level: at Farasgaon in Bastar, within a family one brother was the circulation agent as well as stringer for *Deshbandhu*, his younger brother who hadn't managed to finish school was gainfully employed as a hawker for the same newspaper. Circulation, editorial, advertising and distribution all under one little roof!

But more often than not, the news was collected rather than reported by this multi-purpose human being. A general store owner in a village called Bhanpuri on the Kanker–Jagdalpur highway had a sign up on his shop: 'Come and give your news here', it said in Hindi. At Kondagaon, a long distance telephone booth owner had a similar sign, he was the agent for *Nava Bharat*. He said people came and gave him press releases. The more you carry local news, the more local people buy newspapers, these stringers said. Their job was to collect the tiny, inconsequential items of self-publicity that filled local news columns and drew readers to these pages. Precisely the sort of news items that sharp-eyed news editors in self-respecting metropolitan newspapers would circle with a red pen and term a plant.

Localisation democratised media access and abolished gatekeepers. Since its logic was that local gentry should be able to read about themselves in the next day's papers it encouraged its stringers and circulation agents to forward all the local handouts they received. The citizen walked with his news to the place of receipt, it was stamped and forwarded with no alteration, and liable to appear on the next day's pages without much alteration either. It was received by a shopkeeper, transported by a road transport bus, free of charge, to a mailbox in a district town bus terminus. Sometimes, if the paper or an interested party paid the fax charges, it was faxed to a modem centre, scattered across districts. A modem centre was a district-level newspaper bureau where local pages were made up and transmitted by modem to the town where the edition for the region would be produced. Even in a bigger place such as Jagdalpur the full-time reporters in the *Nava Bharat* bureau would happily accept handouts and thank the bearer for them.[6]

In a place like Chhattisgarh, those availing themselves of the proffered hospitality of a newspaper's columns ranged from organisers of local school events to the Naxalites (leftwing guerrillas) who terrorised government functionaries. Members of this extremist group had embarked in the summer of 2002 on an 'image-building strategy' which involved issuing press notes, sending letters to the editors of newspapers, and responding to articles that appear in the press. They sought to explain their position and apologise for excesses by gaining access to the local pages of the Hindi press, much as the rest of the citizenry was doing. The difference was that their handouts were not delivered personally to the newspaper bureau or to the stringer. They were handwritten, on the letterhead of the People's War group, and were mailed to newspaper officers or bureaus, since the group chose to remain underground. Their press releases were issued by different levels of the organisation, both the special zonal committees as well as the central committee. Like all other levels of press notes received by local newspapers, they were eagerly accepted and used.[7]

The-come-and-give-your-news principle applied in different parts of Rajasthan as well. In Banswara district where a great deal of religious news originated on account of pilgrimages and religious fairs, one way of ensuring coverage was to pay the fax charges of the local shopkeeper who functioned as a stringer cum circulation agent. It also helped if he belonged to your community. In Ganoda, 30 km from Banswara town the *Dainik Bhaskar*'s man also happened to be a Jain. 'We are Jains so when I send a story on a Jain event, the Digambhar Jain samaj of Ganoda pays the fax charges. People say, you send our news we will pay fax charges.'[8]

Those who facilitated media access in far-flung corners of the country would dignify their corner shop enterprises by calling themselves news agencies. The appellation was adopted because they were circulation agents for newspapers as well. They would solemnly stamp news items received with the name of their news agency before sending it on to the newspaper through a bus driver or over fax. Thus Vastupal Jain of Ganoda called himself Paras News Agency.

In Kothda, in Udaipur district, Ramesh Chandra Jain, a circulation agent who had been selling *Rajasthan Patrika* for 40 years, sat in a shop in the market square of Kothda, a largely Muslim *tehsil* headquarter town, and diligently stamped handouts brought to him. He kept file copies of these: a press note from a chief veterinary officer, a handout from a school principal, an item on a local Ganesh festival. News items on local problems were sent on to be delivered by a road transport driver to the mailbox *Patrika* had installed at the city bus stand in Udaipur, precisely for this purpose. He was also the distributor for the 120 copies of *Patrika* sold here.[9] Lately he had acquired competition, the *Patrika* appointed a shopkeeper who was the member of the local Rashtriya Swayamsevak Sangh (a right wing Hindu nationalist organisation) to also collect news for the paper from that town and its surroundings. And *Dainik Bhaskar* appointed a local Muslim youth to be its circulation agent and collect the news that people chose to give. That included political handouts from the local Bharatiya Janata Party. He would put a 'Shahid News Agency' stamp on each item and send it on.[10] In addition to these three men, local people also gave news items directly to the bus driver who could be relied upon to put these as well into the *Rajasthan Patrika* mailbox at the Udaipur bus stand.

Why did newspapers want to make their pages quite so accessible to all and sundry? In Bihar Y.C. Agarwal, the vice president of *Hindustan Times* whose Hindi edition *Hindustan* was the leading newspaper here, said it was because the reader was smart and knew what he wanted. 'If he wants to know what is happening around his area, I fulfil that need.' But if you had to fill two pages of news for very small semi-urban areas, you would be able to do it only by being open to all kinds of news being fetched or delivered.[11]

At his competition, *Dainik Jagran*, they put it a little differently. It was as a matter of creating readership loyalty, they said.

> We cover a local Ram Lila because in producing it in a locality so many people are involved. Those who give donations to make it possible, those who make arrangments for the poles or act in it. They would all want to read their names in the paper.[12]

It was in a sense, the local community version of the 'Page 3' culture. *Jagran* was at this point also appointing students as stringers in local schools, who would inform the paper if there was a function in the school. They were creating a cadre of informants, they said. As the news base widened, Hindi newspapers encouraged information gathering of a highly democratised and decentralised kind.

Mirzapur's Media Men

The quality of the public sphere being created in small town India had to do with the quality of news which found its way into the pages of the local press. But when stringers did the reporting themselves, many complexities coloured their output. Interviews with them and with citizenry at the local level highlight both the potential and limitations of stringers or citizen journalists as newspapermen. Whether in Uttar Pradesh or Jharkhand or Bihar, such a person tended to be upper caste, male, and a part-time scribe. The rest of the time he could be a farmer, small entrepreneur, politician, lawyer, teacher or shopkeeper. How well he reported had to do with whether or not he also collected advertising, what his caste and professional background was, why he had come into the profession and how much gumption he had as an individual. It also had to do with how keen his management was to have him display any journalistic derring-do.

Interviews done for this study in 2003 with stringers, correspondents, local government officials and readers drawn from various segments of society in Mirzapur district in eastern Uttar Pradesh shed some light on both the quality of journalism in these parts and on reader expectations from newspapers. The most widely circulated papers here were all in Hindi: *Aj, Hindustan, Dainik Jagran* and *Amar Ujala*. Covering nearly 5,000 sq km, the district is known largely for its carpet weaving and mining industries and the attendant negatives of child and bonded labour.

Several had been stringers for many years. A few were full-time journalists, bureau chiefs in charge of stringers. Several were conscious of the limitations of their journalistic potential, given their circumstances. R.N. Jayaswal, a 65-year-old graduate in political science, was the Mirzapur-based bureau chief of the Vindhyanchal division of the *Amrit Prabhat*, the Hindi edition of the Calcutta-based *Amrita Bazar Patrika*, and published from Allahabad. He was

also the local bureau chief for *The Pioneer,* published from Lucknow
and Varanasi, and a social worker who had helped found the Bandhua
Mukti Morcha, an organisation that worked to free bonded labour.
Reporting in such areas often meant close interaction with agitations
mounted by landless agricultural labour, with Naxalites and the non-
literate population in the district. Given the international focus on
issues of child labour as well as rescue and rehabilitation of bonded
labour, he thought that local print media had a catalytic role to play.[13]

However, he said, such reporting was based on a personal commitment and unlikely to be rewarding. On the contrary, as a caste Hindu,
he had faced social boycott from family, friends and acquaintances.
Wealthy landlords as well as the erstwhile owners of large carpet-
making units initially tried to buy him off, he said, but when that
failed, *goonda*s were sent to beat him up. In time, as attention and
donor funds were channelised towards this issue, the local district
and state-level functionaries were more supportive of the efforts of
activists and journalists alike. According to Jayaswal the Hindi print
media was significantly responsible for exposing cases of bonded
labour, including child labour in the carpet industry, and for formu-
lating the well-established proposition that the carpet industry pro-
duces an army of uneducated people.

Ram Murthy Pandey, a school graduate at Halliya in Mirzapur,
reported for *Hindustan* which is published from Varanasi and has a
bureau office at the Mirzapur district head quarters. He was 45 years
old and between him and his two brothers they owned 15 *bigha*s
(measure of land varying from a third of an acre to an acre) of land.
He had been a stringer for 11 years, working for *Prayag Darpan,
Amar Ujala, Samay* and *Dainik Jagran* before he came to *Hindustan.*
He had been a Congress party office bearer in Halliya and Lalgunj,
and had also been a district-level secretary as well as organiser of
the district unit for the party. That was when he began writing for
newspapers on rural issues and problems.

Pandey earned Rs 500 a month irrespective of the number of stories he wrote, another Rs 105 with which he had to subscribe to the
Hindustan, and got a commission on the advertisements he collected
for the newspaper. He was aware that this commission which added to
his income made him dependent on the block authorities and traders.
'That means I cannot take a stand against either the government or

the trading community.' But he seemed to think it was possible. 'The trick is to get past them all, and yet contribute to enhancing people's awareness.'[14] He used the term 'good story', like any regular journalist. A good story he said, was typically about problems facing rural people: handpumps that have fallen into disrepair, food stocks that have found their way out of the public distribution system and into the market, and other news of corruption involving local officials such as the BDO (Block Development Officer) using the government vehicle for private use. 'I have had to face boycott by him whenever I write such a piece.' Any more analysis than that, he thought, was unnecessary since readers tended to lose interest.[15] He had a useful source in the head clerk at the block office who got him all the local news on inside developments.

After the land reforms were enacted in this area the Patel community has become extremely powerful, Pandey said.

They are more in number and have easily got control over the land here. We Brahmins have to fight to defend our honour and dignity which these fellows are bent on ravaging. They have been troubling us for quite some time now in this part of Halliya block. Being a correspondent allows me to contain their oppression.

Rajiv Ojha, with *Aj* for the last 20 years, started out with *Jagran*. A 39-year-old advocate, he was also a supplier of raw materials such as china clay and plaster of Paris for Chunar's crockery industry. He lived in Chunar. His law degree and his post graduate diploma in journalism helped him write news with a lot of analysis, he said. 'I think that was problem with the management in *Jagran*, but it is an asset in *Aj*.' He admitted that it was depressing to read some of the news that got published. According to him most news items tend to be events-centric, not processual or analytical. These are mostly of the *teen marey, terah ghayal** variety, which merely passes on information.

*Literally, three killed and thirteen injured, referring to the overwhelming focus on mishaps and single events, which do not always have any impact on the development outcomes of people's lives.

This was not only to do with the stringer's lack of formal training or of their backgrounds, he said.

There is so much competition between newspapers themselves to be the first to report that often the quality of the news item itself is missed out. How can you expect the person to analyse any news when he is simultaneously pressured for advertisements and to send stories fast so that the particular issue of the newspaper can get published fast.[16] [Multi-edition papers sent by train to other parts of the state closed their pages fairly early in the evening.]

He was candid enough to say the income from advertising was an important incentive for becoming a stringer. 'Each advertisement means a commission of 5–10 per cent. That supplements the apparently low income of stringers.'

His fellow stringer for *Aj* at Lalganj in Mirzapur, Shashi Bhushan Dubey, had been working with the print media for the last 25 years. He was earlier with *Jagran*, *Amrit Prabhat* and *Rashtriya Swarup*. A 45-year-old post graduate in journalism from Mirzapur, he belonged to a family that owned 700 *bigha*s of land. People become stringers he said because it brought them a lot of clout. If you were a contractor or transporter, being a stringer conferred respectability, and could be extremely beneficial. It gave them a cover to carry on their business, clout with the local administration and politicians, and brought them a respectability that distracted public opinion from their underhand dealings. They develop the right connections and contacts so they even got encouragement. 'You see, it is not only about officials not interfering with your work. It is also about them supporting what you do.' Of himself, he said that he was in this profession because he wanted to be. 'Inspired by ideals of social work, and by a willingness to expose corruption and injustice we have taken on these roles.' He was also the circulation agent for *Aj*, but was not responsible for collecting advertisements. While he was reimbursed for fuel expenses incurred while reporting, he only got an honorarium for the work he did. 'Let me tell you, in this profession and at this level, no one is salaried. Anyone who claims he is, is lying.'[17]

A stringer-transporter from the district of Gorakhpur confirmed this cynical assessment, dwelling on the advantages of this part-time calling.

I am not into this trade for any altruistic reason. Rather, it is the press *ka billa* [clout] that interests me. I have a taxi and sumo service that operates between Sonauli border and Gorakhpur. Putting a press tag on them saves me from harassment by the police. They know that if they touch anything of mine, it will be a big story about the kind of activities they are into. That helps![18]

Nor were newspaper managements keen on any journalistic derring-do being displayed. Stringers were hired to increase the presence of local gentry on the paper's pages, not to embarrass them with revelations. This stringer-transporter did his reporting around the Nepal border.

I did a story on the RAW–ISI nexus [India's Research and Analysis Wing and Pakistan's Inter-Services Intelligence]. A couple of RAW officials met up their ISI counterparts at Kathmandu. My management was appalled. I irritated them further by doing up a story on the involvement of the border police with smuggling. Each story I wrote was like a nail in the coffin. I was finally pulled up and told, '*chup chaap se pade raho*' [keep quiet]. I was instructed to report ordinary news. So that is what I do. Who killed whom, who got robbed, you know that kind of stuff.[19]

Many of the stringers in Mirzapur were older men with a fairly long innings in their second profession. Siddhanath Singh, a 52-year-old cultivator who owned 5 acres of land, was a stringer for *Jagran*, at Kalhat Bazaar when he was interviewed, and said he had been with the print media for the last 26 years. In 1977 when the Janata wave swept the north he was a member of the Jan Sangh (the precursor of the Bharatiya Janata Party), keen to be more actively associated with the process of building up a new society. He was a graduate, and *Jagran* accepted his offer to cover news for them. He has had no formal training in journalism. Those were heady days he says, when everyone wanted to be part of something. He was looking for an identity, he said, which he found while reporting for *Jagran*. Since 1980, when he got the agency for this paper he has been its circulation agent for a radius of 5–7 km around Kalhat Bazaar. He also collected advertisements for the paper. He was paid a monthly remuneration, irrespective of the number of stories he did.

Like Ram Murthy Pandey, above, Singh saw his primary task to be that of bringing the attention of the bureaucracy to handpumps that were non-functional and to school buildings, roads and bridges that had fallen into disrepair. It was also essential to inform people through the newspapers about different welfare schemes that were announced and about news related to panchayati raj institutions. 'People are very keen to know about these. I think that is due to the new-found "power" that at least some people have got (after the 73rd Amendment), and everyone wants to know how to use it.'[20]

It is useful to contrast the perceptions of those who do the reporting with the views of those who were implementing the government's development schemes in these parts. Every one of them lamented the lack of context or analysis. Gyaneshwar Tiwari, a BDO at Pahadi thought that given the range of government programmes being implemented, ranging from development to welfare, the reporting he saw in the newspapers barely skimmed the surface of the activity going on, and was unsatisfactory in quality.

> There was this article the other day on how the wells have dried up. Just that—the number and the location. But is it not a responsibility of newspapers to also analyse why these wells have dried up? Surely the *sarkari karamchari* [government worker] has not gobbled up the water? Why is there no discussion on water-tables, on ground-water run-offs that happen because there are no trees? And who has cut away these trees? Unless the newspapers, especially the local papers explain these issues, how can they say they are doing responsible reporting?[21]

Shiv Kedar Singh, a former block *pramukh* (president) at Narayanpur, was more damning. To begin with, he said, his experience with the media, especially the Hindi-speaking print media, had been such that he could never be sure that any news was factual.

As far as possible, I have to corroborate what I read with my own eyes, which is possible only at the district block level. For example, recently *Hindustan* reported that the Pontoon bridge at Chunar had got damaged due to heavy rain and storm. When I went to the specified site I saw there was no problem, and the people there told me that there never had been any such problem. Any such news that is found to be inaccurate should be corrected by the concerned newspaper, and apologies issued.

Nor did stringers or reporters follow up on a news item. News for them is just a 'story', an event, which has neither context, nor a subsequent process. For instance, he said, there were regular stories about grains in the public distribution system being poor.

But is that all there is to it? Did it not link up with corruption in the bureaucratic system? Does it not tell us that grain is rotting in our godowns? Those are the gaps in our knowledge that we would expect an honest and re-sponsible media to fill.[22]

Chandra Shekhar Shukla had been BDO at Rajgarh (Mirzapur) block for six months when he was interviewed. He was 35 years old and a keen reader of Hindi newspapers which gave him an opportunity to try and understand what was happening in his district and block. 'However, I often feel dissatisfied because I feel I am not able to lay my hands on any analysis,' he said. Not only did the local newspapers give only information, they focused entirely on negative aspects. He gave the example of a monitoring meeting for the Jawahar Rozagar Yojana which he had organised in his previous posting. *Gram sabha*s (village general bodies) are supposed to monitor this scheme in the presence of the BDO. At one village where the quorum of 10 per cent required for such meetings was not reached he opted to hold the meeting nevertheless, since many people had come. The next day it was all over the newspapers: that he had gone ahead with a *gram sabha* meeting without quorum and was encouraging despotism. The reporter had not tried to get his side of the story. His point was that if they had not gone ahead with the meeting that day, the villagers who had made the effort to come would have been de-motivated. What guarantee was there that they would turn up the next time?[23]

And he too thought that the frequent reports about tube wells were pointless without saying why they had gone dry:

> There are usually two reasons for this. One, that the pump has not been bored according to the standard set by the government, so instead of being 150 feet deep, the pump is only 120 feet deep. This indicates that the contractor has pocketed cash. The second reason could be—and this has longer-term implications—the level of ground water, and people's callousness towards the environment in general.

In Gorakhpur a BDO mourned the 'web of negativism' that local reporting spun.

> While I was in Chamoli, it was such a common sight to see little girls running uphill to their schools in so much excitement. But not once did I see newspapers there write a story or do an analysis of how and why communities and people there were so enthusiastic about school.

To Santosh Srivastav, the Press Trust of India (PTI) correspondent in Mirzapur, the fault lay with both reporters and ordinary citizens. He says most local reporters look at journalism as a means to get close to the government. For them, this is just a smart career move that brings them clout as well as respectability. As a consequence, serious coverage—especially coverage of development issues—suffers. And they and their newspapers get away with this because actually readers are quite uninterested. 'They are indifferent to issues of democracy, governance and development. Both feed into each other.'[24]

Srivastav and Shamshed Khan, Secretary of an NGO called CREDA in Mirzapur, also blamed stringer reporting for the perception of Naxalism that the newspapers perpetuated. Srivastav said:

> The identity of the Kol tribes in this locality, especially in Halliya, is getting sharper. This identity-formation is directly linked with

Naxalism and its fury. However, police and the bureaucracy insist on referring to this problem as a 'law-and-order' issue. This is not a 'law-and-order' issue, it is a 'development' issue. But since the administration sees it as a law-and-order problem, the local media follows suit.

Shamshed Khan, has his own reading of what makes a stringer less independent than he could be.[25] They belong to a social strata and a given caste group that is involved in perpetuating poverty, exploitation and malfunctioning in both the bureaucracy as well as society. At the local level, it is difficult to report serious issues of development due to pressure from within the social or caste group that stringers belong to. Dalit (an untouchable, in the Indian caste system) issues, land issues and human rights issues are not covered at all he said, since the stringers and the exploiters belong to the same caste. Most stringers in Mirzapur belong to the Brahmin community. Most of the land mafia were also Brahmins.

The caste profile of stringers did not make them the voice of down-trodden anywhere in India's Hindi belt, though there were individual exceptions. By and large local editions had middle-class concerns: power supply, water, crime, development infrastructure. Not caste atrocities or exploitation of labour or subjugation of women. Injustice did not move the local news machine. In Varanasi Shekhar Tripathi, the resident editor of *Hindustan*, confirmed this: 'Upper caste string-ers likhte hain police ke khilaf, afsaron ke khilaf. Social aur eco-nomic issue par nahin likhenge. Eastern UP mein crime ka samachar zyadatar'[26] (Upper caste stringers write against the police, against officers. They will not write on social and economic issues. In Eastern UP crime news dominates).

Readers in Mirzapur also proferred perceptions of what con-stituted local news and how much impact it could have. Tejbal Chaturvedi, a 52-year-old cultivator in Halliya educated up to high school, was a subscriber to *Dainik Jagran*. To him the local news pages were crime chronicles that did not even bother to investigate the crime stories they chronicled! From the conditions in the rural areas it would be difficult to believe that the bureaucracy has taken note of the negative daily reports, he felt. Roads continue to be bad, and hand pumps are never repaired. Yet he read the paper for the crisp and easy-to-read format in which the news is presented, and because he was a particularly enterprising cultivator, he also headed a local NGO. 'Reading *Jagran* also helps me to know about government requiring NGOs to implement their projects. In fact that's the kind of news that I am most interested in these days.'[27]

Mohammed Karim Ansari, a private practitioner at Chaudahawan found the reporting on property disputes unsatisfactory because they never refer to the social causes that underline these disputes.[28] Readers were aware that stringers also collect advertisements and in the perception of some this role constricts their independence as journalists. Chandra Mohan Prasad, the son of a landless labourer, with a recent post graduation degree from Kanpur, was a keen readers of newspapers, with a preference for *Jagran*. He said there was practically nothing reported on wider issues that had widespread socio-economic implications. Reading the newspapers, one did not easily get a feel of the extent to which landlessness continues in this area. That meant there were no obvious references to child labour, bonded labour, agricultural labour as well as to discrimination against *chamar*s, *musahar*s and *kol*s.*

He also rationalised as to why this was so.

I don't blame reporters and managers of newspapers either. Such news is hardly interesting, especially for the landed and urban social groups who read the newspapers. It also embarrasses the government, which is something local reporters would not want to do. Think about it, reporters depend on BDOs for advertisements. They would also want to be on good terms with the sarkar.[29]

Representatives of the sarkar thought so too. Chandra Shekhar Shukla, referred to the the 'consumerism of the advertisements that propel their newspapers' which was why stringers they do not touch private traders, or for that matter even bureaucrats like himself.

---

*Chamar*s and *musahar*s are scheduled caste communities, while *kol*s are the most important scheduled tribe community in Mirzapur.

'They know they will have to come back to us for their advertise-ments, which they get a commission for. That perhaps accounts for the events-based negative news that we hear and read.'[30]

Sanju Agrahari, a businessman in Halliya town kept all important newspapers such as *Aj*, *Hindustan*, *Jagran* and *Ujala* at his cloth shop.

> I keep newspapers in my shop simply so that customers can read them. I do not have the time to read any, frankly, I find them most irrelevant. They are full of political news. In fact, that is another reason I keep newspapers here. My brother is an activist of the Samajwadi Party so he needs to know what is happening in the vicinity. These newspapers are for him.[31]

As local news proliferated, its consumers developed a sharp sense of its limitations, and the nexuses that coloured local citizen journal-ism. The most pointed comment on what local journalism lacked came from a shopkeeper in a village called Markundi in Chitrakoot district of Uttar Pradesh. '*Yeh log bhanda phod nahin karte*', he said of the correspondents of the big Hindi newspapers. *Bhanda phod* was the local term for an exposé. What he was saying was, such re-porters never did exposés.

Positives of Local News Gathering

In a village called Sabla in Rajasthan, bisected by the national high-way in Dungarpur district, an uncle and nephew, serving the two rivals *Dainik Bhaskar* and *Rajasthan Patrika* between them, demon-strated an awareness of the pitfalls and possibilities of their avocation which transcended the stereotypical, commonly disparaged image of the rural informant. The uncle had, that day, booked eight obituary notices wearing the hat of a circulation and advertising agent. Then he donned his reporter's hat and described succinctly what a village offered by way of blackmail potential, to a canny scribe who might be so inclined.[32]

If a shop was selling medicine without the owner having the man-datory pharmaceutical degree he could be exposed unless he bribed the local stringer. He said he wrote about corruption at the level of the police and the local *patwari* (village land records officer) who always demanded a bribe to issue a certificate, but didn't quite manage to expose them. The *Patrika* wanted proof to print his allegations, but how was he to provide proof? In that village there were indigenous medicine practitioners running clinics without a license, who needed to be exposed. And the road that ran through it had been routed differently from what was shown on paper. The *patwari* knew where the road should be but the public works department had built it differently to mollify people who would lose their house or land. People had taken compensation to surrender their land for the highway but still did not give up the land.

Down the road and inside a lane lived his nephew, son of a shopkeeper but a lad with well-honed journalistic instincts. Four years ago he has taken on the distribution agency for *Dainik Bhaskar.* Then he started sending stories. With a nose for news and rapidly acquired technological savvy, Dipak Patel demonstrated what a stringer could grow into. He acquired a digital camera, computer and modem, and kept the four-page district supplement supplied with stories and colour photographs as newsy as any city reporter might produce. He covered crime, tree felling, water logging and administrative neglect. He sent photographs of Adivasi children in school, all sporting school uniform trousers supplied by the government, which did not even reach their ankles. When he covered the annual fair held there, he did a feature on the pickpockets who operated there. He modestly described his news sense as God's gift.[33]

On Republic Day the local *tehsildar* or revenue officer bestowed state recognition on 22-year-old Dipak, for service to his district, the first time such an honour had been conferred in that area for journalism. He was still paid the princely sum of Rs 10 per column centimetre.

Thanks to localisation the village-level bureaucracy in the Hindi belt was rapidly becoming *au fait* with the media universe. In Jharkhand, Anil Kumar Singh, the circle officer of Patan in Palamau district was an unusual man who claimed to have been a newspaper reader for 30 years, but now he had more choice than ever before. He subscribed to three newspapers daily, *Hindustan, Hindustan Times* and *Prabhat Khabar*, as well as magazines like *India Today*. When he could, he also looked at *Rashtriya Navin Mail, Dainik Jagran* and *Ranchi Express*. He not only found them '100 per cent useful' but also valued the fact that you could rebut what appeared in the press more than you could a sensational report on television. What he missed in his current posting was access to *Jansatta* which did not reach his division. He missed its language, news and coverage.[34]

He found newspapers a useful means of dissemination: 'Like today, 800 aged people have come to collect old age pension; I gave this information in newspaper ... in the village, people read newspaper and tell each other.' And he thought their coverage could be constructive: if the information they gave about people's problems was useful, it was easy to act on them. He had also learned to deal with the damage they could do. During his administrative tenure, he said, he had given rebuttals 17 or 18 times to the newspapers.

Overall, some members of civil society were beginning to acknowledge, a more aware population also helped them catalyse development. Newspapers were now being read for a variety of purposes.

> The additional page on Raisen that is brought out by *Nava Bharat* is useful for people as it gives them information on local issues. Information related to politics, the cost of food grains, news about various rallies and meeting organised in Bhopal and Raisen, all this.[35]

But resident editors of local editions in places as varied as Varanasi, Patna, Raipur and Udaipur, were clear-eyed and sometimes cynical about the stringers who filed for their editions. From the mid-1990s to mid-2000s, as the number of local pages grew, as four-page locally printed colour pull-outs began to be launched from districts, replacing the initial one or half page of news for each district, stringers went from being circulation agents with added responsibilities to something more potent. A resident editor described his stringer as 'not only our representative, he is the editor of that region. He sells 200 copies and he is a stringer for 10 years. No one is a bigger journalist there than him.'[36]

Editors concurred that the more newspapers were read, the more the local stringer mattered in the pocket from where he reported. They quickly developed clout. Sanjeev Kshitij, resident editor of *Amar Ujala* in Varanasi, observed:

> To become a stringer is to become a member of the existing power coterie. Every day you get three requests to move the

existing one. I have 400 stringers. I get 20–30 complaints about them every day. I have to verify if the complainant is an interested party or a genuine case. If there is a caste conflict between Yadavs and Thakurs I have to see what caste my stringer is and check his story accordingly. Caste complications make the appointment of a stringer more complicated than the appointment of an editor.[37]

In Bihar, the resident editor of *Hindustan* would say succinctly, 'I have an army of content providers. It is the content developers who are missing.'[38] And in Raipur the resident editor dismissed them as blackmailers.[39]

A few years down the line, across states, stringers continued to evoke a range of emotions from those with whom they came into contact. Government functionaries, social activists, politicians and resident editors presiding over these armies of stringers—everybody had their own perceptions of them, their abilities and usefulness, their motivations and their predisposition. Moreover, the self-perception of a stringer was often at odds with the perception that the resident editor of the edition he was filing for, had of him. He saw himself as an honest soul simply trying to put his village on the news map, and getting pilloried by local vested interests for exposing corruption and misgovernance.

Delocalisation

After the initial flush of localisation a reaction set in to the indiscriminate flow of miscellaneous news. Newspapers were creating separate pages to cater to what circulation executives believed was a growing demand for local news, but editors were hard put to find news that could be dignified with a place on a news page. *Dainik Jagran*, which used to have three pages for Kumaon, now had nine after Uttaranchal became a state, and in a hill area with limited reporting staff, found filling them a major challenge. In Varanasi, Shashank Shekhar Tripathi, the resident editor of *Hindustan* observed about his own paper, 'We put out 11 editions, do blanket coverage. But there is a side effect to this. We give seven pages of city news, but there simply is not so much news in a city like this. Substandard items get flashed, as a result.'[40] Moreover, every half an hour an edition was being released and quality control was difficult to achieve.

In a sense he was echoing what a resident editor in his own group, posted in Patna, had said two years earlier. According to Naveen Joshi:

> Stringers file any rubbish, like a cow has overturned an egg cart. The emphasis is on volume. The resident editor comes into office and counts: We have 110 news items, fewer by two compared to *Jagran*. The pressure comes from the circulation department. Carrying anywhere from 25 to 40 stories per page is our USP. Put three lines on page 1, and carry over. If the circulation manager says I cannot sell this paper, the resident editor is gone.[41]

It was a succinct summing up of what local news came to mean: keep it local and voluminous, never mind if it scarcely deserved to be termed as news.

The resident editor of *Hindustan* in Bhagalpur in Bihar described much of what was going into his paper as stuff that did not deserve to be called news.[42] The former said he was also forced to carry substandard news on days advertising fell short. He was beginning to come round to the view that even if people wanted to see their names in print, readers were also beginning to tire of the kind of news they were being fed. After experimenting with separate pages for Banka and Kalgaon, neighbourhood areas of Bhagalpur, this was stopped, said the editor, so that they 'did not have to take rubbish'.

At this point Bhagalpur was putting out seven editions covering 19 districts, six of them in Jharkhand. In four of these districts—Katihar, Purnea, Sahibgunj, Deogarh—there were full-fledged centres, where pages were made. Saharsa sent four pages. A chief subeditor was deployed to vet all the news that went in, both in the locally made pages and those that came from other centres. He screened what stringers sent and would say sagely, 'unless 10 or 15 people have died it is not news for Patna'.[43]

Fifty-three stringers fed the Bhagalpur news centre, 10 of them had the potential to become very good, as the editors put it. These were now told that if the district magistrate and policemen were doing their job, that was not news. And that some adjectives were not necessary. If a professor was mentioned he did not have to be described as learned. The subjects which figured most frequently were crime, sex and education. Farm-related news was not a priority. When you saw the problem from the perspective of one of the stringers who fed the Bhagalpur edition it became clear that for him this was a volume game. Amrendra Kumar Tiwari gave four items a day, a 100 a month, out of which he estimated about 70 got published. It was bad enough photocopying all the stories he said, but what was worse was that the paper then paid by cheque and the bank charged for clearance. But he was enamoured of his part-time profession nonetheless, he wanted more training in writing, and wanted to use fewer words and acquire a better style.[44]

At the end of a month-long review the chief subeditor concluded that localisation had led to a drop in standards. The language used had deteriorated and the paper had become crime-based with even small local brawls being reported. Planted news was frequent, and political parties wheedled their way on to news pages with what was often no more than internal party news.[45] He decided the paper would not use news of disputes in which both side were not quoted.

When *Hindustan* began to delocalise at Bhagalpur in 2003 it was the start of a process of introspection by the big multi-edition dailies. By 2005 *Dainik Jagran* in UP and *Dainik Bhaskar* in Jaipur were asserting that the stringers they employed to report were not required to book advertising any more, or function as circulation agents. Complaints of pressure from stringers to give advertisements if a politician wanted coverage-led proprietors to seek to remedy the situation. At *Jagran,* one of them asserted that separate people has begun to be employed to book advertising.[46] And when the paper set up a school of media management in Noida, it began to send out teams to train journalists at its small town and district editions.

By the end of 2005 at least in some areas of the local news universe there was enough introspection to lead to soul-searching in editorial offices about the quality of news being peddled as well as the negative consequences that were becoming apparent in the local edition approach. *Dainik Bhaskar* began to appoint state editors, one for Chandigarh, Punjab and Haryana, and another for Rajasthan. Their job was to focus more closely on editorial quality. The Rajasthan appointment was spurred partly by the fact that *Rajasthan Patrika* had overtaken *Dainik Bhaskar* in 2004 to become No. 1 again in this state. When N.K. Singh moved from Bhopal to take on this job in mid-2005 he began a major exercise in quality control of district news and professed concern at the consequences of localisation that were becoming manifest. 'For me the issue is the fall in intellectual standards of newspapers because of localisation.' He also acknowledged that *Dainik Bhaskar* had a credibility problem in the state because of the kind of news it had been peddling.[47] There was at last recognition at the top that journalism in these parts had been led by the market with runaway consequences.

In September 2005 if you were to wander into the Jaipur office of *Dainik Bhaskar* at mid-morning you would see in a glass enclosure half a dozen men poring over newspapers at a long table. The paper had created a review cell comprised of senior subeditors to give feedback on the quality of news which had appeared in local editions across the state the previous day. What they would blue pencil was later collated into a power point presentation, prepared edition by edition to be presented at monthly meetings of resident editors. These dealt with missed stories, story structure, factual mistakes, blunders, repetition, and made comparisons with the same day's editions of *Rajasthan Patrika*. Competition first led to degradation of the editorial product, and subsequently to its improvement.

And in Ajmer in 2005 the *Bhaskar* resident editor undertook to try and improve qualitatively, the kind of journalism that came from the 80 plus stringers that this edition had. To take care of the allegations of blackmail frequently made about the professional functioning of stringers, this edition began to insist that only stories where the version of the person being written about had been obtained, would be used. Its resident editor, a young PhD from the city, held up copies of paper, with stories displayed to prominently give the version of the other side in quotes.

We do not carry any story without the other person's version. We give both sides. If the version is not available I say stop the story. Where possible we give a credit line to the stringer for getting the version. He must also feel he is a part of the paper.[48]

The second thing he did was to start separating the advertising and reporting functions. Till a year back stringers did both, but that was ending. 'Once a stringer gets an advertisement from someone he will not write against them. For Rs 200 he sells the paper.' The practice of having circulation agents as stringers was also ended. And finally the paper began to be choosy about whom it appointed to provide news. 'We do not have shopkeepers any more, we want to weed out such stringers. Nor can I use *panwalas* (people who sell *pans*) as stringers. He is my brand ambassador. Priority is a retired headmaster.'[49]

This weeding out was accompanied by an effort to strengthen the desk to turn the volume of news to advantage. Here as well as elsewhere localised newspapers were learning to collate inputs from different editions to organise them under issues. 'We can do it if we plan. Drought, water problems, midday meal, rural health system. Do the overall story properly, get the administration version, and display it. Then when we carry the whole thing we get terrific response, and instant action.'[50] Elsewhere too the scattered nature of local news coverage was being reorganised to become more purposeful. Whether it was *Prabhat Khabar* in Ranchi or *Hindustan* in Varanasi, increasingly the local news *fauj* (army) was being deployed to survey the state of governance region wide. As newspaper localisation evolved it began to develop its own strengths and the charge that local news was inconsequential and incapable of having impact began to lose its sting.

Conclusion

As urban and rural local self-governance took root in India, as local communities become more vocal and more conscious of their rights, as local commercial interests came forward to make viable the publications that could engender such a space, the emergence of a local public sphere became inevitable. But once the paper began to reach smaller places, the news network also had to encompass these places, to deliver incident-based, problem-based reporting that would draw readers. As newspapers in Hindi-speaking states expanded their circulation base they invited circulation agents to send news about their areas.

As the amount of space given to local news grew, the local news network also grew beyond the circulation agent to the advertising agent, as well as other interested individuals in the community. When the paper involved was a large and influential one, a household name all over the state, the visiting card conferred status upon the local stringer. He became the local gentry's passport to figuring in the newspaper. An important agent of localisation was thus emerging.

Localisation democratised media access and abolished conventional gatekeepers of news as stringers, and circulation agents competed to forward to the page-making centres all the local handouts they received. In a place like Chhattisgarh, those availing themselves of the proffered hospitality of a newspaper's columns ranged from organisers of local school events to the Naxalites who terrorised government functionaries in these parts.

But when stringers did the reporting themselves, many complexities coloured their output. How well he reported had to do with whether or not he also collected advertising, what his caste and professional background was, why he had come into the profession, and how much gumption he had as an individual. It also had to do with how keen his management was to have him display any journalistic derring-do. It was plain to village level civil society that while newspapers were anxious to be local and to be read, they did not always have a sense of how to use their forum to provide purposeful coverage. Yet their stringers quickly developed clout and began to matter in the pocket from where they reported. They became a member of the existing power coterie, and their caste influenced their reporting.

As localisation evolved, local reporting came under the scanner, and a process of delocalisation was initiated so that newspapers stopped creating separate pages for localities which simply did not generate that much news. Basic news ethics was revived, planted stories eliminated, and circulation, reporting and advertising functions separated. Once there was recognition at the top that journalism in these parts had been led by the market with runaway consequences, newspapers moved to restore their own credibility. They became watchful of whom they appointed as stringers, and began to insist on basic reporting ethics being adhered to.

With the cleaning up and professionalising of local news collection, its advantages became evident to those who participated in the local public sphere. Those working in the training of panchayats in rural areas sensed the change newspapers were bringing about was in the nature of politics. They brought transparency in the dynamics of political parties with the reporting they did. The army of local stringers was also being deployed to survey the state of governance regionwide. As newspaper localisation evolved it began to develop its own strengths and the charge that local news was inconsequential and incapable of having impact began to lose its sting.

Notes

1. Yadvesh, general manager *Hindustan*, interviewed by author, Varanasi, 15 March 2005.
2. 'Mirzapur: Micro Media, Minimal Impact', 29 July 2003. http://www.thehoot.org/story.asp?storyid=Web61113226hoot52519%20PM865&pn=1&section=S13.
3. Rajeev Harsh, interviewed by author, Udaipur, 2 December 2004.
4. Babulal Sharma, interviewed by author, Jaipur, January–February 2002.
5. Satish Shukla, bureau chief and subeditor, *Dainik Jagran*, interviewed by Indrajit Roy, Nautanhwa, Gorakhpur, 20 June 2003.
6. Author's observation, Jagdalpur, May 2002.
7. Sevanti Ninan, 'The Naxals and the Press'. http://www.thehoot.org/story.asp?storyid=webhoothootL1K0914023&pn=1 (accessed 29 May 2005).
8. Vastupal Jain, Paras News Agency, interview with author, Ganoda, 1 December 2004.
9. Ramesh Chandra Jain, interviewed by author, Kothda, 28 November 2004.
10. Mohammad Shahid, interviewed by author, Kothda, 28 November 2004.
11. Y.C. Agarwal, interview with author, Patna, 3 June 2003.
12. Shailendra Dixit and Anand Tripathi, *Dainik Jagran*, interview with author, Patna, 4 June 2003.
13. R.N. Jayaswal, interviewed by Indrajit Roy, Mirzapur, 13 June 2003.
14. Ram Murthy Pandey, Halliya, interviewed by Indrajit Roy, Mirzapur, 14 June 2003.
15. Ibid.
16. Rajiv Ojha, stringer, *Aj*, interviewed by Indrajit Roy, Chunar (Mirzapur), 15 June 2003.
17. Shashi Bhushan Dubey, stringer, *Aj*, interviewed by Indrajit Roy, Lalganj (Mirzapur), 14 June 2003.

18. Stringer for *Rashtriya Sahara* who pleaded for anonymity, interviewed by Indrajit Roy, Sonauli, Maharajganj, 20 June 2003.
19. Ibid.
20. Siddhanath Singh, stringer, *Jagran*, Kalhat Bazaar (Mirzapur), 15 June 2003.
21. Gyaneshwar Tiwari, Block Development Officer, interviewed by Indrajit Roy at Pahadi (Mirzapur), 13 June 2003.
22. Shiv Kedar Singh, former block *pramukh*, Narayanpur (Mirzapur), interviewed by Indrajit Roy, 15 June 2003.
23. Chandra Shekhar Shukla, Block Development Officer, interviewed by Indrajit Roy, Rajgarh (Mirzapur), 13 June 2003.
24. Santosh Srivastav, interviewed by Indrajit Roy, Mirzapur, 13 June 2003.
25. Shamshed Khan, interviewed by Indrajit Roy, Mirzapur, 15 June 2003.
26. Shashank Shekhar Tripathi, interviewed by author, Varanasi, 15 March 2005.
27. Tejbal Chaturvedi, interviewed by Indrajit Roy, Mirzapur, 14 June 2003.
28. Mohammed Karim Ansari of Chaudahawan, interviewed by Indrajit Roy, Mirzapur, 14 June 2003.
29. Chandra Mohan Prasad, interviewed by Indrajit Roy, Devripurab, 14 June 2003.
30. Chandra Shekhar Shukla, Block Development Officer, interviewed by Indrajit Roy, Rajgarh (Mirzapur), 13 June 2003.
31. Sanju Agrahari, businessman, interviewed by Indrajit Roy, Halliya town (Mirzapur), 14 June 2003.
32. Tulsi Ram Patel, interviewed by author, Sabla, Dungarpur, 1 December 2004.
33. Dipak Patel, interviewed by author, Sabla, Dungarpur, 1 December 2004.
34. Anil Kumar Singh, interviewed by Vasavi, Patan, 24 April 2003.
35. Sudeepa, programme coordinator with Aarambh, interviewed by Sushmita Malaviya, Raisen, 3 April 2004.
36. Shashank Shekhar Tripathi, interviewed by author, Varanasi, 15 March 2005.
37. Sanjeev Kshitij, resident editor, *Amar Ujala*, Varanasi, interviewed by author, 17 March 2005.
38. Naveen Joshi, resident editor, *Hindustan*, interview with author, Patna, 1 June 2003.
39. Anal Shukla, resident editor, *Nava Bharat*, interviewed by author, Raipur, May 2002.
40. Shashank Shekhar Tripathi, interviewed by author, Varanasi, 15 March 2005.
41. Naveen Joshi, resident editor, *Hindustan*, interviewed by author, Patna, 2 June 2003.

42. Vijay Bhaskar, resident editor, *Hindustan*, interviewed by author, Bhagalpur, 5 June 2003.
43. Praveen Baghi, *Hindustan*, interviewed by author, Bhagalpur, 6 June 2003.
44. Amrendra Kumar Tiwari, stringer, *Hindustan*, interviewed by author, Bhagalpur, 6 June 2003.
45. Praveen Baghi, *Hindustan*, interviewed by author, Bhagalpur, 6 June 2003.
46. Mahendra Mohan and Sanjay Gupta, interviewed by author, Noida, 2 September 2005.
47. N.K. Singh, state editor, *Dainik Bhaskar*, interviewed by author, 16–17 September 2005.
48. Indu Shekhar Pancholi, resident editor, *Dainik Bhaskar*, interviewed by author, 15 September 2005.
49. Ibid.
50. Ibid.

6

The Universe of Local News

*'We do not need to go hunting for news,
news finds its way to the paper.'*

On 10 June 2002 the Palamu edition of *Prabhat Khabar* reported
that a herd of 12 wild elephants was causing havoc in villages in the
Gopikandar division. It listed village by village the number of houses
that had been destroyed. Two days later on 12 June there was another
story. For a single column-story it was remarkably vivid. Fear of elephants was driving people to sleep in their fields, there was no help
as yet from the government; forest officials were doing nothing. *'Van
vibhag ke pad adhikariyon haath pe haath ghare baithe the'* ('the
employees of the forest department were sitting at home'). Enraged
tribals had, the previous day, beaten up a forest guard in the Dungarpur
forest office. Now they were planning to block the Dungarpur–
Dumka–Pakud road to draw attention to their plight.

The same day there was a background piece on the issue across
four columns: *'Junglee hathiyon ke bekabu uthpat pe prashasan ka
nazar nahin'* (the administration is not tracking the unrestrained
destruction caused by wild elephants). It recalled earlier incidents in
the year, with 17 people killed. For two years, said the story, elephants
had created havoc in Palamu, destroying property, making people
spend nights outside their houses in fear, until it became a political
issue. Earlier in the year Chief Minister Babulal Marandi came to
Dumka to distribute compensation among affected families.

When 11 people were killed in one night in January (*kuchal kar
maar dala*—trampled to death) it led to statewide mayhem. A decision
was taken to kill the elephants and a shooter was requisitioned, but
nobody could decide who should give the orders to kill. The state of

Jharkhand had declared the elephant the state animal (*Jharkhand ka rajkiya pashu ghoshit kar diya gaya*). How could the state animal be killed by the state government? As the newspaper account told it, the government then decided not to kill them, gifted them to the neighbouring state of West Bengal, drove them to the border and left them there. But their tusker was killed so the herd came back into Jharkhand. The government's dilemma was that it was unable to create a sanctuary for the state animal.

And now things were back to square one. By 15 June the story had moved to page one, after 27 houses had been destroyed. Another four-column story. And then a few days later when 11 more homes were destroyed, and 43 rendered homeless, yet another four-column story. By 20 June the elephants had moved on to another division, Kathikund Prakhand, and on 21 June one death by trampling was reported from there. *Prabhat Khabar*'s local rival, *Hindustan*, was tracking the same story.

Or take another story: On 30 November 2004, the Banswara edition of *Dainik Bhaskar* in Rajasthan, reported in graphic detail the forest department manoeuvres set in motion after a panther growled at 5.30 A.M. in the upper reaches of the forests near Pratapgarh. The man-eating panther had killed two girls over the previous three weeks, and a cage brought from Kota was standing by as four teams of forest guards, accompanied by a tranquilliser gun master and a shooter, scattered to surround the Khankhora forest area where the animal was. The panther did not oblige before the story went to press that night, but the newspaper and its rivals were at hand, to track it blow by blow.

The universe of local news is not dull. It resonates with action, fear, frustration and suspense as it brings alive the daily struggles of a level of citizenry who simply did not figure in the news earlier. It has demonstrated, over the periods monitored, that these struggles were not always mundane. If you lived in a forested district in India in the 21st century, neither wild animals nor the Naxalites were distant enough for comfort.

In Palamu where the elephants wrought their havoc, the bureau chief of the *Ranchi Express*, Surendra Singh Ruby, described terrorism as the most important category of news.

We do not need to go hunting for news, news finds its way to the paper ....We constantly focus on various aspects of terrorism, most specifically, why there is a steady rise in such activities. There are also drinking water problems to cover, both urban and rural. Power problems, forest problems. The railway line is held up because people are afraid the government will not relocate them.[1]

As Don Fry writes in 'What Makes Local News Really Local', local papers write about what people are talking about: they make it news. He added that local papers regarded normal things that happen to a lot of ordinary people as news.[2] And without any precedents around them to follow, this was the formula instinctively adopted for the local public sphere which came into existence in the Hindi belt. It gave voice to both the existing and emerging middle class and reflected a public preoccupation with law and order, infrastructure and governance. For the first time the spotlight was turned on the quality of governance at the most decentralised administrative levels. Because of the faithfulness with which it documented every blip as it were on the civic radar, local news was an effective barometer of systemic breakdown. It both increased the accountability of local government functionaries and made them less faceless. In the panther story in Banswara described earlier, the reporter took care to name all the forest department personnel who took part in the operation, including forest guards.

Local news was more urban than rural in focus, even if it served rural areas. It reflected a mystifying neglect of agriculture which even farmers who doubled as scribes would complain about. It was less concerned with issues of livelihood than you would expect newspapers in states with low per capita incomes to be. Whether male or female, urban or rural, the newsmakers tended to be middle class. Local news pages reflected the vibrancy of grassroots panchayat politics as well as the percolation of party politics down to the panchayat level, even as the panchayats represented the emergence of a rural middle class. Poverty existed in the local public sphere, and was taken note of. But there rarely was a subaltern perspective.

For this you had to turn to a small segment of uncommodified media with a grassroots perspective, made possible, ironically, by Indian donor funding. In the Bundelkhand area of Uttar Pradesh a fortnightly newspaper called *Khabar Lahariya*, brought out in the

Bundeli dialect, was demonstrating that you could focus on the
bottom rung of rural society and find plenty to write about. The
publication was catalysed by an educational resource centre in Delhi
called Nirantar, and run by group of rural and small town women,
some of whom were Dalits. Almost all their stories originated in villages, and a steady focus was maintained on news about Dalits and
Adivasis. A monthly eight-page paper called *Ujala Jhadi* published
from Jaipur and covering the districts of Rajasthan, also focused on
rural news, but had a more activist approach to coverage, focusing
on issues that were agitating civil society in the region (Figure 6.1).

FIGURE 6.1 *Khabar Lahariya* from Uttar Pradesh and *Ujala Jhadi* from
Rajasthan, the uncommodified press, focused on village news

The local news universe created by home-grown chroniclers also covered education and health fairly prolifically because these affected the majority's aspirations and their quality of life. The sorry state of hospitals and schools in semi-urban and rural schools came under the scanner. In addition, every local occurance of disease, death or accident made news, but was only occasionally followed up for the patterns it might yield.

Unless panchayat elections were imminent, local news priorities reflected a marked depoliticisation and gave space to new categories of news which reflected the area's cultural calender. Religious news became such a significant category that there were times of year when it could be the main news of the day. Overall the news was miscellaneous in nature partly because that was how the chroniclers understood their job. And it resonated with crime coverage because sales agents conveyed that there was demand for this category of news. Local news judgement too developed its own clear characteristics, the chief of which was unpredictability.

Sampling

This chapter is based on a sampling of local news and advertising from 2002 to 2005. Four month-long monitoring exercises of local news pages or sections were undertaken in Palamu and Santhal Parganas in Jharkhand, and Betul and Hoshangabad in Madhya Pradesh in 2002, employing the quantitative content analysis method. The districts were chosen to give representation to tribal districts (Betul and Santhal Parganas), high literacy (Betul, at 67 per cent), one with the majority of its population below the poverty line (Palamu) and non-tribal areas in two states (Palamu and Hoshangabad).

Local editions in Gurgaon in Haryana were picked for monitoring to provide a contrast to these four districts. While being semi-rural on one hand, and an extension of the capital city of New Delhi on the other, Gurgaon had become by 2005 the outsourcing capital of India, housing call centres for major multinationals. Its public sphere was beginning to reflect these contrasting realities. It was covered by major Hindi dailies publishing from Delhi, Chandigarh and Noida. One week-long comparitive monitoring of local coverage in four

Hindi dailies was undertaken in Gurgaon in 2003 and another longer period was tracked in the same district in 2004. A convenience sampling of local editions of varying newspapers, published from Patna, Varanasi, Bhopal, Lucknow, Raipur, Indore and Banswara between 2002 and 2005, has also been used for the analysis.

Nothing is too Small

For Faiyaz Ahmed, at this point the only English correspondent in Palamu, what constituted news for the *Hindustan Times* was fairly straightforward. 'All things that disrupt peace are covered by me. Anything that becomes news—a Hindu boy marrying an Muslim girl or vice versa. Background of leaders and an analysis of their speech are my favourites.' He listed other issues that mattered: paucity of grain, water problems, illiteracy. None of the towns and villages in Palamu had adequate health and clinical facilities. 'None of these issues is small.'[3] His colleague at *Hindustan* had his own grading of what was fit to print: 'Naxalism, tribals converting to Christianity, the mafia world, illegal activities, the middlemen menace. When it comes to the representative of a district judge taking a bribe, that can only be written in form of allegation.'[4]

As the reporter put it, none of these issues was small for the people who lived in that district. It affected their quality of life. For the first time a local discourse was being created around them. This was so geographically circumscribed that it shut out what might be happening in the neighbouring district, barely 200 km away. (The consequences of that will be discussed later in this book.) But within the district's towns, villages and *kasba*s, civic life came under the scanner.

Civil construction in rural India is a permanent scandal. But now every single road and building in which shoddy materials were used, was a potential subject for newspaper coverage. Nothing was too small or inconsequential for the day's local edition. If there had been better governance in India's districts—if salaries were paid, if Harijans and tribals had access to housing schemes floated in their name, if schools had roofs and teachers, if citizens got their pensions, if clean drinking water was available in every village and municipal locality—much of this news would lose its bite.

When a local small farmer or shopkeeper acquires a press card it does perhaps open the door to blackmail as is frequently argued by critics of newspaper localisation. But infinitely more, as competition among newspapers brought checks and balances, it shone the light of exposure on the myriad petty scams that permeate every sphere of local governance in democratic India. As politicians, bureaucrats and journalists themselves said repeatedly in the course of researching this book, 'khabar nahin rukhti' (literally, news cannot be held back; figuratively, wrongdoing has nowhere to hide). Anil Swarup, a senior bureaucrat in UP would add wryly, 'It is true, but unfortunately since some of us are saleable, kuch khabar rukhti hai' (some news can be stopped).

He also had an unusual take on the response of the administration to these news items on local scams.

> I used to take them seriously, then I found that if you ordered inquiries the journalists become very important. And their blackmail capacity increases. So what one began to do was to get an informal factual ascertainment of what is happening. You can just ask for the files. Files speak for themselves.[5]

Whose voices could be heard in this local public sphere? Nobody was too inconsequential to figure in it, but governance rather than inequality was on the local reporter's agenda. The actors were ordinary people as well as local politicians and a variety of government functionaries whose names are faithfully listed in any story about government or political activities. But apart from such worthy gentry, small-time lawbreakers became newsmakers, as crime topped the reader's list of local news most in demand—'400 telephones dead because of robbery.' 'Man sent to jail for stealing a duck.' A village water supply pump operator employed by the public health department in a village called Aichwadi in Gurgaon whose salary had not been paid by the panchayat for three years merited a double-column story with highlights.[6] Teachers and students figured regularly.

In summer a village with a water problem would figure prominently on the local news page. And when the edition had a photographer and news editor who knew their job local news ceased to be inconsequential and faceless. As local editions went colour, they featured large colour photographs of people who never before would have newsmakers, such as a five-column colour photograph of village women gathered for a ceremony in memory of a *havaldar* killed on duty; or of a line of prisoners awaiting their turn for a check-up at a health awareness camp inside jail; or a picture of diggers uncovering a gaping hole in mainline water supply pipe, a wordless explanation for why 150,000 people went without water in their taps the previous day.[7]

Local News Judgement

Local news judgement had one distinctive characteristic: it was usually completely unpredictable. As *Dainik Bhaskar*'s state news coordinator in Jaipur, Ramesh Agarwal, put it, news judgement varied more in local editions because there was no hard and fast criteria for local news. The first lead could be the arrival of the monsoons, the local presence of a celebrity, or the opening of a religious fair.

> We can make wrong decisions also. In choosing the first lead we could take wrong decisions at local level, depending on the quality of the desk in-charge. Journalists here are not so educated. Public interest is main criteria, but our reading of that interest may vary.[8]

But it was mostly event-based news based on a gauging of reader interest. Local crime and accident were important. As for the day's lead, the criteria had changed.

Dainik Bhaskar's state editor for Rajasthan N.K. Singh said that back in 1975–76, when he planned the front page as a subeditor, if the prime minister made a speech you knew you had the day's first lead. That was no longer the case.[9]

> Ten years ago political news was big. Statements by big guys would be news. Now the big guy need not be a politician. Could be Bipasha Basu. Lata Mangeshkar, a poet, anyone can be first lead.[10] If I carry a speech by minister ten people will read. If a minister trips and falls, a hundred will read.[11]

In an earlier age news judgement was independent of the principle of demand and supply. A paper did not look at what was in demand, it gave reader what it thought he should read. But now with competition in every local news arena, you needed to understand what the demand was for.

In a large multi-edition paper such as the *Dainik Bhaskar* constant transfers ensured that the man deciding the day's edition need not be from the region at all, so the challenge became greater. In different parts of Rajasthan, for instance, different festivals rated reader interest. How much should the *Teej* festival be played up in Jaipur? Or the Urs mela in Ajmer? Primarily the reader was interested in what affected him or her. And that included coverage of rain in Rajasthan, the only Indian state with a desert within its boundaries. No matter how much destruction excessive rainfall might do, in that state, said the paper's state editor, you had to be careful not to be negative in reporting rain.[12]

Some categories of news which had barely existed in newspapers a decade or two earlier were now emerging as local news staples. News related to religion was one such category. In November 2004 the resident editor of *Dainik Bhaskar*'s Banswara edition in southern Rajasthan would assert that for his edition the major news was religious as such activities took place all year round.[13] Banswara had a huge amount of religion-related news. *Rajasthan Patrika* even printed posters related to the Beneshwar mela, an annual tribal fair, and when it took place it generated a number of local advertising supplements. The paper's chief of bureau said they started covering the event 25 years ago.

When news was defined as anything the reader was interested in, religion scored high as a priority with the local populace (Figure 6.2). *Hindustan*'s Bhagalpur edition in 2003 had a designated page which featured religious news. In Varanasi the resident editor of *Hindustan* said that there were nine different temples devoted to the Navratras (a festival of nine nights of worship) and the paper had to do 'proper coverage' of the activities at each one because the reader was keen on such news.[14] And the Charkha survey of local news in Jharkhand, Uttaranchal and Chhattisgarh made special mention of the fact that the trend of having a separate beat for religion/spirituality has been

FIGURE 6.2 Religious news: *Nayi Duniya*'s Diwali special issue and *Punjab Kesari*'s weekly supplement, *Dharm Sanskriti*

started in every paper. Festivals and observances apart, temple-building or administration is regularly reported on. In June 2002 in *Prabhat Khabar* in Palamu there were a number of stories that assumed reader interest in contentious issues of temple management. *Dainik Bhaskar* went one better: one of its editions, Ujjain, had a godman as resident editor, who was abroad for some months in the year giving discourses. He doubtless ensured that his edition did full justice to the coverage of things godly.

Through the 1990s, with reader interest beginning to define news priorities, the presence of reports and columns relating to religion and spirituality grew in both the English language and regional language press. *The Hindu*, which had traditionally carried a sermon on its inside pages, would be joined by *The Times of India*, and then *Indian Express* and *Hindustan Times* in having a regular column on spiritual matters. On television the number of 24-hour channels devoted to religious matters grew to four by 2005. So it was wholly predictable that when local editions came, furiously competing to cater to the interests of small town, semi-urban and rural India, they would reflect in their pages the year round calender of festivals and observances that define cultural and spiritual life in the country.

The editions of *Dainik Jagran* and *Dainik Bhaskar* in the month of March 2002 in Hoshangabad, Madhya Pradesh, reflected this: on 17 out of 30 days in the *Bhaskar*, and on 18 out of 30 days in *Dainik Jagran* religious observances rated space in the local pages, through photographs and coverage. In addition to the festivity related to Mahashivratri and Holi, there were reports conforming to the increasingly common trend of carrying sermons of local godmen and holy women. When Krishna Devi spoke on Bhakti during a five-day *pravachan* (sermon), *Dainik Jagran* carried reports with pictures on all five days. A reporter in Faizabad in UP would describe how the holy men of Ayodhya had taken to having press releases of their *pravachan* delivered to newspaper offices, along with a thousand rupees as *dakshina* (offering), to ease the sermon's passage into the next day's edition.[15]

A Swedish anthropologist who attempted an ethnography of *Dainik Jagran* described how the Lucknow newsroom assigned festival stories out of a desire to take the newspaper closer to the common man, but how the journalists executing them produced idealised and stereotyped coverage because for this genre of journalism they had no models to follow (Stahlberg 2002: 161–62). Depoliticisation of news was beginning to make commercial sense but had yet to acquire journalistic rationale.

A Comparitive Exercise

An exercise undertaken for this book compared news judgement across four local editions over seven days in Gurgaon in Haryana. 11 March 2003 was a rare day when three local editions led with the same story, datelined Gurgaon, of the Haryana Urban Development Authority demolishing the large house of a former Congress minister because it violated building laws. The *Gurgaon Bhaskar* found the story so compelling that it carried four pictures of the incident, *Amar Ujala*'s Gurgaon News ('Newj') three and *Punjab Kesari* three.

On the second day, 12 March, it was still a first lead for *Amar Ujala* but not for *Dainik Bhaskar*. A more typical day would be 10 March when not a single story was common to all four front pages of the local editions/pages: *Amar Ujala, Punjab Kesari, Hindustan* and *Gurgaon Bhaskar*. A story on the construction of a Sheetal Mata temple figures in three of the four editions, two other stories were carried in two editions each; there were no stories common to all four editions. There were very different front pages for each edition on 13 March and on 14 March *Gurgaon Bhaskar* and *Amar Ujala*'s *Gurgaon News* actually had the same lead, on a man arrested for selling forged certificates. *Punjab Kesari* however led with a feature on sanitation workers getting stepmotherly treatment from the government and *Hindustan* with the demolition of some encroachments. But of the total stories carried that day on page one—eight each in *Bhaskar* and *Ujala*, 10 in *Punjab Kesari* and 12 in *Hindustan*—there were not more than three that appeared on two front pages each.

The variety of stories on these pages demonstrated that just about anything can go on page one of a local edition. A change in the school syllabus made for a prominent four-column story in *Dainik Bhaskar*, but no other edition carried that story either on page one, or on any other page that day. Nor did anyone else carry '18 cows saved before slaughter' (*Amar Ujala*, 14 March). On the 15, 16 and 17 March it was the same. No story was common to four editions, and no one had the same lead story as any body else. The spectrum of what local news can cover was so wide that newspapers were constantly evolving their own news judgement. It could touch on local self-governance, political strife, power theft, blocked drains, stray cows, school functions, a local protest or simply a large donation to a local temple.

A local edition for a district like Gurgaon which borders New Delhi covers the gamut from local–rural to international and reflects a culture which is at once traditional and modern, regressive and aspirational. International Womens Day is observed as a political and social ritual in the district but there is also a story tucked away on page three of *Amar Ujala*'s *Gurgaon News* which talks of the continuing scourge of female foeticide, thanks to a mushrooming of amniocentesis clinics. The sex ratio for the district which houses India's fastest growing city dropped from 927 women per 1,000 men in the year 2000 to 780 per 1,000 men by 2004 according to the local census office.

What was significant was that in many ways the news in Gurgaon was no different from those items which fill local pages in Palamu in distant Jharkhand. Trees were illegally cut, liquor was illegally brewed, the Lok Jan Shakti Party in Gurgaon was rallying for the rights of Dalits, labourers and farmers. Teacher transfers were an issue here as much as there, drinking water was a problem, urban and rural roads were a mess, and crime was a big ticket item as a news category. Illegal arms were being confiscated in both places. A photograph of women thronging a village secondary school corridor for a health camp could also quite easily belong to a Palamu newspaper edition.

Local scandals played well, and if riveting enough could occupy much of page one in the local pull-out. On 17 March 2004 the *Dainik Bhaskar* devoted the top half of a page to a local controversy involving a *mahant* (temple head), and a foreign national, a Canadian woman, claiming to be his wife. He said she was like his daughter. The headline was snappy: '*Maria kahe pati, Mahant kahe beti.*' (Maria says husband, Mahant says daughter).

The headlines that were relatively absent in Gurgaon were the plethora of items relating to corruption which could be found in Palamu. And some headlines which one would be unlikely to find in Palamu related to golf tournaments and the fact that Chinese apples were affecting the sale of Indian apples. Or a report on Arabian Nights at a local starred hotel. Also unlikely would be a large front page item on the Punjabi pop singer Mika and his fusion music. Gurgaon was both urban and rural and its urban part was a fast growing satellite of the county's capital, New Delhi.

The newspapers here may have been in Hindi but the upwardly mobile, liberalising economic climate infected the newsroom which cheerfully sprinked its Hindi with English. News figured in the masthead as 'newj'. On 14 March 2003 the *Gurgaon Bhaskar* used both the English word syllabus and the Hindi word *pathyakram* in the same story. On the same page it talked of fieldworkers, certificates, and used the phrase, 'crimes against women' in the Devanagari script. Words of daily usage just slipped into the vocabulary: elsewhere you came across master plan, personality, act, diocese, test, season and brand ambassador. And the chief minister was always a 'CM' (*Seeyam*).

Politics at the Grassroots

Despite the trend towards depoliticisation, panchayat elections feature as a major event in the local news calendar. In January 2005 in Madhya Pradesh and then again in August 2005 in Uttar Pradesh, the panchayat elections which were held established that local editions have learned to make the most of this exercise of grassroots political power. Their marketing departments induced candidates to advertise themselves, and their reporters fanned out to do blanket coverage.

Panchayat elections have grown in importance with decentralisation of power which gives elected village office bearers sanctioning power over government schemes. They have become lucrative, and money power has become a factor in elections at this level. In 2005 it was observed that spending on panchayat elections reached a new high—the sale of liquor went up across the state and muscle power was deployed for the first time in a panchayat election.[16] Both bureaucrats and journalists in Lucknow used the same cynical phrase to describe what panchayati raj now stood for: decentralisation of corruption. As Mahesh Pande the news coordinator at *Hindustan* put it, winning a panchayat election gave the village panchayat a sanction for five years of corruption. Reports filed by his local stringers reflected the increased money power in what used to be a village-level grassroots exercise, he said, adding that they would write about the wining and dining of rural voters. People now even came from abroad to vote in panchayat elections because the stakes were so high.[17] The paper gave plenty of space to printing thousands of panchayat results, as did *Dainik Jagran*, which had a later closing deadline every night.

These were very closely fought elections: people were known to win or lose by a single vote. On 27 August 2005 *Dainik Jagran*'s Gonda edition reported that six dozen policemen were being deployed at every counting centre, and that the administration had disallowed mobile phones at these centres. From the reports filed on polling day it was evident that newspaper stringers were going around from one polling booth to the other to report what percentage of votes was cast by what hour of the day.

In Jharkhand in April 2002 with panchayat elections imminent, political coverage at the local level was substantially panchayat-related, though much of it from the perspective of political parties. In theory panchayati raj implies local self-governance without political party affiliation, in practice all recent panchayat elections in the Hindi speaking states have demonstrated political party affiliations. *Prabhat Khabar*, through the month, had 80 items of local political coverage, of which 33 were directly related to the preparations for or the prospects of panchayat elections. *Hindustan* had some 50 items of political news in the same month of which 17 were related to panchayat elections. The majority of items in both newspapers related to party-affiliated panchayat politics.

National–Regional–Local

The local public sphere was shaped not just by the local pages or pull-outs that it carried, but by the entire package that arrived in the morning at the reader's doorstep. Apart from the district-level pages a local edition brought with it news from the outside world. On any given day the front page of a local edition (as opposed to the pull-out) was likely to be an apt illustration of the triumphs, tragedies and banalities which move a country like India. Take for instance the front page of the Sitamarhi edition of *Hindustan* in Bihar on a single day, 2 June, in the year 2003. There were 15 stories and nine briefs. The first lead that day was filed by the editor of the paper, Mrinal Pande, from Lausane in Switzerland recording the prime minister's success in getting five major nations to support India's position on cross-border terrorism emanating from Pakistan. She was in the journalist contingent accompanying the prime minister. It was displayed with a common headline along with a story filed by PTI in London which said that the Pakistani foreign minister had acknowledged that there was cross-border terrorism.

The second lead was a story on a train that had created rail history within Bihar by taking 14 hours to traverse 140 kilometres on account of a rail accident affecting track clearance. A box item said that the passengers had gone without food and water for that period. Immediately below the Lausane story were three stories: a one-and-half-column item on the kidnapping and murder of the brother of the district chief of the Dalit Sena, a single-column news item on a Supreme Court ruling regarding the cricketer Ajay Jadeja, and a single para report on the murder of a forester's wife in Patna. Beneath the Jadeja item the paper took note of an arrest warrant issued in Navada for a former minister in the state.

Elsewhere on page one you were told that nine independent legislators in neighbouring Uttar Pradesh had declared allegiance to the coalition government's Chief Minister Mayawati, that the election to 24 seats of the Vidhan Parishad in Bihar had been notified, that a scuffle over recovering parking charges had led to stoning and *golabari* (firing) at Tatanagar station resulting in the death of one, that a Shia–Sunni clash had killed two in Ghosi and that the agency of a consumer goods multinational company in Patna had been broken into, leading to firing within the premises. Beneath all this mayhem was a four-column bottom anchor on the highest paid company executives in India, which told you that the Wipro chief took home a salary of Rs 48 million a year. The fruits of liberalisation in India, the frustration of daily travel in Bharat (India), a transient Indian diplomatic triumph over Pakistan, a sprinking of violence, mayhem and crime, and one more election. All of this jostled for the attention of the newspaper reading public in *mofussil* (district) Bihar. The nine briefs originated outside the state. There were no local stories on this page one.

If you moved on to the same day's Santhal Parganas edition of the paper printed from Bhagalpur and intended to cover parts of Jharkhand, a distinct geographical shift was visible. Of the 10 stories on page one, five were datelined Ranchi. The prime minister's Lausane triumph was banished to a brief. But the top salaries story held its ground. The first lead was five deaths in a fire in the house of a forest warden in Ranchi, along with a picture of police in the house, the second a well laid out three-column listing of bureaucrats shifted in a statewide shuffle.

The news that the prime minister was visiting Bihar for 340 minutes (as the paper put it) two days later was only front page news for the *Nagar* (city), *Nagar Star* and *Star Nagar* editions coming out of the state capital Patna. In the further reaches of the state—Bhagalpur, Santhal Parganas, Magadh, Champaran, Sitamarhi—it did not figure on page one. But with the exception of Bhagalpur city, every other front page had the same bottom anchor on chief executive salaries, with the same photographs featuring three high-fliers. And without exception, every single edition of that day's paper (they were 24, printed from three centres) had cutouts of Ally McBeal and Serena Williams on the ear panels (Figure 6.3). Both told you something about what Indians in small town India wanted to read about. In all the editions on this day, truly local stories were tucked into the inside pages.

And what did one edition of a multi-edition paper pick up from other districts for its state page, which could be one page or two? In the case of *Dainik Jagran* in Patna stories picked up from the district bureaus for the state's page can either be read as a reflection of the law and order situation in Bihar at that point, or a reflection of the newspaper's news priorities, based on its understanding of a reader's interest.

FIGURE 6.3 Serena Williams and Ally McBeal adorn the masthead of the
Champaran edition of *Hindustan* in Bihar

The *Apna Pradesh* page, the only page in the Patna edition to find
space for news from the rest of the state, had on Monday, 2 June
2003, 14 news stories from different districts, not counting the briefs:
one on the shooting of a village *mukhiya* (head) in Raxaul, another
on tension following shooting in Siwan, three different stories related
to kidnappings one of which announced the release of three kidnapped youth, and various other stories relating to murder, death in
custody, police nabbing extremists and so on. Not a single one of the
14 news items was unrelated to crime. The next day's state's pages
(3 June 2002) had 16 stories, 14 related to crime and killings. On a
third day the mix was an improvement, eight items were offence-or
crime-related, four were not.

In an articulation of news strategy, one editor said that the soul of
localisation lay in changing what people were willing to read about
first thing in the morning. Was is something that had shaken their
country, a major development in state politics, or an event far more
circumscribed, which had perhaps shaken their town? Harivansh,

the editor of *Prabhat Khabar*, recalls the first time he decided to break with the convention of what constituted the page one lead in a city newspaper. In November 1989, on the eve of national elections, a dacoity took place in the house of a widow at 5 P.M. in the evening in the city of Ranchi. The family's possessions were looted and the two daughters molested.

> I made a lead story of that incident. Now what was my mentality behind highlighting that? It says something about Ranchi society, if we live in such an insecure city that a widow cannot live safely in our midst. That lady said I will leave, I cannot live here. So we decided to make it the lead. That was the turning point. Local crime became an issue in that election. A year ago I saw that *The Telegraph* had made a lead story of a boy falling into a manhole. But we did that kind of thing years ago.[18]

A News Board

Miscellany was the defining characteristic of the local news universe and tended to comprise the largest category in month-long periods of monitoring undertaken. In Santhal Parganas and Palamu it was by far always the single largest category of news items in both papers monitored, *Hindustan* and *Prabhat Khabar*. These were made up of protest *bandh*s, electricity and water crises, cultural programmes, property disputes and such gems as an MLA (Member of Legislative Assembly) and MP fighting over the foundation-stone-laying programme of a school. The stories concerned unutilised funds, cultural programmes, truck collisions, hunger strikes, seminars, even someone creating a record by playing a tabla for over 25 hours. And when an 85-year-old married a 38-year-old widow, he made news.

A collection of headlines with datelines from the *Champaran Star* edition of the *Hindustan* in Bihar[19] illustrates the pell-mell clubbing together of disparate news that attracts the label miscellaneous.

- Pulse polio campaign speeded up, Narkatiyaganj;
- Farewell function (to principal), Narkatiyaganj;

- Accused jailed in a loot case, Majholiya;
- Terror over abduction incidence, Sikta;
- Injured in land dispute, Gownaha;
- Labourers migrating towards Ladakh, Lauriya;
- Students of Dhobeen Middle School receive education under tree; Lauriya;
- Preparations for Congress conference, Mainatand;
- Boys and girls of rural areas have won (in a Sanskrit competition), Ramnagar;
- Panchayat meeting, Mainatand;
- Seminar organised, Valmikinagar;
- Business of selling illegal liquor in Sathi going on fearlessly;
- Literacy workers took lamp in place of food, Narkatiyaganj.

And yet within that miscellaneous list are telling headlines. Labourers migrating towards Ladakh is one, students of Dhobeen Middle School receive education under tree, is another, literacy workers took lamp in place of food, is a third. They told you something, however cursorily, about the quality of life in India.

The purpose of this bunching together of disparate news, most of which got no follow up at all in subsequent editions, was to create a news board which recorded civic life so minutely that every citizen would be tempted to subscribe to the paper and advertise in it.

The second largest category of news in most local editions was crime. Why does crime get so much coverage in local news the world over? Partly because reader and viewer feedback indicates an interest in crime news and partly because it is a regular beat for even the smallest of newspapers. Then again, it is a regular beat because newspapers assume a demand for crime coverage. Regional editors across the Hindi belt acknowledged the pride of place crime reporting had on their pages, and certainly circulation and marketing confirmed that they gave editorial feedback from their newsagents indicating that people wanted to read about crime in their localities.

About apprehension of criminals or reporting of crime? About neighbourhood crime, quality-of-life crimes, business crime, or effects of crime (including victims and prisons), or family and juvenile crime?[20] As far as one could gauge such a systematic approach to crime reporting had not evolved in the local Hindi press. But it was definitely a beat, perhaps the most important one. As the resident editor of *Hindustan* in Varanasi put it, '*crime kuch bhi ho jaye*, highlight.' (whatever crime takes place highlight it).[21] And Sunita Aron the resident editor of *Hindustan Times* in Lucknow would say, 'For Hindi newspapers crime is important. We are careful about crime. The minute you start investigating you know it will go all the way up.' Meaning, in Uttar Pradesh, crime had the patronage of the highest levels of the political hierarchy.[22]

But certainly for newspapers in Bihar crime was very important. Whether in Bhagalpur or Patna the management cadres in *Hindustan* made it clear that they were keen to give their readers all the crime coverage they could. 'Crime is on top of everybody's concern, crime has to be there.'[23] Journalists and managers in Uttar Pradesh would joke that in Bihar the role models available were all associated with crime, that is why there was so much demand for crime coverage. In Patna, journalists who found that home truth more depressing than funny would confirm that crime got the biggest coverage in the state, partly because it had become such a pervasive industry. The number of kidnappings rose from 212 in united Bihar in 1990 to 387 in the state after the separation of the state. And the number of gangs operating in kidnapping had risen from 12 or 13 in 1988 to an estimated 70 in 2003.[24]

The Diara *chetra* (division) of Bhagalpur, sandwiched between Kosi and Ganga, was so crime-ridden that the *Hindustan* stringer for the area would confidently assert that 90 per cent of those who lived there were offenders. The region was covered by a *jyotish maharaj* (vedic astrologer) called Sri Ram Pathak, whose yeoman service as a crime reporter was so much in demand that the resident editor of the paper, according to him, had come to his house to enlist him. He was paid Rs 10 per crime story in addition to a stipend of Rs 200 per month, so there was an incentive to produce volume: '300 to 350 I used to send, 100–125 would be printed, now I send 125 to 150, 60 to 80 get published.' He was a stringer for *Jagran* when the *Hindustan* wooed him away; in the process they inherited a defamation case that had been filed against him when he had reported some years earlier for *Aj*. This was for reporting on an incident of gang rape which occurred during a residential training camp organised by the department of education. The accused was a local mafia don he said, who then filed a defamation case against him.[25]

The superintendent of police for that region would confirm that the area was crime-prone, partly because the dimensions of the land changed whenever the rivers flooded, leading to disputes over boundaries. He would offer his own take on crime reporting: 'Reporters are so friendly, *hamari galti nahin chapte, hamari achievements chapte hain*' (they do not write about our mistakes, only about our achievements). They also do excessive crime reporting, he said; some stringers go to the spot and write, others find out on the phone. He added that they were fond of publishing a crime story on the front page, though all stories did not necessarily belong on page one.[26]

There was no localised Hindi newspaper which did not ride the crime bandwagon. At *Jagran* a marketing executive would cite his paper's USP (Unique Selling Point): 'We give stage two of the crime.'[27] When the paper launched its Hindi news channel on TV in 2005 it advertised its crime coverage thus:

> Channel 7's Crime Time has a range of shows covering the entire gamut of crime in the country. From scams or financial frauds to the savagery of a love turned sour, from a look into the world of juvenile crime, an insight into the world of forensics— Channel 7 has it all.

But unlike television crime reporting which in India through 2005–06 developed into full-scale daily evening crime shows employing actors as anchors, local crime news coverage was too itemised for the most part to dwell too long on crimes. However it was voluminous, conforming with a trend common in local news coverage in countries like the United States of America.

And this was because it was a beat. The 'excessive crime reporting' that the police official above complained of is explained thus by a crime news analyst:

> Newspapers have a lot of crime coverage because they have reporters designated to look for it. This may seem self-evident,

but consider how the police beat works on most newspapers, large and small. Each day the police reporter—or reporters in the case of metro—checks in with anywhere from a half dozen to two dozen law enforcement agencies seeking an answer to the question, 'What's going on?'

On a metro with a morning and evening cop reporter that question will get asked more than once a day. Do the maths: metro police beat reporters are asking cops 'What's going on?' as much as 40 or 50 times a day—a guaranteed way to produce stories.

Does that happen on any other beat? No, but imagine if it did. Imagine how the content mix would change if health or education or arts reporters made 20, 30 or 40 phone calls a day looking for stories.[28]

In Rajasthan, in a village outside Banswara a self-taught young stringer described how he would ring the nearest police station for his area and check as to whether any crime had occurred in its jurisdiction, particularly one that lent itself to a photograph. He would then go along, take a picture with his digital camera and transmit it to the local edition in Dungarpur by modem.[29] But even if there was no picture, he was guaranteed one crime story a day, he said. Citizen journalists over time developed as sharp a nose for crime news as any city reporter on the beat. A *Ranchi Express* correspondent in Palamu said that he had to respond to public demand, 'People here want to read anything related to crime', and admitted to occasionally sensationalising news.

I would be lying if I said I do not sensationalise at all. There was a mini gun factory in Chanepur. The police was completely unaware. But when I hyped up this story and added spice to it, the police became alert. They raided the factory and destroyed it completely. The headline of the article was, 'Mini gun factory operating just ½ km from police station. Govt has no clue.' This is what reader wants to read. It increases the market of the newspaper.[30]

There was however, a positive side to this market-dictated fondness for reporting crime. The resident editor of the *Amar Ujala* in Varanasi could recall a time when journalists were on the mafia payroll. They never reported crime.[31]

Reflecting Insurgency

Distinct from everyday crime was the shadow of insurgency that loomed large over some parts of the Hindi belt and figured in daily discourse. In Jharkhand, Chhattisgarh and parts of Bihar the more than two decades old Naxal insurgency is sufficiently entrenched for its proponents to be significant actors in the daily life of the region. And as a manager of *Rashtriya Navin Mail* put it, 'without news of the extremists, our paper looks incomplete. Our readers are dissatisfied.'[32]

In Bihar and Jharkhand the daily reporting on the activities of insurgents had a matter of fact tone. Its frequency suggested that the Naxalites were active on a daily basis, and the nature of items in both papers under review suggests that the news source was usually the local police. A month-long analysis of the local news items in the Santhal Parganas edition of *Hindustan* in April 2002 shows that news relating to Naxalites construed the third largest category, after miscellaneous and political news (41 items). A similar break-up of the local news over the same period, for the same district, in another newspaper, *Prabhat Khabar*, shows that here too, news relating to this group makes up the third largest category. The majority are single-column reports: beating, burning bombing prevail. In the course of the month there is one analytic report, displayed over seven columns, a feature on why the group known as Peoples' War Group (PWG) directs its actions against the establishment.

In the *Hindustan*, when the accused in a bomb blast case was arrested, the story got a five-column spread, and the reporter took a byline (on 13 April 2003). The news was about encounters, arrests, attacks. The Naxals figured as both perpetrators and victims, but usually the former. One four-column bylined report told you that in Lohardaga in Palamau, Naxals are running the village. Another three-column bylined story reported that the villagers lived in fear due to the activities of the PWG (20 April). And then, over three columns, 'Gadhwa residents living in fear of People's War naxals' (*Hindustan*, 30 April 2003). It may be an outlawed group, but they were treated like political actors: their meetings and campaigns were reported, as were the accusations that the PWG periodically made against the police. It is significant that reporters were not afraid to take bylines: there was a sense that the Naxals were not averse to having their depredations reported.

The *Prabhat Khabar* published 15 stories in the same month on Naxal actions ranging from bombing, killing, kidnapping conducting a people's court, having a meeting, to running a village, launching a poster campaign. In comparison there were only three on actions by state, two of these on encounters. This paper had more long analytic stories, including an eight-column look at why ruling party politicians were being targeted, published the same day that an attack on a BJP politician took place. An analysis was generated with remarkable speed. It gave the recent background of Naxal activities, asserting that they had come under pressure and fear for their life and their weapons. Yet at the same time it said that after a certain police officer was transferred the pressure on Naxals had lessened. The police investigations in earlier incidents, said the backgrounder, had produced nothing.

According to an old hand at *Ranchi Express*, brought back from retirement to help fight the competition in Palamu, terrorism was the single most important category of news. 'There is a whole lot of news in Palamu, we do not have to work at all. We focus constantly on various aspects of terrorism, and why there is a steady rise in such activities.'[33]

In Chhattisgarh when the state's formation was followed by a burst of media proliferation, the Naxalites were quick to seize the opportunity to use the media to counter the pressure put on them by the country's armed forces, deployed in Bastar. They mounted a carefully calibrated image-building strategy, seeking through press notes, letters to the editor columns, and even press tours, to co-opt a media used to taking its version of events from the police. Press releases were issued by different levels of the organisation, both the special zonal committees as well as the central committee of the organisation known as Peoples' War. And they designated spokespeople at different levels.

The then resident editor of *Deshbandhu*, a newspaper headquartered in Raipur, said their strategy at that point was to be seen as a political party.[34] Meanwhile *Highway Channel*, a local evening paper affiliated to *Deshbandhu*, published from Jagdalpur in Bastar, frequently investigated incidents perpetrated by Naxalites and became known for its courageous reports on exposing both their operations and the Congress party's calculations vis-à-vis the extremists, as well as the Congress state government's paralysis in these areas. As a social worker operating in the area put it, local newspapers like this one 'brought transparency in the dynamics of political parties, enabling discussion on why parties follow a certain policy.'[35]

Market Driven Priorities

If crime and insurgency figured high in the categories of news believed to be demanded by readers, so did education and health. Both these areas of development news were assiduously covered because the newspapers sensed that education was related to people's aspirations, and health to their quality of life.

The reporting on education in *mofussil* India runs the gamut from humdrum to stark and poignant. On 31 March 2002 in *Prabhat Khabar* you could find a report on a school in the Santhal Parganas division of Jharkhand which has not had a principal since 1976: the Netarhaat Adivasi Dayboarding School. Against 46 sanc-tioned posts there were 28 teachers, and no principal.[36]

This was a world in which textbooks remained unavailable, where the principal was arrested for siphoning off a teacher's salary, where an unthinking transfer policy ensured that Bengali and Hindi language teachers were sent to an Urdu medium school, and where there were schools with three teachers for 600 students, though Jharkhand's official teacher-pupil ratio was 1:26 (*Jharkhand Development Report 2006*: 50). A small newspaper headline would record that the answer booklets for a board exam did not arrive in time for the exam to be held. Or that students could not join a school because the person who had to sign their form had been transferred and not replaced.

Unlike farming, migration and hunger, the education sector does get covered. Often routinely, but sometimes painstakingly. The coverage usually falls into the following categories: individual accomplishments, infrastructure, education as a cottage industry, events such as training camps, results, speeches, and institutional stories. In Palamu in the month of June 2002 there were 47 stories in the course of a month on the local pages, more than one a day; eight related to events, and there were 15 qualitative reports.

A five-column story on a literacy programme in Dumka took a detailed look at the financial neglect and disruption caused by the irregular flow of funds. A four-column Bokaro story looked at shrinking curriculum choices, many schools had stopped offering humanities subjects in this township. One reason for the steady coverage was that there was a Chhatra Chetna Sangathan (Student Awareness Association) in this region, with a spokesperson who held press conferences on these issues. That helped to focus the attention of the press.

A small two-column story filed by a representative from Godda narrated that the district education officer's (DEO's) absence from office (because he was transferred and no replacement had joined) meant that students who had made it successfully to Navodaya schools (goverment-funded public schools) but needed the DEO's signature on their papers could not complete their admission. Meanwhile an employee there was demanding Rs 200 from each student for a signature. All kinds of administrative hitches led to the harassment of students in these parts.

Prabhat Khabar's reporting often stood out. On 13 June 2002 a four-column story datelined Bokaro reported that 18 students tried to immolate themselves in front of the house of a politician heading a technical institute. This could have been an one-column item saying 'students immolate themselves'. Or it could have been just a sensational story. Instead it went into the whole vexatious issue of affiliation , with the High Court overturning previous judgements on the matter, and what that was doing to the students' future. The college had been built with this MLA's constituency funds, but it never did get affiliation to the All India Council for Technical Education.

A quantitative survey done over three months for Jharkhand found that out of 1,671 news items there were 289 on education. However these did not contain any discussion on the quality of education. Much of the news related to higher education or of the activities of the English-medium schools. The agitation of college or university teachers got more space than primary education in rural areas, or even the actual state of education-related schemes.[37]

At the time of year-end school and college examinations, stories on cheating become endemic in Haryana, Bihar, Madhya Pradesh and Uttar Pradesh. The ultimate irony is the coexistence on newspaper pages of a steady volume of advertising from the education industry, promising quality education in rarified surroundings along with a veritable rash of stories on academic corruption. Even as the demand for private education swells the volume of educational advertising, the examination system for private and public education is under strain everywhere in small town and rural India.

In the month of March newspapers everywhere in the Hindi belt have their crop of stories on cheating. In 2005 the *Hindustan* in Varanasi published a pageful of photographs taken in Balia and Azamgarh districts. Seventeen photographs with mocking captions and the headline '*Ise pariksha nahin mission kadachar kahiye sahib?*' (call this mission cheating, not an examination). It observed sardonically that the Uttar Pradesh Madhyamik Shiksha Parishad which claimed to conduct the world's largest board exam had a lot to answer for. The photographs showed some youths hanging from the windows of halls where exams were being conducted, they also showed groups of students sitting on grassy lawns writing answer papers. On page seven of the same edition a six-column top of the page story detailed the complex of factors responsible for turning copying in exams in schools across the state, into an organised industry.[38]

On 19 March 2004 the *Gurgaon Bhaskar* had this intriguing headline, '*Bhiwani ko chod, har par laga nakal ka control*' (except for Bhiwani everywhere copying is under control). It referred to the assertion of the chairman of Haryana school education board that this year cheating in exams, or copying, was substantially under control except in Bhiwani. The official acknowledged the support of the print media in accomplishing this. At the same time, the story said that the Class 10 board exam in Mathematics had seen 54 instances of cheating in Gurgaon district.

In March 2003 one could pick out the following stories that illustrated the same point. A 10 March four-column story in *Amar Ujala* on the fact that teachers encouraged cheating, and another story in the same edition reporting that a special task force that had been formed to prevent cheating had got a mixed response. *The Punjab Kesri* of the same day had three stories relating to the shifting of examination centres and cheating. On 11 March the *Gurgaon Bhaskar* had this either outrageous or reassuring item, depending on your point of view, 'Cheaters will not instantly be given zero marks: Haryana State Education Board.'

In the month of March in 2002 the *Dainik Jagran* and *Dainik Bhaskar* local pages for Betul district in Madhya Pradesh carried eight lead stories and five second leads between them, related to school exams—on security, administrative procedures, mismanagement and six of them specifically on cheating.

Local health reporting is primarily related to disease and medical infrastructure but as an overall category it does get more space than agriculture, poverty or labour-related issues. Health issues do make news in district editions. In the month of April on the local pages of *Prabhat Khabar's* Santhal Parganas edition there were 19 reports in this category. Four related to health camps, and three related to the poor state of health facilities including the place for conducting post-mortems. The rest was a miscellaneous mix: 198 people receiving hepatitis B shots was news. The same month the *Hindustan* had 15 stories on health including camps and drives against various diseases. There was enough reporting on anthrax to indicate that this disease which afflicts animals was an issue at the *mofussil* level.

In June in Palamu the same year there were 16 health-related news items in *Prabhat Khabar*, and 21 in *Hindustan* including one on a region where there was one doctor for a population of 60,000. Sometimes the local correspondent did an outstanding health story. *Prabhat Khabar* published in this month the compelling story of one coal miner's struggle to get his employers to recognise that working in their colliery had caused his blindness. And in Palamu a local cloth merchant who thought newspaper reporting had an impact gave the example of a published report on the hospital in Chanepur distributing expired medicines. A raid conducted following this story found that all the medicines in the hospital stock had exceeded their expiry date. A case was filed against the doctor in charge.[39]

The Charkha survey mentioned earlier, on social development issues in the media, looked at the following issues: poverty, health, women, education, panchayat, agriculture, livelihood, corruption, environment and crime. In the state of Chhattisgarh it found that over three months of scanning these subjects constituted a mere 2 per cent of the overall news. Of this 2 per cent, health-related stories constituted as much as 23 per cent.

> But a closer inspection reveals that over 65 per cent of the news items are from the urban areas, and that too related to strikes by doctors and bad administration in hospitals. It is evident that the coverage given to rural areas on health related issues are the minimum.

The same survey did a detailed scanning of the poorest districts of Chhattisgarh, namely, Bastar, Koriya, Kanker, Raigarh, Jashpur and Devtada, and found that these regions received 4 per cent of the overall coverage, and out of this 4 per cent while crime-related news got a coverage of 62 per cent, health got a coverage of 4 per cent.

In Jharkhand the Charkha survey found that of out of 1,671 news items there were 223 on health. But the deteriorating state of rural health or investigations into where the money sanctioned for health was going, did not figure. Most health news related to camps organised by different organisations. The survey observed that in a state where more than 20,000 children die of malaria and diarrhoea every year, the government's priority was spending on publicity and AIDS awareness though there were at this point no cases of AIDS in the state.

Apart from Chhattisgarh and Jharkhand the disease-and-camp-related nature of health reporting was true of Bihar as well. One day's health stories from different editions of the same newspaper, the *Hindustan* in Bihar, on 3 June 2003 went like this:

- Health ministers agitated on seeing the mismanagement (doctors were absent);

- Vaccination camps organised;
- No medicine (in a hospital);
- Snakebite;
- Pulse polio campaign speeded up;
- Rotary's free medical camp organised in forest area;
- One died of diarrhoea and dozens afflicted
- Heat's effect on polio campaign;
- Polio drop given to 7,031 children;
- Medical system is proving to be useless;
- Three health workers released from services;
- One dozen ill due to contaminated water;
- Heatstroke and heat calamity continues;
- Two AIDS patients found in Katihar jail.

The last, about the AIDS patients, was considered sensational enough to be picked up by four different editions.

Missing Dimensions

When a local public sphere is market-driven those who remain outside its market do not figure in it, unless the newspaper is driven by a sharp social conscience. In its eagerness to cover everything that moves local news often misses what might be termed important by observers of news coverage. Going by the percentage of people living below the poverty line, Palamu is one of the three poorest of Jharkhand's 18 districts (*Jharkhand Development Report 2006*: 75). The perception of those who cover this district too is that poverty is one of its main problems. Yet its local news coverage does not reflect any sustained attention to either the manifestations of poverty or to the administration's specific efforts to tackle it.

A total of 776 items scanned over one entire month's *Hindustan* clippings for Palamu (June 2002) yields one story on hunger, one on exploitation and one on untouchability. Of 740 items scanned in the *Prabhat Khabar* of Palamu, in the same period, there were no stories related to hunger or migration, and just six which even mentioned Dalits or labour, or isssues of caste, and three of these were political. The local editions of these two papers for the Santhal Pargana division, monitored in April 2002, had between them less than six stories looking at poverty or labour issues and none dealing with migration.

A year later interviews with correspondents in that district showed that there were aware of the linkages between poverty and Naxalism, and of the extent of migration.[40] One of them observed that 50–60 people migrated every day from that district.[41] Yet properly reported migration stories are rare in local editions, including that of *Hindustan* in Palamu. Also, as later studies of coverage in this region show, there is no constructive focus on the poorest districts of Jharkhand in newspaper coverage.

One 10-day study in 2003 of newspapers available in Ranchi for instance found that amongst 113 news of development and poverty only four were of the poorest districts. News in the Jharkhand page of the newspaper had confined itself to Bokaro, Jamshedpur, Dhanbad and Hazaribagh. News from the poorest districts—Dumka, Devghar, Pakud, Godda, Sahibganj, Palamu, West Singhbhoom, Lohardaga, Gumla, Giridih—was not there in the capital's newspapers.[42]

A later detailed report on Chhattisgarh, Uttaranchal and Jharkhand looked at three months of coverage in three Hindi newspapers—*Hindustan*, *Prabhat Khabar* and *Ranchi Express*—and two English dailies—*The Telegraph* and *Hindustan Times*—appearing in Ranchi, from 5 August to 25 October 2004.[43] It studied how food, security, health, women, education, panchayat, agriculture, migration, mining and land were covered. It found that though distribution of news-papers has increased after becoming a state, though more pages had been added so that no paper now had less than 16–18 pages including four to eight in colour, there was minimum coverage of these issues, and indeed of the poorest districts in the state. Of a total of 59,675 local news items scanned only 1,671 or 3 per cent related to the subjects mentioned earlier.

Of these 39 per cent were in *Prabhat Khabar*, 27 per cent in *Hindustan*, 23 per cent in *Ranchi Express*, 8 per cent in *Hindustan Times* and 3 per cent in *The Telegraph*. And what of Chhattisgarh and Uttaranchal? It scanned the leading newspapers such as *Amar Ujala*, *Dainik Jagaran*, *Shah Times*, *Hindustan Times* and *Himachal Times*, published from Dehradun and found that only 5 per cent coverage was given to issues of food, security, health, women, education, panchayat, agriculture, migration, mining and land. When scanned for news items that focused on these issues in the six poorest districts of Uttaranchal, it was found that out of 5 per cent of the total coverage given on these issues, a mere 9 per cent was from these six districts. So out of total news items, it was even less than 0.5 per cent. Out of the 9 per cent a remote district such as Chamoli had a mere 1 per cent, whereas Champavat and Bageshwar have been given a space of 6 per cent and 3 per cent respectively.

Similarly a detailed scanning of the poorest districts of Chhattisgarh, namely, Bastar, Koriya, Kanker, Raigarh, Jashpur and Devtada, showed that these regions have received a total coverage of mere 4 per cent. Out of this, crime-related news was given a coverage of 62 per cent while poverty a mere 4 per cent; health, 4 per cent; education, 13 per cent; panchayat, 4 per cent and corruption, 13 per cent. Issues of women, environment, agriculture and livelihood received no coverage in these six districts.[44]

The contrast comes from the fortnightly *Khabar Lahariya*, mentioned at the beginning of this chapter. Over 10 weeks ranging from 1 February to 30 June 2006 it had five first lead stories on page one relating to water scarcity for irrigation. Four of these were block-level surveys of water problems, done by *Khabar Lahariya*'s women reporters who report, produce and distribute the paper themselves. Of the remaining lead stories one each were from Dalit and Adivasi localities. And a memorable one was a lead feature on a man who had paid Rs 15,000 for a pregnant cow. The local veterinarian had certified it as being pregnant but it later turned out that the foetus was a stomach tumour. The man filed a complaint against the vet, but the administration pronounced him not guilty of causing a loss to the cow owner from incompetence. Doubtless a story that village audiences would empathise with.

The overwhelming majority of *Khabar Lahariya* stories had village datelines. And the major focus of stories on its panchayat page related the public distribution system—stories about ration shops without rations and tales of woe of those who failed to get ration cards. Out of 30 stories on this page over 10 weeks, 14 related to these fair price shops which were meant to be a welfare measure for ordinary people.

Hunger

When the state of Jharkhand observed its fourth anniversary of formation *Prabhat Khabar*, the newspaper which had become a self-appointed conscience keeper for the state, commissioned a research agency to assess its socio-economic progress both in comparison with other newly formed states, as well as the neighbouring states of West Bengal, Bihar and Orissa. One table in that study looked at the percentage of households without food sufficiency in the year 1999–2000, relying on the National Sample Survey Organisation's 55th round. The new states were formed in the year 2000.

'Households without food sufficiency' is an euphemism for hunger. And in comparison with eight other states in the country including the newly formed ones of Uttaranchal and Chhattisgarh, Jharkhand topped the list of states with households which did not get two square meals a day. Compared to its mother state of Bihar, where the percentage of households without food sufficiency was 3.5, the figure for Jharkhand was 12.5. Indeed hunger levels in Jharkhand were the highest among all Indian states. One out of eight residents was going to bed hungry every day.

But if you were looking for a reflection of that hunger in the local news pages of the Jharkhand press, you would have had to search very hard indeed. Hunger is pretty much absent from the local news canvas unless there is a hunger death. And not because they are unaware of it. Perhaps they lacked the skills or direction to bring it into their reporting.

Agricultural distress found little space in the climate of steady economic growth that pervaded Indian media discourse in the mid-2000s. Overall local newspapers tended to neglect agriculture just as national newspapers coming out of metropolises did. But there were occasional exceptions. On 14 February 2005 the *Dainik Bhaskar* in Indore published prominently on page one what it called its 'Monday Mega Story'. It was titled '*Kisano par Karz ka Kahar*' (the grip of indebtedness on farmers) and it took a detailed look at the distress caused by rural indebtedness, and the role played by the banking system in driving farmers off their land. From villagers in Neemach it brought tales of debt recovery that was forcing farmers to sell or mortgage the land for which they had taken agricultural loans in the first place. It carried a survey of the extent of indebtedness in the districts of Khargaon, Ujjain, Shajapur, Dhar and Dewas. And it carried in a front page box the names of farmers who had been driven to suicide by their debts (Figure 6.4).[45]

FIGURE 6.4 *Dainik Bhaskar* Indore's Monday Mega Story on rural indebtedness, 14 Febraury 2005

In a state like Rajasthan the importance of irrigation drew the *Rajasthan Patrika* to attempt an act of media activism. It initiated a campaign on water issues to endear itself to the local population. While celebrating its 50th year of publication in 2005 it began a daily campaign in the paper called 'Amritham Jalam' (water is nectar) where people were urged to come forward and clean up all traditional water harvesting systems that were lying unused and dead. In a span of 60 days beginning May and through June, 155,038 citizen volunteers worked on as many as 388 water harvesting structures.

(A variety of sponsors as well as local area development funds of members of parliament and the state legislature were mobilised to underwrite the costs.) The impetus for launching this statewide movement came from a similar small effort in 2004 when the newspaper appealed to people in Jaipur and surrounding areas to clean up water harvesting systems, and got an encouraging response.[46]

But these were exceptions. One rural denizen conspicuous by his relative absence was the farmer. Stories on agriculture were few and far between. Also absent for the most part was unorganised labour, and those truly on the margin. When people in rural India migrate, they do not become a subject of investigation for the local newshound. Perhaps because he is himself usually drawn from the local urban gentry and they do not figure on his radar. Or perhaps because those on the margins are not newspaper readers. As localisation grew, reader interest became its abiding criteria. Though some farmers reported for newspapers, and others delivered them, yet others said that in a rural agricultural economy newspapers provided little information of relevance. Farmers interviewed in both Palamu and Devghar districts invariable mentioned seed and fertiliser availability at affordable prices as their major problem and added in the same breath that newspapers never dealt with these issues.

Numerically agriculture-related stories figure very little in district editions. For instance one week's newspapers across four editions in Haryana's Gurgaon district, part of a farm belt, produced a total of less than 25 stories on agriculture, many of them to do with irrigation. In comparison, on a single day the number of stories on local administration across four editions was 34. Local editions were urban crime and governance-centred in their focus.

Monitoring of one month of *Dainik Bhaskar*'s pull-out for Itarsi–Hoshangabad in March 2002 yielded 11 items on agriculture, compared to 17 for religious observances. And *Dainik Jagran* in that district over the same period had nine agriculture-related stories. The two papers were also monitored for their coverage of Betul, and here *Bhaskar* had five stories related to agriculture in one month; and *Jagran*, two. And in Jharkhand, two editions each of two newspapers over two months yielded negligible coverage of farm-related issues. As a youth said in Sindho village in Devghar district, 'If they start publishing potato, onion and garlic rates in newspapers every farmer will be interested in reading them.'47

While the rural newspaper revolution in the Hindi belt did reach villages connected by major roads, the majority of readers of district editions were urban. And the majority of stringers were based in urban areas. In Bhagalpur in June 2003 people at the *Hindustan* desk were admitting that agricultural news went out of the window when they stopped getting their feature pages from Patna and began getting them from Delhi. Before that the Patna office used to generate agriculture-related features. Local editions, said the senior subeditor in charge of stringers' copy, were becoming crime news based.[48] In the hinterland of Bhagalpur lies prime farming area from where corn and bananas go in trucks to distant parts of the country. But farmers at Maheshkund which is a big village as well as a newspaper distribution centre, said that there was very little farm reporting in newspapers, and very little impact as a result of whatever was written.[49]

Covering Women

The way women are covered in local editions is indicative of a society in transition. Even as they figure overwhelmingly as victims, there are frequent public pronouncements, faithfully covered by local stringers, which urge economic and social uplift of women.

In Palamu during the entire month of June 2002 in *Hindustan* there were 56 items related to women. Fifty-five featured them as victims: of marital violence, of rape, murder and hounding for being witches. One item from Sarath, Devghar said a woman had been killed for having a dusky complexion, another from Palajori said women were increasingly being harassed after being called witches and devils. There were three or four suicides. And there was a single two-column item about a training camp being organised for women.

Prabhat Khabar that month had around 35 items relating to women. One said that rural women did not know what AIDS was about; another that a youth cultural forum had formed a women's board; a third said that an Ekta Nari Manch (a platform for women's unity) had been created in Jharkhand; and a fourth news item was an exhortation to women to step forward and demand their rights. A fifth item originating in Godda said women would campaign on civic problems. A seminar on a women's development programme was also reported as was a statement that no more violence on women would be tolerated. Apart from these seven the remaining 28 items related to women as victims. That month there were five cases of women committing suicide. The rest related to murder, sexual harassment and rape.

In April 2002 in *Prabhat Khabar*'s Santhal Parganas edition there was news relating to three women being elected to panchayat posts. Another datelined Chandva said a tribal woman was to head Sairak panchayat. Nine items related to crimes against women, some of which are worth noting. A man kidnapped his mother and daughter, and a husband killed his wife over food. The same month *Hindustan* recorded that a tribal woman was most likely to be the head of the pachayat in Chandra, in Latehar. Another news item from Daltonganj said members of the Chero tribe had been motivated against dowry. In a column called 'People Speak' the paper published an interview with a woman who said that if women did not step out of their boundaries there would be no problem. Eight items related to women as victims of violence, others were miscellaneous.

Foeticide was not reported from Jharkhand; it was from Haryana. Out of some 35 news items relating to women in four local editions of Gurgaon over a period of seven days there were two reports relating to the problem of amniocentesis-enabled foeticide being discussed. The rest of the news was not easily categorised. There was an unusual case of an attempt to burn a son-in-law in his wife's home. There were cases of suicide and rape, and there was an item which said bribes given and taken resolve cases of violence against women. The fact that International Women's Day was observed just before the monitoring period began resulted in a clutch of positive exhortations. The local Rotary Club claimed it had trained 200 women and given loans to a 100, and a camp was organised in another instance to train women in the domestication of animals. The point to remember about coverage of issues related to women in the local press is that the news force deployed is usually 100 per cent male.

And the Outside World...

Finally, how much did the outside world percolate into the local news universe? Events like the General Budget, or the riots in Gujarat in 2002, or an India–Pakistan cricket match filter down, often to the village level. In early March 2002 a Dalit tea stall owner in Sindho village of Santhal Parganas in Jharkhand told an interviewer that at that point the Budget was the most important news because it informed him about the decrease and increase in prices of different things. And the same month that year in Madhya Pradesh the events in Godhra in the previous month had their repercussions. *Bandhs* organised in reaction to the events in Gujarat affected daily life in both Betul and Hoshangabad districts in March 2002, and were reported in *Dainik Jagran* and *Dainik Bhaskar* in both districts.

An Indo-Pakistan cricket match does not leave life in any corner of India untouched. On March 2004 when the India team went to Lahore to play against Pakistan local news pages everywhere did their bit to forage for the local angle to this event. *Gurgaon Bhaskar* on 24 March said in its lead, '*Countdown shuru ho gaya*' (the countdown has begun) and carried interviews of 10 residents from their district, with their pictures, on what they thought India's chances of winning were. The following day the newspaper decided to check out how the Muslim majority region of Mewat in Gurgaon was reacting to the first day's win and reported that it was untrue that Pakistan's defeat would plunge residents here into mourning. '*Yeh sarasa galat nikla. Mewat wasiyon ka utsah dekhne layak tha*' (This turned out to be patently untrue. The enthusiasm of Mewat residents was worth seeing). The paper then named the Indian Muslim cricket fans it had interviewed.

For a winsome vignette of what cricket fever can do to rural India you had to turn to a 10 March 2003 brief in *Punjab Kesari*, around the time that India was playing in the cricket World Cup, and had already defeated Pakistan. It said, '*Tigri gaon cricket ke bukhar mein duba hua hai*' (Tigri village is immersed in cricket fever). It went on to say that the elders and women of this village were doing a *havan* (a religious ritual) to celebrate the team's success against Pakistan. *Sarpanch* Jai Bhagwan told the *Kesari*'s stringer that on account of the handsome victory of the Indian cricket team he was thinking of renaming the Shiv *mandir* (temple) in the village as cricket Shiv. He added that he had watched the match on television wearing a pad, a guard and a helmet.

Conclusion

Local news gave voice to both the existing and emerging middle class and reflected a public preoccupation with law and order, infrastructure and governance. It was more urban than rural in focus, even if it served rural areas. It reflected a mystifying neglect of agriculture. It was less concerned with issues of livelihood than you would expect newspapers in states with low per capita incomes to be. Whether male or female, urban or rural, the newsmakers tended to be middle class. Local news pages reflected the vibrancy of grass-roots panchayat politics as well as the percolation of party politics down to the panchayat level. The panchayats represented the emergence of a rural middle class. Poverty existed in the local public sphere, and was taken note of. But there was rarely a subaltern perspective.

Miscellany was the defining characteristic of the local news universe and tended to comprise the largest category in month-long periods of monitoring undertaken. As for local news judgement, it had one distinctive characteristic: it was usually completely unpredictable. The definition of news was also changing. Some categories of news which had barely existed in newspapers a decade or two earlier were now emerging as local news staples. News related to religion was one such category. In an articulation of news strategy, one editor said that the soul of localisation lay in changing what people were willing to read about first thing in the morning.

Notes

1. Surendra Singh Ruby, *Ranchi Express*, interviewed by Vasavi, Palamu, 15 April 2003.
2. Don Fry, 'What Makes Local News Really Local', Poynter Online, 22 July 2004.

THE UNIVERSE OF LOCAL NEWS 183

3. Fayaz Ahmed, interviewed by Vasavi, Palamu, 15 April 2003.
4. Vasudev Tewari, *Hindustan*, interviewed by Vasavi, Palamu, 15 April 2003.
5. Anil Swarup, commissioner rural development, interviewed by author, Lucknow, 30 August 2005.
6. *Gurgaon Bhaskar*, p. 14, 17 March 2004.
7. Examples drawn from *Gurgaon Bhaskar*, March–April 2004.
8. Ramesh Agarwal, state news coordinator, *Dainik Bhaskar*, interviewed by author, Jaipur, 17 September 2005.
9. N.K. Singh, interviewed by author, Jaipur, 16 and 17 September 2005.
10. Bipasha Basu is a popular Bollywood actress; Lata Mangeshkar a very popular singer.
11. Ramesh Agarwal, interviewed by author, Jaipur, 17 September 2005.
12. N.K. Singh, interviewed by author, Jaipur, 16–17 September 2005.
13. Anuj Khare, resident editor, *Dainik Bhaskar*, interviewed by author, Banswara, 30 November 2004.
14. Shashank Shekhar Tripathi, resident editor, *Hindustan*, interviewed by author, 16 March 2005.
15. Suman Gupta, *Jan Morcha*, interviewed by author, Faizabad, 27 August 2005.
16. Sunita Aron, resident editor, *Hindustan Times*, interviewed by author, Lucknow, 26 August 2005.
17. Mahesh Pande, *Hindustan*, interviewed by author , Lucknow, 30 August 2005.
18. Harivansh, editor, *Prabhat Khabar*, interviewed by author, New Delhi, 27 October 2005.
19. 3 June 2003.
20. Classfications discussed in 'Cheap Shots on Crime Coverage', 13 November 2003, www.timporter.com/firstdraft/archives/000223.html.
21. Shashank Shekhar Tripathi, resident editor, *Hindustan*, interviewed by author, Varanasi, 15 March 2005.
22. Sunita Aron, resident editor, *Hindustan Times*, interviewed by author, 26 August 2005.
23. Y.C. Agarwal, chief executive, *Hindustan*, interviewed by author, Patna, 3 June 2003.
24. Nalin Varma, *Statesman*, interviewed by author, 2 June 2003.
25. Sri Ram Pathak, interviewed by author, outside Bhagalpur city limits, 6 June 2003.
26. S.K. Singh, interviewed by author, outside Bhagalpur, 6 June 2003.
27. A.S. Raghunath, general manager brand development, *Jagran*, interviewed by author, 31 March 2005.
28. Classfications discussed in 'Cheap Shots on Crime Coverage', 13 November 2003, www.timporter.com/firstdraft/archives/000223.html.

29. Dipak Patel, *Dainik Bhaskar*, interviewed by author, Sabla, Banswara district, 1 December 2004.
30. Dharmendra Jaiswal, *Ranchi Express*, interviewed by Vasavi, 16 April 2003.
31. Sanjeev Kshitij, interviewed by author, Varanasi, 17 March 2005.
32. Om Prakash Amarendra, interviewed by Vasavi, Palamu, April 2003.
33. Surendra Singh Ruby, interviewed by Vasavi, Palamu, April 2003.
34. Sevanti Ninan, 'The Naxals and the Press', thehoot.org, http://www.thehoot.org/story.asp?storyid=webhoothootL1K0914023&pn=1 (accessed 29 May 2005).
35. Amitabh Singh, Debate, interviewed by Sushmita Malaviya, Bhopal, 31 January 2004.
36. *Prabhat Khabar*, 31 March 2002.
37. Charkha survey, unpublished, details in Aman Namra, 'New Boundaries, Old Limits', http:// www.indiatogether.org/2005/mar/med-newstates.htm.
38. *Hindustan*, Varanasi edition, p. 13, 18 March 2005.
39. Sanjay Prasad, interviewed by Vasavi, Palamu, 15 April 2003.
40. Vasudev Tiwari and Subodh Kumar Pathak, *Hindustan*, interviewed by Vasavi, 15 April 2003.
41. Subodh Kumar Pathak, interview by Vasavi, 15 April 2005.
42. Sudhir Pal, 'The print media and the poorest districts of Jharkhand', http://www.thehoot.org/story.asp?storyid=Web210214166229 Hoot92230%20PM977&pn=1 (downloaded April 2006).
43. 'Detailed report on Chhattisgarh, Uttaranchal and Jharkhand Media Scanning', Survey done by Charkha, unpublished, 2005.
44. Ibid.
45. *Dainik Bhaskar*, 14 February 2005.
46. Ramesh Menon, 'Media campaign brings hope to desert' (16 July 2005). indiatogether.org.
47. Mangal Soren, interviewed by Aloka Kajoor, Sindho village, March 2002.
48. Praveen Baghi, *Hindustan*, interviewed by author, Bhagalpur, 6 June 2003.
49. Interviewed by author, Maheshkund, Bhagalpur district, 7 June 2003.

7

Media and Commerce

'We did not believe that people actually do this. Cut out a coupon, then stand in a line to redeem it. But people did it.'

There are few really new ideas in the old game of financing news-papers and persuading people to buy them. When Hindi newspapers sought to energetically develop classified advertising relevant to local pages and began to woo new readers with gift schemes and price incentives, they were simply drawing upon old tricks developed by some of the world's best-known newspapers. And doubtless giving them an original spin. It is difficult to imagine either the *Daily Mail* or *The Times* tempting newspaper subscribers with a plastic chair, as the owners of *Danik Bhaskar* spent Rs 15 million doing,[1] in the state of Chhattisgarh, to gain a 30 per cent circulation increase.

But it was the one-time owner of the *Mail* and *The Times*, Alfred Harmsworth, later known as Lord Northcliffe, who back in 1889 launched what was possibly the first newspaper-related gift scheme, intended to excite reader interest. Shortly after he had launched a new weekly which was not doing brilliantly he and his brother en-countered a man begging for the price of a meal as they strolled down the Thames Embankment. As they chatted with him the subject of prize competitions came up. To which the man said what he really wanted was a prize that would give him a pound a week for life.

Acting on that idea, *Answers to Correspondents*, as the weekly was called, began offering its readers the chance of winning a pound for life. All they had to do was guess the exact amount of gold coinage in the Banking Department of the Bank of England at the close of business on a certain date. The Christmas number of *Answers* which announced the results sold 205,000 copies, a considerable improve-ment over its pre-contest circulation of 30,000 copies. And the winner was sent a pound a week for the eight years that he lived after that (Canning 2001: 296).

When Hindi newspapers in the 21st century came up with their prize coupon schemes the contests and the gifts they offered were more mundane, but the outcome could be dramatic. When *Hindustan* in Bihar launched a gift scheme with a Maruti car as a grand prize it was won by a farmer in Madhubani. Before he could claim it, however, he was kidnapped and the kidnappers approached the newspaper to have the car transferred to them. Negotiations led to a compromise, the kidnappers gave the farmer a motorcycle and kept the car.[2]

Incentivising the Reader

Expanding the market for Hindi newspapers has meant that by 2005 all the lead players were following the strategy of price wars, and schemes with which to woo readers with gifts or coupons. In Dehradun in 2002 *Amar Ujala*'s 'Election Dhamaka' a contest that the paper ran, which offered a Maruti Esteem car as first prize, drew a stag-gering response running into 1.44 million participants. When *Dainik Jagran* launched its Holi (the Hindu festival of colour) scheme in March 2005 it was a three-month campaign to publish coupons which could be redeemed for gifts. It covered 16 editions of the paper. Both small town and big city readers were being enticed with a pro-motional campaign that promised 60,000 prizes worth Rs 30 million. If you subscribed to the paper you could end up winning a gift. Into the list of prizes the newspaper's management threw in everything it imagined an aspiring middle-class heart might desire: car, motor-cycles, home theaters, DVD players, fridges, colour television sets, cellular phones and gift vouchers from a jeweller. A scheme simply meant that a coupon would be published on the front page of the newspaper till 29 May, which a reader had to cut and collect on a coupon form published in the paper.

The coupon clipping culture among readers was growing. Marketing schemes were an idea *Dainik Bhaskar* adopted from other people. When its owners moved into Jaipur in December 1996 with a 500 strong army of market surveyors, offering gift coupons was not part of their strategy. But three months after they came into Jaipur, *Rajasthan Patrika* did a plastic chair scheme in Alwar. *Bhaskar* borrowed the idea to boost its circulation in Raipur in Chhattisgarh. It got them a 30 per cent jump in circulation for a three-month period. Then they tried it in Gujarat. Says Girish Agarwal of *Dainik Bhaskar*:

> When we were going to Gujarat *Gujarat Samachar* gave a plastic bucket. They said, the cover price of our paper is Rs 80 I will give you a gift for Rs 90. It was the coupon system. We did not believe that people actually do this. Cut out a coupon, keep them everyday, then stand in a line to redeem it. But people did it. We found that the conversion of coupon into gift, the ratio of those who converted as high as 85 per cent. We did the same scheme there after 6 months.[3]

Television had made the Indian media consumer into an incentive freak before newspapers did. In the early 1990s contests began to blossom on Doordarshan (India's state-owned public broadcaster) as well as on the satellite channels. By 1994, Zee TV was claiming that contests on its channel were attracting 800,000 entries a week. And by 2003 a contest on Aaj Tak was generating 1.32 million smses in four days.[4]

Circulation schemes helped to expand a paper's reach, but the entry level incentives offered usually took the form of price wars. Every launch of an edition from the *Bhaskar* group meant a price incentive for readers it signed up. And *The Times of India* in Delhi demonstrated how an invitation price could give a circulation boost even to an established edition. In addition to price wars gifts for first-time subscribers helped to draw them into the circulation net. When both *Patrika* and *Bhaskar* started their Banswara edition in June 2004 a gift was guaranteed for those who subscribed: 250 gm tea from *Bhaskar*, while *Patrika* gave a bucket. The second circulation drive saw *Bhaskar* give a big plastic jar, while *Patrika* gave toothpaste. A Banswara circulation agent was cynical about the schemes. Only city people get the draw, he said. '*Bada inam gaon mein kabhi nahin khula*'[5] (the big prizes are never won by village folk).

By 2005 circulation schemes were an everyday affair. A general manager in Varanasi[6] explained how the economics of price wars and circulation schemes worked. Newspapers made money primarily through advertising which depended on circulation. Unless a paper was close to number one in its territory its claim on advertising was likely to be tenuous. So you tried to expand sales through gift schemes. The duration of the scheme was carefully pegged to how long it took to change a subscriber's reading habits. That required an exposure of at least two months. That is why papers gave coupons for at least 60 days of a 90-day trial scheme. And to make people feel they had a chance of winning a prize or gift the scheme needed to touch large numbers. If you offered a car as first prize, down the line you also needed to give a 1,000 T-shirts.

Some newspapers devised the assured gift scheme whereby every subscriber would get something. A scheme might cost Rs 100,000 to implement. And the highest growth you could expect from it was 25–30 per cent of your base. You might be able to retain 50 per cent of this growth after the scheme ended, so in the long term it could mean no more than a 12–15 per cent growth in circulation. But the newspaper benefited in two ways. If you developed the quality of your product further you might retain 80 per cent of the sampling readers. Increased circulation translated into an increased rate of government advertising. The Directorate of Advertising and Visual Publicity which fixed government advertising rates linked these to circulation certified by the Audit Bureau of Circulation (ABC). Higher circulation also enable a newspaper to present better numbers to the advertiser. In the Indian market by 2005 it was established wisdom that only number one and number two could expect to get advertising. So a circulation jump brought in that most valuable commodity of all: advertising. The additional bonus was that since your increase was at the expense of your competitor, the distance between your and the competition widened. Your coming into the advertiser's net could mean your competition falling out of the same net. A scheme made a volume growth possible in a space of six months.

All calculations in this game were so finely calibrated as to keep marketing departments permanently on their toes. Competition grew and grew between 1995 and 2005, hundred of local editions blossomed across Hindi-speaking states, chasing the competition. *Jagran* followed *Hindustan* to Bhagalpur and Muzaffarpur in Bihar in 2003 and 2005, *Bhaskar* beat *Rajasthan Patrika* to Banswara in Rajasthan in 2004. Proifts were not easy to come by. In its third year in Varanasi, *Hindustan* was still in the red. But the incremental numbers which the new editions added to the overall circulation helped with numbers to present to advertisers. The competition was frenetic. And advertisers had fairly foolproof ways of confirming whether a paper was delivering the market it promised. There were two or three categories of advertising that a local edition got, and one of them was for coaching institutes. If a coaching institute spent Rs 20,000 on an advertisement and did not get enough response from applicants, it was unlikely to put in further advertisements. If LG, Samsung or Nokia were offering a gift announced only in your newspaper they would be able to tell how effective the insertion had been from how many customers visited their showroom. The response an advertiser got was the clearest indication of which segment of the market the advertisement was reaching.

Apart from readers, hawkers were also being incentivised with gift schemes and enhanced hawker commissions if they increased sales. Since distribution was totally hawker-based their role in increasing circulation was invaluable. In Ranchi, early morning interviews with hawkers showed how good competition was proving to be for them: if *Prabhat Khabar* was giving refrigerators, *Jagran* was giving motorcycles. This was in Jharkhand's capital city. At the district distribution centres the bait was considerably more modest: airbag, wall clock, tiffin box, raincoat. If you wanted to up the ante, you gave cycles.[7]

Price wars also brought in new readers, and while you waged these you had to protect the hawker's commission. However, if the commission was disproportionate to the price of the paper, you risked attracting the wrath of the ABC which would consider it an unfair trade practice.

Price incentives helped *Dainik Bhaskar* enter new markets. When it entered Jaipur, *Rajasthan Patrika* was selling at Rs 2.25, so it priced its paper at Rs 2. Its pre-launch offer was Rs 1.5 for six months, if the customer signed up early. Customers bit, the paper launched in 1996 with 172,000 copies. Five days later, on 25 December, *Patrika* reduced the cover price from Rs 2.25 to Rs 1.5. That too, according to Girish Agarwal, helped *Bhaskar*, because it helped create two-newspaper households. Now, to buy two newspapers, all a customer had to do was pay only 75 paise more than what he had been paying all along for *Patrika*.[8]

At the *Rajasthan Patrika* Nihar Kothari would say that lowering their price to match the competition helped them increase their circulation substantially: 'We never imagined that a rupee would make so much difference. Hawkers became our champions. We dropped the price and hawkers played the role of taking the paper to all sorts of readers.'[9] Subsequently *Dainik Bhaskar* lowered its price when it entered Haryana in 2000, Gujarat in 2003 and Mumbai in the English newspaper segment in 2005.

Again, the idea is an old trick in the international newspaper trade: In *The Powers That Be* David Halberstram describes how Adolph Ochs dropped the price of the *New York Times* in 1898 when the superior coverage of the Spanish-American War offered by his rivals threatened the paper's circulation. He dropped its price from three cents a copy to one cent, and its circulation soared (Halberstram 1979: 209).

Local Advertising

Price wars only served to increase the dependence of newspapers on advertising. Typically for English language newspapers the break-up between advertising and cover price revenues was 80:20. When *Jagran* published its numbers in the run-up to its public issue it showed its revenue break-up as 63 per cent advertising and 37 per cent from cover price. *Jagran*, given its size, was an exception. For other regional language papers the break-up was more likely to be 50 per cent advertising and 50 per cent from circulation revenue. Regional papers depended on cover pricing to a greater degree than the English language press did. *The Times of India*'s profit per copy was bigger than the revenue per copy that a paper like *Dainik Jagran* was making.

The lion's share of commercial advertising went to the English press in cities like Delhi and Bombay. But this began to change as privately owned satellite TV channels grew in number and viewership. First the Hindi language general entertainment channels began to attract advertising, then the Hindi news channels. Mrinal Pande, editor of *Hindustan*, said that she thought the change was catalysed by a news channel like Aaj Tak launched by the Living Media group.[10] Its viewership ratings grew very fast, and advertisers realised it was being watched in the smaller towns and villages that they wanted to reach with their consumer products.

When commerce goes from being a by-product of journalism to becoming its driving force, newspapers begin to look and sound rather different. If you were to open a newspaper in a state capital on the morning of the chief minister's birthday, a raft of congratulatory advertising would leap out at you. Just the party faithful and favour seekers demonstrating their fealty to the current chief? Perhaps, but with a little encouragement from the newspaper itself. In 2002, in the new state of Chhattisgarh, *Hindustan Times*, a new entrant to the state, decided to bring out a marketing supplement pegged to Chief Minister Ajit Jogi's birthday and solicited advertising for it.

Nor were displays of fealty to the ruling head confined to his birthday. Wherever he travelled in the state, felicitation advertisements were taken out to greet him. In Bastar, Pavan Dubey, the editor of the lone evening paper, *Highway Channel*, said of the flood of Jogi-centric advertising, 'If the CM comes ten times the people have to greet him. Earlier the chief minister was far away. He wouldn't have noticed if people had greeted him from here.'[11] So statehood made newspapers more important, more solvent and more benignly disposed towards the government.

Advertising was the spur which underwrote the localisation exercise. The more editions you had the greater numbers you could offer a pan-Indian advertiser. There were national and local advertisers to be wooed, and new categories of advertising to dream up, such as cashing in on a tradition of political sycophancy. The internationally established principle that cornering classifieds makes a paper more invincible to competition was in evidence here as shrewd managements tried to develop their classfied sections by introducing all manner of categories. The increased commercial activity that a country growing at 8 per cent a year saw led to regular supplements being introduced which could cash in on such advertising. Weekly property supplements blossomed in Hindi dailies such as *Dainik Jagran* as did career supplements which carried a huge amount of educational advertising.

The creation of new avenues of local advertising was one of the early consequences of localisation. *Dainik Bhaskar*'s entry into Rajasthan in 1996 was followed by rapid localisation, which *Rajasthan Patrika* copied. In the 2000s in Rajasthan, both *Patrika* and its rival *Dainik Bhaskar* had begun to get three levels of advertising—corporate, retail and local—compared to just corporate a few years back. The increase in retail advertising was facilitated by the introduction of a split rate which enabled an advertiser to reach a narrow segment of the paper's audience if he so chose.[12]

A proliferation of district editions increases the overall readership or circulation numbers that you could give all-India advertisers. In 2003, advertising for *Hindustan* in the state of Bihar was coming primarily from national advertising. The entry of corporate advertising into district supplements was very visible by 2005. Manufacturers of consumer durables used these newspapers to enter the semi-urban and rural market and the universe of local news expanded to accommodate them. If Hyundai took out a full-page colour advertisement to promote its Santro in Patna it would also appear in the farthest reaches of the state. The more innovative national advertisers localised their advertisement campaign. Motorcycles were a major advertising category for Hindi newspapers because so much of their sales was in the semi-urban and rural areas. Yamaha's three-column advertisement in the Itarsi–Hoshangabad *Bhaskar* featured photographs of local youth in Bhilai who had taken part in a contest to promote the mileage given by its bikes.

With the spread of localisation in the new and old states, local advertising gradually blossomed. It was category that needed nurturing. And as innovatively as possible. At *Hindustan* in Bihar in 2003 the company's vice-president proudly flourished a tiny advertisement put in from a small town called Ara by a widow who wanted to sell her cows. It told you that you could get 6 kg of milk from the animals, at each milking. She paid Rs 50 for that advertisement which was collected by the local stringer.[13] He had the freedom to negotiate

advertising rates according to what people could afford to pay. Stringers all over the country for that matter, were booking advertising
until the middle of the decade of 2000 when some newspapers began
to separate the two functions to counter charges of blackmailing.

In Bhagalpur, Bihar, the marketing manager for *Hindustan* had,
in June 2003 a Rs 0.9 million target for local advertising but he also
had a problem. In a state where kidnapping was a flourishing industry
retailers were loth to advertise their showrooms in his paper, which
would mean drawing unwelcome attention to their business. They
were reluctant to advertise, he said. As for ordinary people, the concept of local classifieds was news to them; if they wanted a tenant
for their house they merely spread the word among their extended
family. Rural display advertising rates were therefore pegged fairly
low at Rs 80 per column cm, and you could get a double column advertisement for price of a single column.[14]

As the idea of very local advertising gained currency local quacks,
computer institutes, property dealers, and buyers and sellers began
to use these columns. Nomenclature in the advertisement sections
of these papers often used English words in the Devanagari script.
Display classifieds in the Indore *City* section of *Dainik Bhaskar* were
called just that, and the classifications within this section were called
Tours and Travels, Classes, Medical, Pets, Computer and General
(Figure 7.1). The only Hindi classifications used were for rentals:
Kiray se Lena Dena, and for buying and selling: *Kharidna/Bechna
hai*. In Varanasi a small classified advertisement could present a bi-
zarre juxtaposition of modernity and tradition: a girl with a plunging
neckline advertising a family vegetarian restaurant.[15]

A category that grew fast in southern Rajasthan was classifieds
for *badhai* and *shok*, or advertisements greeting people on business
or academic or political successes, and condoling with them when
they were bereaved. In southern Chhattisgarh, in Bastar, it became
fashionable for those with disposable incomes to put in congratulatory advertisements for their children, with their photographs, on
their birthdays or if they did well in school! In December 2004 the
resident editor of *Dainik Bhaskar* in Udaipur and his advertising
manager were estimating that in Banswara district the income from
such display classifieds was Rs 3–3.5 million a year.

FIGURE 7.1 An advertising supplement in the Indore *Dainik Bhaskar* on
14 February 2005 intersperses advertisements from local outlets
with Valentine's Day messages

Another category of advertising was political in nature, related to elections, ranging from panchayat elections to state and national elections. *Dainik Bhaskar* in Madhya Pradesh evolved packages of advertising to sell to candidates for every level of election. An MLA, Suneelam, charged that if you did not take their packages, it affected the level of enthusiasm with which the paper would cover your contest. Moreover there was an insidious category of advertorials called Impact Features which *Bhaskar* was introducing at the local level. They looked like news stories, but were carried in the advertising columns. In Bhopal the paper's resident editor said the difference in display was clear, but Suneelam contended that rural readers were not yet sophisticated enough to tell the difference.[16]

The panchayat elections whenever they came around were very lucrative for newspapers. Thousands of candidates in UP and Madhya Pradesh used the local editions of newspapers to tell their voters what their election symbols were. In theory no party affiliation was permitted for panchayat elections but candidates were wont to affix photographs of state or national leaders to advertisements featuring themselves. Some gave their mobile numbers in the advertisements, others made promises to develop their villages as model villages. The charges for such advertising were between Rs 500 and Rs 1,000 per display advertisement.

But the truly pervasive and lucrative category of advertising that began to sustain local pages and supplements, was educational. These related to schools and coaching institutes and were visible whenever one picked up a local edition. S.S. Public School and Hostel took out in Varanasi a large colour advertisement for its English medium co-educational institutes, with a boys' hostel, close circuit camera in each room and laboratories.[17] *Dainik Jagran* carried front page advertisment in English from the Aakash Institute offering a two-year coaching course for medical exams.[18] The J.P. Aacademy (ISO [International Organisation for Standardisation] certified) in Meerut was advertising its 40-acre campus with separate hostels that offered cooler, geyser, television and telephone, a hospital on campus, security and back-up power generation. It asked for Rs 250 to be sent for a prospectus.[19] And so on. No wonder TAM Media Research's division AdEx India was showing in its compilation of print media advertising figures at year end 2004 that educational institutions spent Rs 2,090 million to emerge as the top category in print.[20]

The new states generated more advertising for the newspapers publishing from there. This came from companies shifting there, from investors being invited in, from new infrastructure projects undertaken by the state governments, apart from the traditional Congress sycophancy mentioned earlier. According to the *Dainik Bhaskar*'s controller of advertising, the paper saw a 42 per cent increase in revenue over the corresponding period the previous year. The story was repeated in the other two states. In Dehradun, the *Doon Classified*, which exists only to carry advertising and be inserted in the city's broadsheets, had, by 2002, acquired a circulation of some 30,000 copies a week, sustained by heavy advertising for property sales and rentals, and miscellaneous categories. With a sleepy city transformed into a state capital, all kinds of commercial activity received a fillip.

After the creation of the new state *Dainik Jagran*'s circulation saw a four-time increase. Earlier Dehradun was a retired people's city. 'Now after becoming a *rajdhani* (state capital) its commercial importance has gone up.' The state government has its own advertising budget, and the flow of banks, financial institutions, branch offices of major companies, and of shops and showrooms into the city has meant a substantial jump in advertising available.[21]

Marketing

The Hindi newspaper revolution may have owed something to growing literacy, political awareness and rising rural incomes. But above all it was a marketer's revolution, and the sons of Ramesh Agarwal, the owner of *Daink Bhaskar*, led the way in pioneering direct selling of newspapers to readers by launching the market survey approach to booking orders while entering a new territory. Somewhere along the way Sudhir Agarwal would certainly have learned something from Samir Jain, the scion of the Bennett Coleman group, whom Sudhir, according to a journalist who worked with him for many years,[22] frequently visited, coming back each time full of accounts what Jain had said. By the time the Agarwals came to launch in Jaipur in 1996 where they deployed their personal contact approach to newspaper selling for the first time, *The Times of India* had under Samir Jain become an out and out marketer's newspaper. It had launched a price war to take on *Hindustan Times* in its citadel of Delhi, whittled away at its base most successfully, and built up a marketing cadre that was the envy of other newspaper owners.

Post-liberalisation in the early 1990s, as Indian society registered visible change including conspicuous consumption by the better off, journalism began to reflect the interests of upwardly mobile readers. Conventional news broadened to include 'news you can use', not just glossy supplements related to food, fitness, fashion and leisure, but also columns in Hindi newspapers which told you how to improve your English.[23] Newspapers increased their pages and added colour. With *The Times of India* pioneering the *Delhi Times*, they began to incorporate city supplements which focused on society events and local personalities. Page 3 journalism, as this began to be known, had a clear commercial logic. In noting that the 'icons of Socialist India were being replaced by the heroes of Socialite India', *The Economic Times* spelt out the linkage between industries which rarely advertised their wares and the emergence of a Page 3 culture. The wine and couture industries and designer restaurants had all been built by the exposure they received when they threw parties for the city's visible set.[24] A couple of years down the line several regional newspapers had city supplements celebrating the good life and the people who lived it (Figure 7.2). Among them were *Punjab Kesari*, *Hindustan* and *Dainik Bhaskar*. The trend was conspicuous by its absence in leading Bengali newspapers like the *Ananda Bazar Parika*. But Page 3 became a part of India's vocabulary.

The 21st century drive for profits brought a new pragmatism to the news business. In January 2003 it was reported that Bennett, Coleman & Co. (BCCL) was charging for coverage in the nine city supplements columns of *The Times of India* through its online company called Medianet. The Medianet CEO clarified that paid features were limited to the lifestyle sections of the metro supplements of the two papers.[25] Even as the report triggered a huge debate in the media, across the country, the paper stopped indicating which items were paid for. Initially these features would carry the attribution 'Medianet' below the article in a minuscule point size. The following year it was reported that photographs published in the *Bombay Times* were being charged for.[26] Companies were warming up to the idea of paying for feature articles and photographs so Medianet was being able to move away

FIGURE 7.2 Weekly supplements with English titles: *Dainik Jagran*'s *Property*; *Hindustan*'s *FEST*, the same paper's classified advertisement section *Search Engine*, and its *Metro Remix*; *Dainik Jagran*'s *Jagran City*; *Navbharat Times*' *Hello Delhi* and *Amar Ujala*'s *Career*

from the fashion fraternity and switch to covering corporate events. Later that year BCCL extended the practice to its TV oper-ation by introducing a rate card for its TV channel called Zoom, listing charges for in-programme placement.[27] While this was dubbed the most controversial idea in the annals of journalism, advertising industry executives saw it as the coalescing of brand and content which had become fairly common on television.[28] Sponsored cover-age, a television concept, was also coming into print. In 2003, *India Today* published a sponsored cover story and during the World Cup series, some of the coverage in the *Indian Express*, NDTV.com and *India Today* was sponsored.[29]

Part of the shift in the way goals were set for journalistic enterprises had to do with who was now running the ship. Management in newspaper establishments had been the preserve of home-grown, family-appointed managers. But Samir Jain was possibly the first to bring graduates of India's top management schools into the business, and the management of newspapers began to become professional-ised. In early 2006 it was possible to look around and name people associated with *The Times of India*, the Ananda Bazar Patrika Group, and *Business Standard* who had at some point been top-ranking employees of India's premier mulitnational consumer goods company, Hindustan Lever. It accounted for the pragmatism which now affected decision making, not just the selling of editorial space but also com-promises with advertisers which sometimes affected the reporting of business journalists. Listing of newspapers on the stock exchange and the need to publish quarterly results had affected newspapers in other parts of the world. That aspect of publishing culture was set to come to India.

The change in management personnel was reflected in the degree of reader responsiveness which newspapers were rapidly developing. Multinationals after all were accustomed to eliciting consumer feed-back. Apart from *Dainik Bhaskar*'s house-to-house surveys which preceded every launch to find out what readers wanted from their newspapers (taken to an unprecedented 1.1 million households in Mumbai), newspapers wooed readers with gift schemes and invited them to send in feedback or complaints on their mobile phones. *Dainik Jagran* began soliticiting sms feedback by publishing phone numbers on its front page. One for complaints, another for readers to call and get the latest ball by ball news when a cricket match was on. Said its brand development manager, 'Who has time to write a letter to the editor?'[30]

Readers of the Future

Brand-building as an exercise for the future means catching readers young. By 2004–05 the more ambitious newspapers were strategising to cover the youth segment. *Dainik Bhaskar* had a supplement for school-going children called *School Bhaskar*, and one for younger children called *Bal Bhaskar*. In March 2004 a newspaper agent in Pipariya in Madhya Pradesh was confirming that strong youth and children's supplements were an effective entry point into a family that did not take newspapers.

> From what I see and understand, parents are forced to buy newspapers by children. For instance *Nava Bharat*'s *Phulwari* and *Dainik Bhaskar*'s *Bal Bhaskar* are a big hit among children. So children convince their parents to buy the paper. And parents often buy the newspaper hoping that it will help increase their children's general knowledge. I would easily attribute 30 to 40 per cent of the increase in newspapers to this trend. It is so evident that since *Nava Bharat* packed *Phulwari* (their children's supplement) into their main edition, there has been a 20 per cent drop in their circulation here.[31]

The preference was also for pull-outs, rather than pages in a broadsheet.

On 9 December 2004 *Dainik Jagran* launched *Junior Jagran* in the National Capital Region (NCR) for the teenage segment, shrewdly using a bilingual name and several pages in English to make a bilingual pitch to young people who were not Hindi readers. Every week a few pages were produced by students of a handpicked school, with a marked bias towards English-speaking schools.[32] It had already test-launched the product in Punjab two months before that. The paper's brand development department conducted focus group discussions among young people. Like its rival *Bhaskar*, *Jagran* was gung-ho about understanding its reader, be it an adult or child.

This 16-page Hindi-English supplement was also localised for four of its pages, with *Jagran*'s editorial team reaching out to schools in Noida, Ghaziabad, Delhi and Gurgaon to get students from different schools each fortnight to write, edit and paginate. The paper's editor and CEO Sanjay Gupta was asserting that the newspaper was filling the void created by the gradual disappearance of school magazines.[33]

> Our aim is to revive the glorious tradition to educate and entertain teenagers in order to encourage and inculcate the reading habit amongst youngsters through *Junion Jagran* by providing them a forum to express. Simultaneously I do believe that the tabloid will act as a catalyst in nurturing journalism among teenagers.

The same press release was clarifying that the unique feature of *Junior Jagran* was that it was available to advertisers for the entire Delhi and NCR region in the city split formats, and that the paper would be undertaking school and college distribution in addition to household delivery. Newspaper owners were clear: they wanted to serve the community but marketing and advertising had to pay for the product they were producing.

Conclusion

Circulation incentives and advertising were the spur which underwrote the newspaper localisation exercise. The more editions you had the greater numbers you could offer a pan-Indian advertiser. There were national and local advertisers to be wooed, and new categories of advertising to dream up, such as cashing in on a tradition of political sycophancy. When commerce went from being a by-product of journalism to becoming its driving force, newspapers begin to look and sound rather different.

Brand-building meant catching readers young. By 2004–05 the more ambitious newspapers were strategising to cover the youth segment. Newspaper owners were clear: they wanted to serve the community, but in a competitive scenario marketing and advertising had to drive their publishing businesses.

Notes

1. Iqbal Singh, 6 August 2001, Interview with Girish Agarwal, agencyfaqs. com. http://www.agencyfaqs.com/news/interviews/data/24.html, last downloaded 30 July 2006.
2. Naveen Joshi, resident editor, *Hindustan*, interviewed by author, Patna, 1 June 2003.
3. Girish Agarwal, interviewed by author, Mumbai, 27 January 2005.
4. Sevanti Ninan, 'Overly Interactive', *The Hindu*, Sunday, 27 April 2003.
5. Vastupal Jain, Paras News Agency, interviewed by author, village Ganoda, Banswara distirct, 1 December 2004.
6. Yadvesh Kumar, general manager, *Hindustan*, interviewed by author, Varanasi, 15 March 2005.
7. Sevanti Ninan, 'Wooing Hawkers', *The Hindu*, Ranchi, 26 October 2003.
8. Iqbal Singh, 6 August 2001, interview with Girish Agarwal, 26 October 2003.
9. Nihar Kothari, interviewed by author, Jaipur, 17 March 2006.
10. Mrinal Pande, interviewed by author, New Delhi, 12 December 2005.
11. Pavan Dubey, editor, *Highway Channel*, interviewed by author, Jagdalpal, May 2002.
12. '*Patrika–Bhaskar* competition leads to localisation, commercialisation in Rajasthan', Sevanti Ninan, the hoot.org, 7 May 2002. http://www.thehoot.org/story.asp?section=&lang=L1&storyid=nitinhoot K057021&pn=2, last downloaded July 2006.
13. Y.C. Agarwal, Vice President, *Hindustan Times*, interviewed by author, Patna, 3 June 2003.
14. Bimal Kumar, marketing manager, *Hindustan*, interviewed by author, Bhagalpur, 5 June 2003.
15. *Dainik Jagran*, Varanasi, 28 February 2005, p. 2.
16. Suneelam, Samajwadi Party MLA, interviewed by author, Bhopal, 19 February 2005.
17. *Dainik Jagran*, Varanasi, 28 February 2005.
18. *Dainik Jagran*, 27 February 2005.
19. *Daink Jagran*, 26 February 2005.
20. 'Print media outpaces TV in advertising: Adex study', *Hindu Business Line*, 5 January 2005. http://www.blonnet.com/2005/01/05/stories/2005010502010400.htm.
21. Ashok Pande, news editor in Dehradun, interviewed by author, May 2002.
22. Mahesh Shrivastava, *Raj Express*, interviewed by author, Bhopal, 18 Februuary 2004.

23. *Amar Ujala* and *Navbharat Times* had such columns at the time of writing.

24. Harihar Narayanswamy and Reshmi Dasgupta, 'The Ultimate P: P3', *The Economic Times*, 30 October 2002.

25. Shuchi Bansal, 'Some Times news smells of money', *Business Standard*, 29 January 2003.

26. *Mid Day*, 11 May 2004.

27. Soumik Sen, 'Want an Office Party on Air? Pay Zoom', *Business Standard*, 30 September 2004.

28. Shuchi Bansal, 'All the News that's Paid For', *Business Standard*, 19 May 2004.

29. Sevanti Ninan, 'Sponsors Ahoy', *The Hindu*, 16 February 2003.

30. A.S. Raghunath, general manager, brand development, *Jagran*, interviewed by author, Noida, 31 March 2005.

31. Ajay Gorkha Maheshwari, interviewed by Sushmita Malaviya, Pipariya, 26 March 2004.

32. A.S. Raghunath, *Dainik Jagran*, interviewed by author, Noida, 31 March 2005.

33. Press Release, New Delhi, 8 December 2004.

8

Journalists and Politicians

*'If you want Rajya Sabha membership you have to show
that your (newspaper's) reach is considerable at the
level of the electorate.'*

In both provenance and evolution, Hindi journalism was a far less
sanitised commodity than English journalism. It soaked in societal
influences and responded to them. Whether cordial or contentious,
it had a closer rapport with regional politicians. The language it used
continued to evolve and respond to both local and market influences.
And its practitioners had pragmatic yardsticks of professional ethics.

What this meant in practice was a cosier relationship with local
politicians, and far more give and take than journalistic ethics might
dictate. The political linkages were useful to obtain land for their
offices and presses as well as for commercial ventures. Media is an
industry, and there is one striking point of contrast between the
leading lights of the English and Hindi press in India. By 2006 the
only major English publication to be still owned by other industrial
interests was *Hindustan Times*. For the others, whether it was the
owners of *The Times of India*, *The Hindu*, *Indian Express*, the *Living
Media Group* or even *The Telegraph* and *Deccan Herald*, the main
business interests were media-related. That was not always the case
with the Hindi press. Though they did not own significant businesses
to begin with, media owners went on to acquire other businesses.

The *Dainik Jagran* was a striking example of a newspaper owned
by a group which began with just a newspaper to its name and then
went on to acquire sugar mills and a shopping mall, apart from other
businesses. As one of its directors put it:

We spent little on the paper and had a lot of profit. With the
power of the newspaper they were making *Jagran* micro motors.

Kalpanath Rai became sugar minister, he gave licenses for sugar mills. Instead of paying for the license we gave coverage to him and printed advertisements free of cost.

Two of the Gupta brothers look after the industries, including the mall, and a hosiery unit. The acquisitions were possible because the group had garnered advertising wealth, he said. *Jagran* was *The Times of India* of UP.[1] In 2005–06 it reported advertising revenue of Rs 3,060 million.

The *Dainik Bhaskar* increased its business interests substantially over the years that it had a growing newspaper. In early 2005 Sudhir Agarwal its managing editor, estimated that of the group's total turn-over of Rs 15,000 million the newspapers and the printing press in Noida accounted for Rs 6,000 million.[2] The rest, then, was accounted for by other industrial interests including a factory in Sri Lanka. The group went into the gold importing business in 2005.

Though the owner of *Nai Duniya* would say that his was the only newspaper without a '*punjipati*' (industrialist) behind its founding,[3] this paper went on to acquire substantial landed assets as well as a few businesses. When a land allotment to it became the subject of a CBI (Central Bureau of Investigation, the Central Government's investigating agency) enquiry ordered by the governor of Madhya Pradesh, the state government's defence was that there was ample precedent: 'Almost all national and regional newspapers have been given pieces of land to build their offices in almost every town in the state.'[4] The *Nava Bharat* group in Madhya Pradesh and Chhattisgarh had ventured into entrepreneurship including a tree farming venture, though not always successfully.

Narendra Mohan, the late patriarch of Jagran Prakashan Pvt Limited which published *Dainik Jagran*, sought to dispel the notion that Hindi newspapers were constant beneficiaries of real estate allotments. He recounted at a panel discussion that when his group wanted to establish a newspaper in Delhi, they were not allotted land, even after obtaining a letter of recommendation from Prime Minister Indira Gandhi.

The government of UP did not allot the land and we had to pay for the land through our nose, 2.7 millions of rupees for the plot and we spent another 8 millions for the building.

Similarly in Varanasi we did not get the land, in Lucknow we
did not get the land, in Bareilly we did not get the land, in
Agra we did not get the land. We did not get the land anywhere.
We did not receive any favour from any government. (Narendra
Mohan, quoted in *Vidura* Roundtable 1992: 13)

Journalists, he added, were much more successful in obtaining con-
cessional housing plots for themselves. But the above statement only
confirms that land was sought, at all these places.

Thirteen years later his son and brother would speak again, in an
interview, of how *Dainik Jagran* was never given land in New Delhi's
press row and assert, 'Bahadurshah Zafar Marg (in the heart of the
capital city of New Delhi) is the biggest bribe that English journalists
can get. We had applied for land in B.Z. Marg in the 1970s. That request is still pending.'

Apart from easing their business expansion, political linkages also
helped to insulate newspaper owners against workers' strikes, and
ensured that they would continue to get government advertising.
Hindi newspapers up until the 1990s got less commercial advertising
than English ones.

Close relations with those who ruled the state also meant that
they became power brokers at the local level, peddling influence, as
Lalit Surjan, the owner-editor of *Deshbandhu*, in Chhattisgarh put
it. He gave examples: a PWD (Public Works Department) contractor
would go to a newspaper owner to arrange a meeting with the chief
minister, or a film producer would solicit their help in getting entertainment tax withdrawn on a particular film. As for localisation
and the increase in district editions, that too was part of a game
plan: 'If you want Rajya Sabha membership you have to show that
your reach is considerable at the level of the electorate. If the chief
minister is going to a particular village and sees copies of a newspaper
he knows the newspaper reaches there.'[5] Surjan's own paper demonstrated considerable editorial support to Ajit Yogi when he was Chief
Minister of Chhattisgarh, but he maintained that as an editor he es-
chewed political ambitions.

He describes the sort of favours political parties could expect from
more solvent newspaper groups: 'Five years ago when Congress had
its conference at Pachmarhi the party approached newspaper houses

to host lunches and dinners for its duration.[6] In turn, chief ministers attended when the children of proprietors or editors got married. And there were occasions when a chief minister would put his state plane at an editor's disposal. The Press Council of India's report on favours given to journalists had described 30 categories of favours.[7] To this Surjan added another category: 'Business houses which owned newspapers also dabbled in pipe supply. You need lots of pipes for tubewells. All the newspapers are into this.' And there was yet another category which the Press Council had failed to note, because its report was prepared before the new states came into existence. That was the obtaining of mining leases in these states. The vice-president of *Hindustan Times* in Patna had obtained a gold mining lease in Jharkhand.[8]

In Bihar, however, Lalu Prasad Yadav's professed disregard for upper-caste journalists who he thought were biased against him, led to a distinct lack of pampering. Unlike Madhya Pradesh, where thanks to Chief Ministers Arjun Singh and Digvijay Singh over the years many prime location government houses were occupied by journalists, journalists in Bihar got no housing from the government.

Numerous Beneficiaries

It was not only the big newspapers who benefited from government largesse. Small time Hindi journalism had its entrepreneurial dimensions. In Uttaranchal, a hill state without much job generation, self-employment was the norm. If you were not running a school or a coaching academy in Dehradun, you were likely to be running a newspaper. In 2002 there were 11 daily newspapers and no less than 84 weeklies coming out of this city and they had a very unique periodicity—neither weekly nor daily, but on demand. Many of these publications were listed with the Directorate of Advertising and Visual Publicity and when required to furnish proof of their existence, from time to time, the proprietors would rush to print copies, with different datelines. To use a term well understood in Dehradun, they printed for the file. Altogether, Uttaranchal had 31 dailies, out of Dehradun, Haridwar, Udham Singh Nagar, Tehri, Pauri Garhwal and Nainital, and 122 weeklies. The majority of both kinds of publications, were four pagers. Why they appear at all may seem a mystery to outsiders who encounter them but in the state everybody seems to understand the economics of this publishing industry only too well.

The fact that most state governments had annual advertising and publicity budgets running into several millions of rupees and a stated advertising policy designed to encourage the existence of small newspapers, meant that they often ended up propping up dud publications. Newspapers were patronised by rotation, and there were some days in the year when everybody got advertising: Republic Day, Independence Day, Uttaranchal Raising Day, when a new government completed a hundred days in office and so on. In Mayawati's UP the list would include Ambedkar's birthday. All of it put together could add up to some Rs 20,000 worth of advertising a year for a publication, and if you owned ten such publications, that was Rs 200,000 of income for doing precious little. The state government was not the only patron of these publications. Public sector giants such as the Oil and Natural Gas Corporation patronised publications such as the *Garhwal Post* and were rewarded with glowing articles about the corporation in the same issue.

It was a trend that Dehradun inherited from the mother state of UP, which had a thriving tradition of small newspapers, with towns like Kanpur publishing even more titles than Dehradun. Madhya Pradesh does not have such a tradition, but Bihar did. Avdesh Kaushal, founder of the Rural Litigation and Entitlement Kendra in Dehradun and a leading social worker in the city puts down the motivation for such publishing to three reasons: for blackmail, for government and public sector advertisements and for newsprint quotas which were then sold in the black. Several would be printed from the same press: you printed a few copies of one masthead, change the masthead and print a few more, and so on. What these papers earn for the proprietor depended on how many of them he owned.[9]

In the year 2005 Uttar Pradesh's public relations department had a total of 1,523 publications registered with it, for advertising. Some 385 of these were dailies. The deputy director of the Directorate of Information explained that if the common man wanted to get close to those in power, he could do so by floating a newspaper.[10]

The Hindi belt politician had a clear and pragmatic understanding of what the media was worth, and what it meant for him. There is a telling anecdote that a retired Lucknow journalist Gyanendra Sharma narrates, about a Chief Minister of Madhya Pradesh in the 1960s, Govind Narain Singh, who was frequently criticised in the national press for his less-than-hands-on approach to governance. One day Singh emerged from a lift in Vallabh Bhavan in Bhopal to see two journalists waiting to go up.

When he saw my senior colleague, he took him by his arm and said : '*Bhai Saab aap bahut acchha likhte hain lekin shaayad aapko yeh naheen pataa ki mere vidhayak aapkaa angrejee kaa akhbaar naheen padhte so aapke likhane se meree sarkaar ke liye koyee khatraa naheen hai.*' [You write very well but perhaps you do not know that my MLAs do not read your English newspaper so your writing does not constitute a threat to my government.] '*Ve Hindi kaa akhbar* [he named one prominent Hindi daily] *zaroor padhte hain aur mujhe yeh pataa hai ki unko kaise khush rakhaa jaaye*' [Ofcourse they do read Hindi newspapers but I know how to keep those people happy]. '*Rahey baat mere kshetra kee, so wahaan ke log to koyee akhbaar padhte hee naheen, isliye wahaan bhee mujhe koyee khatraa naheen hai.*' [As for my constituency, the people there do not read any newspaper so there too I have nothing to fear from you.] His constituency was Rampur Baghelan in Satna district. He said it, laughed and went away without waiting for any response from us. But what he said made a permanent impression on my memory. What the witty CM said then still holds good, probably more than before.

Except that with the coming of localisation people in his rural constituency today would be reading a newspaper.

Sharma adds that it was much easier for the regional politicians to keep the regional newspapers on the right side than the national press. They not only got a security cover and protection from government departments entrusted with the job of enforcing a number of state laws—particularly the labour laws, but also monetary support in terms of advertisements, land at a cheaper rate and facilities for non-newspaper business interests of the proprietors.[11]

Perhaps that is why the political class in this region was wont to demonstrate from time to time that it did not fear the Hindi press. In Chhattisgarh in 2002, the chief minister who was a bureaucrat-turned-politician could recall that when he took over as collector of Indore his predecessor left him what was known as a charge report, a sort of handing-over report. According to Ajit Jogi one of the pieces of advice in that report was that if he wanted to succeed in Indore he would have to talk to Abhay Chajlani (the owner of *Nai Duniya*) every night before going to sleep. He recalled that the paper had a hold on the state of a kind not to be seen any where else in the country. 'They decided everything, even matters relating to sports and lotteries.' Jogi took credit for working to undermine this kind of influence. He said he invited the *Dainik Bhaskar* to come to Indore, gave them land and support, and watched them fight *Nai Duniya* tenaciously till they overtook it in circulation. According to Jogi the Congress party (Indian National Congress) later backed the *Bhaskar* group in entering Rajasthan to take on the *Rajasthan Patrika*.[12]

Some strong regional newspapers had identifiable political affiliations which they did not bother to deny: *Nai Duniya* with the Congress, *Rajasthan Patrika* with the BJP (Bharatiya Janata Party) when Bhairon Singh Shekhawat was chief minister, *Dainik Jagran* also with the BJP. Some had a member of the owning family in the Rajya Sabha with a party affiliation: *Ranchi Express*'s Ajay Maroo was a BJP MP in the Rajya Sabha (Upper House in the Indian Parliament) in 2005, *Nava Bharat*'s P.K. Maheshwari had previously served as a Congress MP in the the Rajya Sabha. Shobana Bharatiya, the proprietress of *Hindustan Times* group which published *Hindustan* accepted a Congress-headed coalition government's nomination to the Rajya Sabha in the eminent persons category in 2006.

The family which owned *Dainik Jagran* was the most pragmatic in this regard. Its proprietor Narendra Mohan is known to have campaigned hard for a Rajya Sabha ticket from the Congress and finally accepted one from the right wing BJP. Some years after his death, his brother Mahendra Mohn Gupta, his successor as chairman of the *Jagran* group of publications, was also keen on the BJP sending him to the Rajya Sabha from UP just as it had sent his brother.

When that did not work out he accepted, in 2006, the offer of a Rajya Sabha ticket from the Samajwadi Party (a democratic socialist party in North India), then in power in the state. From the point of view of the party too, getting the head of the leading newspaper in the state aboard, was a clever move.

The *Dainik Bhaskar* was equally pragmatic. It was seldom inclined to rock the ruling party's boat. In Haryana its rise paralleled the chief ministerial reign of Om Prakash Chautala. Political scientist Yogendra Yadav cites an anecdote to illustrate how careful the paper was to not offend. In 2001 when he took part in a *padyatra* (a long march undertaken for a specific purpose) in Haryana as part of a Jayaprakash Narayan memorial observance. The *Daink Bhaskar* approached him to write a daily diary. On 8 March, International Women's Day, he wrote about how the event did not seem to feature in the chief minister's daily schedule at all, though Haryana was a state notorious for female foeticide. The CM had not paused to take cognisance of it. The comment brought an agitated response from the paper after it was published. Why, the paper's Panipat head-quarters wanted to know, what he writing on such controversial subjects? The diary which had been appearing on page one till then, began appearing on page seven for the rest of the *padyatra*. Yet there was no official rejoinder from the state government to contra-dict the assertion made in his dairy column.[13]

The most chequered relationship that a local press corps had with a chief minister, perhaps, was the one UP journalists had with Mulayam Singh Yadav in his different terms as chief minister. In his first term he was so lavish with handouts of cash and land to journalists that when Mayawati succeeded him and publicised the favours, a Press Council of India committee was set up to look into the entire issue. The second time around he declared a *Halla Bol* (call to attack) on *Dainik Jagran* and *Amar Ujala* for encouraging, he said, a separatist movement in Uttaranchal. Arun Shourie described the consequences of this cry for the papers in question:[14]

Addressing a public meeting on October 12, UP chief minister Mulayam Singh Yadav denounced the two papers, '*Halla Bol*', he exhorted his followers, 'Commence the storming'. Why read them, he told them, you don't have to even see them. No one present had any doubt what they meant: Don't let them be seen, that is what it [sic.] meant.

Knowing from past experience what could be in store for them, many journalists left the meeting post-haste.

Since that call, hawkers and news agents selling the two papers have been beaten up. Journalists of the two papers have been beaten up. Vehicles carrying *Jagran* have been waylaid and burnt. The house of the editor of *Amar Ujala* has been attacked. Advertisements to the papers have been cut. Thousands upon thousands of copies of the papers been torched.

Shourie does not say on what grounds Mulayam Singh denounced the two newspapers. But when an Editors Guild committee inquired into the circumstances, the chief minister produced a letter on file, to show that the *Jagran* group had asked for land to start a sugar factory, a request that had not been complied with. The *Halla Bol* was vicious enough to become a landmark in relations between the press and the chief minister.

When Mayawati became chief minister in 2002 much of the UP press had such a rough time with her that there was relief when Mulayam Singh returned to power in 2003. Two free lance writers recorded the responses of journalists:

Mediapersons in Lucknow were almost jubilant when Mulayam Singh Yadav replaced Mayawati as the chief minister of the country's politically most important state. The same press which had become very hostile towards the government because of Mayawati's attitude towards them, has changed colours overnight—and this is only partly because Mulayam Singh's government is in its initial days ....

They went on to cite gushing headlines in the city newspapers.[15]

This term of Mulayam Singh Yadav, however, was marked by less open access to journalists, and some self-censorship on the part of the latter. When a TV channel, Aaj Tak exposed change of land use to favour some bureaucrats in Mulayam Singh's government, the chief minister hit back by holding a well-televised press conference in which he disclosed how many plots journalists had received from the Uttar Pradesh Government. At the *Hindustan Times* the resident editor noted that newspapers overall were now being circumspect about the excesses the chief minister was lavishing on his constituency in Etawah. 'We have our holy cows.' One of the paper's top executives was himself in the queue for land allotment favours in Lucknow. She also described how the *Jagran* had changed its earlier hostility to the chief minister and begun to hedge its bets with regard to all political parties in the state. 'You can see in *Jagran* careful double-column stories on each party. They will give balanced coverage.' She made the point that UP politicians were now less interested in the print media. 'They ask for TV reporters by name. Now the demand is for the electronic media, not for Hindi or English.'[16] The resident editor of *Hindustan* who had moved to Lucknow from Patna would describe how Mulayam Singh Yadav was latterly reluctant to give interviews to journalists, and distinctly less accessible that Lalu Prasad Yadav used to be.[17] He ascribed the decline in direct access in part to the emergence of Amar Singh, the Samajwadi Party's point man for access to the chief minister.

The self-censorship the Uttar Pradesh press was practising was evident in the coverage until then of Mulayam Singh's tenure, many instances of which were documented. The start of his new tenure was marked by transfers of bureaucrats, something Mayawati had been roundly criticised for. This time around the criticism was muted and the *Indian Express*' *Express Newsline* from Lucknow called it 'a cleansing touch'. The chief minister's support for a former minister, Amarmani Tripathi, against whom the CBI was finding more and more convincing evidence of murder, also called for more stringent criticism than it got. Then the chief minister withdrew the POTA (Prevention of Terrorism Act) case against the Thakur politician Raja Bhaiyya, but there was less outrage in the media than there had been when he was arrested by Mayawati.[18]

When Mulayam Singh broke the record for appointing jumbo ministries with a 98-member ministry, criticism of this was moderate in most mainstream papers. And the *Rashtriya Sahara*, whose proprietor Subroto Roy was allied to the Samajwadi Party, actually justified the large ministry as a compulsion of coalition politics. The inordinate delay in swearing in ministers, it explained, was because the honourable chief minister was busy co-ordinating between the coalition partners. It praised the chief minister for fairly representing all parties, regions, castes and communities, and giving weightage to such factors as seniority of leaders. It even had a word of consolation and advice, rather condescendingly, for those who did not get to become minister. Above all, it said that criticism was uncalled for as previous chief ministers have also had jumbo ministries (Kalyan Singh had 93; Rajnath Singh, 85 and Mayawati, 79).[19]

The Indian Express' Lucknow edition was a franchise edition owned by a Rajya Sabha Congress MP and because the Congress party was supporting the Mulayam Singh government, it too fell in line. *Dainik Jagran*, sobered by its brush with Mayawati, let the *Halla Bol* become a thing of the past. When the chief minister completed two years in office in August 2005 it published a survey that was critical of his achievements, but the induction in the subsequent year of its chairman M.M. Gupta into the Samajwadi Party as a Rajya Sabha MP seemed to suggest that the paper was not viewed as an adversary by the ruling party in the state.

Conclusion

The commercial instincts of the Hindi press were honed early on by developing pragmatic political linkages to procure land and favours. Both big and small Hindi newspapers benefited from government largesse. The relationship between press and politicians in this region was calibrated by the needs of both. Some strong regional newspapers had identifiable political affiliations which they did not bother to deny. But whatever their affiliation, all of them chose to tread carefully with the party in power. When Mulayam Singh Yadav returned as chief minister in 2003 his term was marked by less open access to journalists, and some self-censorship on the part of the latter.

Notes

1. Vinod Shukla, interviewed by author, Lucknow, 30 August 2005.
2. Sudhir Agarwal, *Bhaskar* Group, interviewed by author, 27 January 2005.

3. Abhay Chajlani, interviewed by author, Indore, 15 February 2005.
4. 'Conflict of Interest', *India Today*, http://www.india-today.com/ webexclusive/dispatch/20010524/mishra.html (downloaded 8 July 2003).
5. Lalit Surjan, editor, *Deshbandhu*, interviewed by author, New Delhi, 21 March 2005.
6. Ibid.
7. The Report of the Press Council of India, http://www.nwmindia.org/ Law/Bare_acts/press_council_guidelines.htm.
8. Sevanti Ninan, 'Statehood: Good for the Media?', *The Hindu*, 22 September 2002.
9. Sevanti Ninan, 'Uttaranchal's Dubious Publishing Boom', thehoot.org, posted 6 June 2002, http://www.thehoot.org/story.asp?section=&lang= L1&storyid=webhoothootL1K0990210&pn=1.
10. R.C. Thagela, deputy director, information directorate, interviewed by author, Lucknow, 31 August 2005.
11. Gyanendra Sharma, email communication, 9 September 2005.
12. Ajit Jogi, then chief minister of Chhattisgarh, interviewed by author, Raipur, June 2002.
13. Yogendra Yadav, interviewed in New Delhi, 5 July 2006.
14. Arun Shourie, 'Secular Hypocrisy, Double Standard, and Regressions', *The Observer*, 8 November 1994. http://arunshourie.voicesofdharma. com/articles/19941108.htm.
15. Sachin Agarwal and Shivam Vij, 'For Lucknow Scribes Happy Days are Here Again', thehoot.org, 19 October 2003. http://www.thehoot.org/ story.asp?storyid=web210214166112Hoot8430%20PM942&pn=1.
16. Sunita Aron, resident editor, *Hindustan Times*, interviewed by author, Lucknow, 26 August 2005.
17. Naveen Joshi, resident editor, *Hindustan*, Lucknow, interviewed by author, Lucknow, 1 June 2005.
18. Sachin Agarwal and Shivam Vij, 'For Lucknow Scribes Happy Days are Here Again, thehoot.org, 19 October 2003.
19. Ibid.

9

Caste and Communalism

*'To strengthen your movement, you must
yourself become the media.'*

How much can change in a decade and a half in the mental landscape
of a region? Far more than anyone could have imagined. The backdrop to the spread of localisation was the transformative changes
which took place in the Hindi belt and manifested themselves by the
beginning of the decade of the 1990s. A shift was taking place in the
social basis of political power in northern India. The changes had
set in earlier but became evident with the empowerment of the Other
Backward Castes (OBCs) commonly described as the Mandalisation
of north Indian politics. Prime Minister V.P. Singh in 1990 announced
the acceptance of the Mandal Commission's recommendations, chief
among which was that 27 per cent of jobs in the Central Government
would be reserved for backward communities. What changed is best
articulated by the social scientist Yogendra Yadav in some of his
writings. The 1990s, he says, witnessed greater political participation
and intense politicisation of marginalised social groups. 'While urban
middle classes were busy bashing politics and politicians, the democratic space provided by electoral politics was being used more deftly
by Dalits, Adivasis, women and the poor.'[1]

A parallel development saw a coalescing of the upper-caste constituencies of the Bharatiya Janata Party (BJP). The BJP formed its
own 'social bloc', a coalition that offered enduring support to the
party. The core of this support was a strong allegiance from the upper
caste and well-to-do sections of Hindu society. 'Cutting through the
various local rivalries that divided this segment—the traditional
political rivalries between the Rajputs and Brahmins that dominated
many states before the 1990s—the BJP moulded the upper castes

and the "middle class" into a unified political bloc.'² The emergence
of both new strands of politics was enabled by the shrinking presence of the Congress party. In Uttar Pradesh, for instance, the party
went from 85 (out of 85!) parliamentary seats in the 1984 elections
to 15 seats in 1989, and then to five seats in 1991 and 1996. Its stable
vote banks began to desert it for other political parties that were
emerging.

Both political trends culminated in electoral gains for all the
non-Congress forces in the Hindi-speaking states, with the BJP forming governments in Uttar Pradesh, Madhya Pradesh, Jharkhand,
Chhattisgarh and Rajasthan, and the Bahujan Samaj Party (BSP) representing Dalits, and the Samajwadi Party (SP) representing the inheritors of Mandal, also forming successive governments in Uttar Pradesh.
Political pragmatism also saw coalition governments in the same state,
between the BJP and BSP, and the SP and the Congress. The emergence
of the BSP and the SP in electoral politics as well as the Janata Dal in
Bihar, represents what Yadav describes as a 'democratic upsurge from
below,' and the public sphere began to reflect this upsurge.

The nature of political developments in the heartland was not
just mirrored in the media but in some sense also mediated by it.
The Hindi press was drawn from society, and when caste and communalism shaped discourse, its conduct as media also became part of
that discourse.

Imperatives of Caste in Media

Historically, several newspapers in Bihar have had caste associations.
In 1889 *Kayastha Gazette*, named after one of India's upper castes,
made its appearance from Patna, while *Kayastha Messenger* was
published from Gaya. Others published at the turn of the century
and early in the 20th century were *Dwija Patrika, Kshatriya Patrika,
Kshatriya Samachar, Khatri Hitaishi* (all from Patna) and *Teli
Samachar, Mahuri Mayanka, Bhumihar Brahman Patrika, Rauniar
Hitashi, Kayastha Kaumudi, Madhya Deshiya Vanik Patrika, Rauniar
Vaishya, Kushwaha, Saundik* and others (Kumar 1971).

The Indian Nation, founded by the Maharaja of Darbhanga in
1931, had upper caste origins as did a Hindi daily from the same

stable, *Aryavartha*, which appeared in 1941. Both were predominantly Maithili Brahmin in their editorial composition. And according to a scholar in Patna, if they highlighted floods in Bihar, inevitably those in Mithila got a lot more coverage. *Pataliputra Times* was started by a close associate of a Brahmin former Congress Chief Minister of the state, Jagannath Mishra, and survived briefly. Caste representation within the editorial composition of this paper too was predominantly upper caste.[3]

From the late 1970s, the politicisation of people in the state also reflected the upward mobility of the lower castes here, which began with the rise to chief ministership of a backward-caste politician, Karpoori Thakur. He implemented the Mungheri Lal Commission's Report on reservation for other backward classes, creating a political force which has subsequently won two elections in the state. As in Uttar Pradesh, and earlier in southern states like Tamil Nadu, the lower and backward castes seized political power in Bihar. In both UP and Bihar, the political leadership is not upper caste, whereas the majority of the media still is.

1990 was a watershed year in Indian politics, and in the relationship of the media with backward-caste politics in Bihar. The Mandal reservations were opposed not just by some of the English language press headquartered in Delhi* but also by much of the media in Bihar, as Sukant Nagarjun, resident editor of *Hindustan* in Muzaffarpur points out.[4] And Surendra Kishore, political editor of the same paper adds, 'They (the media) did not treat the issue professionally.'[5] At that point the backwards constituted 52 per cent of Bihar's electorate.[6] And upper castes in the state's media were estimated to constitute something like 80 per cent.

Caste-based politics in the Hindi heartland was throwing up a new generation of leaders who were willing to point a finger at journalists reporting on their parties and label them casteist. The most vocal in making this accusation were Lalu Prasad Yadav of the Rashtriya Janata Dal in Bihar, whose constituency was the backward castes, and Mayawati of the Bahujan Samaj Party in Uttar Pradesh.

---

*Indian Express wrote an editorial urging people to come out amd oppose the reservations, the news video Newstrack produced an inflammatory edition as well. But *Jansatta*, the *Expres*'s sister publication in Hindi, took a pro-Mandal stand.

The nub of their accusations was the same: reporting by the media could not be fair or accurate because it suffered from a pronounced upper-caste bias. In both states, the journalists were overwhelmingly upper-caste, both regular employees in newspaper and magazine offices as well as part-time 'stringers' across the length and breadth of the states.

Attitudes to the media as a player now became a part of political formulations. The Bahujan Samaj Party's founder Kanshi Ram, the Dalit publication *Dalit Voice* and other Dalit articulations have from time to time reiterated the party stand that the mainstream media was *manuwadi* or casteist, and not to be trusted. Ajay Upadhyay, former editor of *Hindustan*, points out that when Kanshi Ram built the party, he side-stepped the mainstream media and reached out directly to Dalits through personal communications, often in the form of letters written to the literate Dalits in a village.[7] But the inheritors of socialism were more pragmatic in their dealings with the media; they used it when they could and spurned it when it did not come up to their expectations. Upadhyay also recalls the socialist politician Ram Manohar Lohia's extended articulations with journalists over coffee. Both Lalu Prasad Yadav as chief minister in Bihar and Mulayam Singh Yadav in Uttar Pradesh have turned their backs on the press from time to time, without it affecting their vote base.

A number of journalists in Patna concede that even though corruption and criminalisation destroyed the economy of Bihar through the many years of Lalu Prasad's and then his wife Rabri Devi's chief ministership, it is because of the media that they faced no real criticism. The media carried little credibility with the electorate, or with politicians. According to *The Hindu*'s man in Bihar, K. Balachand:[8]

All politicians in the state see who you are. If you write against them they will say he wrote this because he is not from my caste. The bureaucrat is also casteist. When you write you may not reflect the whole picture because your source is someone from your caste.

The media seldom confronted the government on the issue of growing criminalisation because newspaper managements urged self-censorship. The *Hindustan*'s and *Jagran*'s editorial policies were not confrontationist.[9] Nor were those of others publishing from the state, even on the issue of corruption when the erstwhile chief minister and ruling party leader was facing investigation by the Central Bureau of Investigation. The story of the Rs 7,000 million fodder scam which implicated the chief minister was broken and then pursued by the small Ranchi-based paper *Prabhat Khabar*.

The caste composition of the media was perpetuated because the media had no fixed norms for appointments, and people were free to hire whom they pleased, so it was difficult for other castes to break in. A Brahmin is likely to hire more Brahmins, and this was demonstrated by the employment pattern in *Indian Nation*.[10] Not all journalists in the state however are upper caste, some Dalits and Yadavs came into the profession in Karpoori Thakur's time. But since the beginning of the process of broadening the media's social base began only then, in the late 1970s, a very small percentage of representation in this profession has been achieved till now.[11]

A freelance looking at the issue of caste in the newsroom in Lucknow found that backward-caste journalists could, in 2004, count their numbers on the fingertips, and then start listing names, 'an exercise which some upper-caste scribes were also able to undertake'. There were not even half a dozen Dalit journalists in Lucknow, most of whom did not handle the political beat, and no Dalit journalist worked for an English paper. As for OBC's, there was in 2003 not more than one in every paper.[12] Even as politics in Uttar Pradesh came to be dominated by the Samajwadi Party which was the party of 'other backward castes' (the Constitutional classification for the intermediate castes between the scheduled castes and the upper castes), and the Bahujan Samaj Party (BSP) which was primarily the party of Dalits or the scheduled castes, both these groupings were vastly under-represented in the UP press, particularly amongst political reporters. The backward caste parties were invariably covered by upper-caste journalists, and overseen by upper-caste editors.[13]

In early 2003, during Mayawati's tenure as chief minister, the relationship between her and sections of the press corps was more than a little strained. Her arrest of the influential Thakur politician Raja Bhaiyya was criticised by the press, whose writing reflected their belief that her days were now numbered. But observers noted that as the weeks after the arrest wore on and the chief minister stayed her course, the newspapers began to change their tune as well. 'They first tried to report in favour of Raja Bhaiyya. But when it became clear that his rebellion (Raja Bhaiyya's) had almost fizzled out, there appears to be a clear signal in favour of Mayawati with the approval of the editors.'[14]

Mayawati's lavish celebrations of her birthday each year became a constant target of criticism, in both the national and local press. One year, at a press meet about the fund collection for the BSP during these celebrations, the Reuters correspondent Sharad Pradhan reportedly asked Mayawati: '*Aapne kitna paisa botore liya ab tak?*' (How much money have you amassed by now?) The question was not irrelevant but its tone provoked the chief minister to flare up at the correspondent. He was dropped from subsequent press briefings, and the information directorate thereafter began to scrutinise the writings and therefore loyalty of journalists, particularly those occupying government housing.[15] Notices were issued to some 70 journalists to vacate for non-payment of rent. BSP politicians were not afraid of taking on the press. Some years prior to this, the party's supremo Kanshi Ram slapped a newsperson at a press conference at his house in New Delhi, triggering a love–hate relationship between the party leadership and the media. This reached new levels during the Mayawati regime in Lucknow. She believed her voter did not read the papers, and was not influenced by them, and so she did not speak to the *manuwadi* (casteist) media.[16]

When Mayawati's government fell, the UP press corps including the aggrieved Reuters correspondent could not hide their relief or glee. Sharad Pradhan's 'Watchdog' column in *Hindustan Times* on 30 August 2003 reflected the mood. Titled 'High expectations from new CM', the column said:

> The reign of terror is now over. Everyone appears to be heaving a sigh of relief—be it the man on the street, the all powerful bureaucrats or the mighty people's representatives. (The) Sixteen months that have gone by will be remembered as that dark patch in the history of Uttar Pradesh when fundamental freedom, enshrined in Ambedkar's Constitution, was eroded by a ham-headed and insolent despot who ironically chose to swear by the name of the architect of that Constitution.[17]

Just before his party lost the state elections in Bihar in November 2005, Lalu Prasad Yadav was to assert again in a newspaper interview his firm belief that the upper-class media did not reflect his true popularity in the state. Exit polls were showing that he would lose the election, but he dubbed them an upper-class media conspiracy.[18] This time, however, the media had got its electoral prognosis right.

Apart from specific encounters between the upper-caste media and caste-based politicians, the larger issue is that of caste representation in the media. The relative absence of Dalits and backwards in the ranks of the media was true of the whole country, not just the Hindi belt. And it was seen as accounting for the relative lack of press concern for issues relating to caste inequality and oppression in the regional media, in particular. If there was an atrocity against Dalits, it was more likely to figure in the national press. In 1996 a foreign correspondent wrote:

> India's 4,000 daily newspapers publish in nearly 100 languages, but one voice is largely absent in the press of the world's largest democracy: that of the lower castes, which account for more than 70 per cent of the country's 934 million people. Not one daily newspaper has made speaking on their behalf its role. Few daily newspaper reporters come from lower castes, and none of the nation's prominent columnists does.[19]

On ambedkar.org, a Website devoted to Dalit discourse, a former journalist at the *Pioneer* who became an academic at the Jawaharlal Nehru University in New Delhi, wrote on the occasion of 'Dalit Diary' completing 100 columns in that paper, that Babasaheb Ambedkar had talked about the abuses hurled at him from the Hindu press. Vivek Kumar also quoted BSP leader Kanshi Ram who had abused the media as *manuwadi*. He had said, 'Dalits don't trust the upper-caste media. To strengthen your movement, you must yourself become the media.' A voice for Dalits in the media was sorely needed, and needed to be celebrated when found.[20]

In the state of Jharkhand, the issue was one of absence of both tribals and Dalits from the ranks of the press, though there were quite a few freelance journalists. Here the reason was complex: in the case of tribals it had to do with opportunity, temperament, and the blurred divide between journalism and activism. Thanks to reservations, tribal people had access to government jobs, and better avenues for promotions. Then there were cultural reasons why a tribal scribe would prefer to be a free agent. If they have to give up their freedom they would rather do so for better security than a newspaper offered. And tribal journalists were often also inclined to be activists on issues of concern to them.[21]

But the Dalit view was different. A Dalit activist from Jharkhand wrote:

> More than 12 per cent Dalits live in this state. The Dalit community itself is living without any able leadership. On every question and problem of Dalits, there is an amazing silence from the media side. Every day Dalit women are being sexually exploited, but for the media it is not news. And if they record such incidents, it is very small news.

He went on to add that there was not a single Dalit staff reporter in the newspapers published in Jharkhand. Most journalists were non-Jharkhandi, and unable to give voice to what he called 'the basic feeling of Jharkhand'.[22]

Journalism and Communal Politics

The events at Ayodhya in 1990 became a memorable case study of the role the print media can play in inflaming a communal situation. There is considerable documentation on the issue. The Press Council of India appointed a sub-committee in November 1990 to examine the role of the press, and the role of the authorities in dealing with the press relating to the coverage of the Ramjanmabhoomi–Babri Masjid issue, and its report was published in 1991. *Dainik Jagran*, *Aj*, *Swatantra Chetna* and *Swatantra Bharat* were the papers named for giving an inflated and irresponsible account of the events of October 1990. The report recorded that *Dainik Jagran* had, in the run-up to the October 30 *kar seva*, along with *Aj*, asked its readers 'through news reports, editorials and published appeals' to take a stand on the *kar seva* (Hasan 1998). Following the firing on the *kar sevak*s it inflated the figures of the dead. Vinod Shukla of *Dainik Jagran* would say later that they were misled by an inexperienced reporter and corrected their figure after they realised they had got it wrong. But he also says that the atmosphere in UP in those days was such that even if you were sitting in a bar you could see people around you greet each other with *Jai Sri Ram*.[23]

The *Dainik Jagran's* use of the Ayodhya issue to establish its supremacy as a newspaper in Uttar Pradesh parallels the Bharatiya Janata Party's sustained use of the Ramjanmabhoomi campaign in Ayodhya to establish itself politically in UP. A party that did not win a single Lok Sabha seat from this state in 1984 was able by 1991 to form a government here. An offshoot of that success was the fact that, between 1989 and 1992, Uttar Pradesh became a communal cauldron. 'Every second family was associated with BJP. So they [*Jagran*] took a pro-BJP policy and established themselves in UP. *Hindutva ke lehar par savar uthke, apne aap ko establish kiye* [They rode the wave of Hindutva and established themselves].' That was a journalist formerly with *Jagran* describing the paper's calculated communalism.[24]

A journalist working for *Dainik Jagran* in 2002 in Dehradun confirmed this in the context of competition. It was the need of the moment, he said.

> In 1992 in UP, there was considerable rivalry between *Aj* and *Jagran*. In that climate *Aj* had turned totally communal. It went on publishing, gaining numbers. It used to be No. 1 then. So because of *Aj*, *Jagran* began retaliating. At that point it was the way forward if you wanted numbers. A Muslim readership was practically non-existent at that point, barely 2 to 3 per cent. The readership came from Hindus.[25]

The point that has been made about the Hindi media is that it was relatively fertile ground for the BJP and its associate, the Vishwa Hindu Parishad, to stir up political support. In *Politics after Television*, Arvind Rajagopal contends that the cultural isolation between the English and Hindi print media worked to the political advantage of the Hindu Right, as forms of expression that were principally religious in character, which were excluded from the English language media, flourished in the Hindi media and helped in organising Hindu nationalist opinion. 'If the English media treated issues of religion ... as peripheral to their concerns, and the Hindi media treated it as a relatively familiar, living presence and as a sociological fact within their purview, the latter could become an organising ground for the Hindu right' (Rajagopal 2001: 160). *Aj* and *Jagran* were by no means the only newspapers pandering to communal sentiment. The attempted *kar seva* at Ayodhya in 1990 and subsequent events led other publications too to ride the wave, as it were. Hindi newspapers in Madhya Pradesh that were supposed to be pro-Congress are also accused of having been blatantly communal in this period. In 1992, a provocative story in *Nava Bharat* led to riots in Bhopal. And for the *Dainik Bhaskar* too, in terms of circulation and overtaking *Nai Duniya*, the turning point according to a journalist working in Madhya Pradesh at that time was Ayodhya. It brought out four special editions in Indore.[26]

A Ranchi-based editor, Harivansh, recounts that even in southern Bihar (Jharkhand was formed later), the atmosphere was so surcharged that he lost readership for having reported the deaths at Ayodhya correctly:

> *Jharkhand RSS ka garh tha* [Jharkhand was an RSS base]. In 1990, my director D.S. Sharma rang up and said there is a pamphlet in the market that ours is a Muslim newspaper. After *Prabhat Khabar* reported that only six Hindus had died at Ayodhya, no cash sales were taking place. Readers who used to pick up their copies in the market were simply not buying. I asked my director Sharma, do you want me to do facts-based journalism or not? He said, stick to the facts. I used to phone Ram Kirpal of *Navbharat Times* and the BBC correspondent in Lucknow to check what was happening.

Harivansh filed a complaint with the Press Council against *Jagran* and *Aj*, accusing them of instigating communalism in Ranchi.[27]

Atul Maheshwari, managing director of *Amar Ujala* would also later assert in an interview that his paper stuck to a figure of 18 people dying following the Babri Masjid demolition and lost subscriptions in that charged period, because it was perceived as anti-Hindu.[28]

The far less noticed change which came about, and which no one till date has documented or quantified, is the saffronising[29] of news-rooms, both Hindi and English. In Rajasthan, *Dainik Bhaskar*, *Dainik Nav Jyoti* and *Rajasthan Patrika* all have journalists sympathetic to the BJP or to the RSS in their ranks. One journalist described how RSS sympathisers infiltrated the ranks of journalists in this state: 'They come to news room with press releases, hang around get to know journalists. They get friendly with them. They keep in constant touch. When a vacancy occurs, they get to know, apply, and get in.'[30]

Meanwhile, insiders in *Jagran* describe an editorial meeting that Narendra Mohan called, perhaps the only known case of a politically aligned newspaper proprietor and editor calling a meeting of editorial staff to tell them that his party affiliation should not reflect on his newspaper's political coverage. *Jagran's vichar dhara* (ideology) was *Bharatiya* (Indian), he is supposed to have clarified, not Hindutva. He also made a stirring defence of Muslims, asking if they were not the paper's readers, and criticising attacks upon them. 'He said, I am a BJP MP but let all remember that *Jagran* is not of the BJP. Ali Mian and Shankaracharya should be treated the same. *Jagran* should not become *Panchajanya*.'[31] But that came after much water had flown under the bridge.[32]

By the mid-2000s, the Muslim reader had also begun to read Hindi newspapers and was seen by identifiably Right-wing newspapers such as *Rajasthan Patrika* and *Dainik Jagran* as potential readers. In a city, such as Jaipur, with a sizeable Muslim presence, a Muslim leader would confirm that the learning of Hindi was fairly universal among young Muslims.[33] In March 2006, Gulab Kothari, the chief editor of *Rajasthan Patrika*, asserted in an interview that the paper was anxious to promote communal amity: 'We motivate people to celebrate Id and Diwali together.' That very day, however, the Alwar edition of *Rajasthan Patrika* had whipped up an issue involving a Christian priest into the lead story of the day, whereas *Dainik Bhaskar* carried it lower down on the front page as a smaller story. And asked about the *Patrika*'s changing attitude to Muslims, the chief qazi of Jaipur, Khaled Usmani, would say dryly, 'Gulab Kothari may have changed his way of thinking, the lower cadres in the paper have not.' He also added that the *Patrika* had taken to asking him when they wrote about Muslims, whether they had got it right.[34]

Dainik Jagran however retained a tough line with regard to Muslim terrorism and Pakistan. This showed up in its reporting. In the first half of January 2006 it carried seven front page reports related to terrorism in Kashmir, compared to two each in *Amar Ujala* and *Daink Bhaskar*, and one in *Punjab Kesari*. A researcher looking at coverage of Pakistan in Hindi newspapers found that both *Amar Ujala* and *Dainik Jagran* carried articles that highlighted negative aspects of Pakistan, not necessarily related to Kashmir or terrorism.[35]

Conclusion

The political public sphere was shaped in discernable ways by the media. A shift was taking place in the social basis of political power in northern India, and the nature of political developments in the heartland was not just mirrored in the media but in some sense also mediated by it. The Hindi press was drawn from society and when caste and communalism shaped discourse, their conduct as media also became part of that discourse. Caste-based politics in the Hindi heartland was throwing up a new generation of leaders who were willing to point a finger at journalists reporting on their parties and label them casteist. As for communal influences, in 1992 in UP the way forward if you wanted numbers was to be communal; a Muslim readership was practically non-existent, the readership came from Hindus. But by the mid 2000s the Muslim reader had also begun to read Hindi newspapers and was seen by identifiably Right-wing newspapers such as the *Rajasthan Patrika* and the *Dainik Jagran* as potential readers.

Notes

1. Yogendra Yadav, 'The Big Picture', *The Hindu*, 20 May 2004.
2. Ibid.
3. Professor Hetukar Jha, interviewed by author, Patna, 4 June 2003.

4. Sukanta Nagarjun, interviewed by author, Muzaffarpur, 8 June 2003.
5. Surendra Kishore, interviwed by author, Patna, 2 June 2003.
6. Sankarshan Thakur, *The Making of Laloo Yadav, the Unmaking of Bihar*, HarperCollins India, 2000, p. 79.
7. Ajay Upadhyay, former editor, *Hindustan*, interviewed by author, 5 May 2006.
8. K. Balachand, interviewed by author, Patna, 2 June 2003.
9. Naveen Joshi, interviewed by author, Patna, 1 June 2003.
10. Nalin Varma, *Statesman*, interviwed by author, Patna, 2 June 2003.
11. Sukanta Nagarjun, interviewed by author, Muzaffarpur, 8 June 2003.
12. Shivam Vij, 'Caste in the Newsroom?', http://www.thehoot.org/story.asp?storyid=Web2196523711Hoot122711%20AM1229&pn=1.
13. Shivam Vij, 'Commerce, politics and caste in UP election coverage', thehoot.org, posted 19 May 2004, http://www.thehoot.org/story.asp?storyid=Web219652282Hoot20652%20PM1189&pn=1.
14. Devsagar Singh, 'Mayawati and the Media', thehoot.org, 25 February 2003, http://www.thehoot.org/story.asp?storyid=Web21965229190hoot2252003722&pn=1&section=S16.
15. Ibid.
16. Shivam Vij, 'Commerce, politics and caste ...', thehoot.org, posted 19 May 2004.
17. Sachin Agarwal and Shivam Vij, 'For Lucknow Scribes Happy Days are Here Again', thehoot.org, 19 October 2003.
18. Manini Chatterjee, 'Laloo Scoffs at Exit Polls', *Indian Express*, Delhi, 21 November 2005. http://www.indianexpress.com/full_story.php?content_id=82405.
19. Kenneth J. Cooper, 'India's Majority Lower Castes are Minor Voice in Newspapers', *The Washington Post*, p. A16, 5 September 1996.
20. Dr Vivek Kumar, 'Social Surgery has been Painful but Worth it'. http://www.ambedkar.org/vivek/Socialsurgery.htm.
21. Sevanti Ninan, 'No Adivasi Journalists in Jharkhand Newspapers', thehoot.org, 16 March 2002.
22. Ramdev Bandhu, 'Jharkhand's oppressed dalits and the media', thehoot.org, September 2002.
23. Vinod Shukla, interviewed by author, Lucknow, 30 August 2005.
24. Shashank Shekhar Tripathi, interviewed by author, Varanasi, 15 March 2005.
25. Ashok Pande, *Dainik Jagran*, interviewed by author, Dehradun, May 2002.
26. N.K. Singh, state editor Jaipur, *Dainik Bhaskar*, interviewed by author, 15 September 2005.
27. Harivansh, interviewed by author, New Delhi, 27 Octobr 2005.

28. Atul Maheshwari, interviewed by Rajiv Raghunath, exchange4media, 31 May 2004. http://www.exchange4media.com/content/content.asp? content id=58 (accessed in August 2006).
29. A term used to connote the spread of the Hindutva philosophy. Saffron is the colour Hindu priests wear.
30. Narayan Bareth, BBC, interviewed by author, Jaipur, 17 September 2005.
31. *Panchajanya* is the mouthpiece of the Rashtriya Swayamsevak Sangh.
32. Vinod Shukla, interviewed by author, Lucknow, 30 August 2005.
33. Khaled Usmani, interviewed by author, Jaipur, 18 March 2006.
34. Ibid.
34. Subarno Chattarji, 'Jagran and Nawai-e-Waqt Stoke Paranoia', 8 March 2006. http://www.thehoot.org/story.asp?storyid=Web5917614171 Hoot121201%20AM1999&pn=1.

10

The Development Discourse

'When a government official retires,
he becomes civil society.'

More newspapers are now being read by ordinary people in
small towns and villages, where the written word and its power
has been a weapon of the privileged. However, the growing avid
readership is now caught, between the desire to seek information and news beyond their immediate confines, and the limited
often narrow interpretation of facts, passed off as the truth itself.
The alternatives offered in the mainstream Hindi press also
miserably fail to reflect the plurality of opinion and the depth
of democratic debate that actually exists in the country. As a
result, most often only one point of view reflecting the dominant
rural middle class positions is presented.[1]

Activist Aruna Roy of the Mazdoor Kisan Shakti Sangathan (MKSS)
was essentially saying in the above extract that the newsprint-enabled
local public sphere which was being created in small town and rural
India did not adequately reflect the grassroots discourse, rather it
created its own shallow priorities. She was speaking on the subject
of public discourse in contemporary India to graduating journalism students. Habermas emphasized the role of the public sphere as
a way for civil society to articulate its interests. This chapter explores
the implications of newspaper localisation for the development
agendas of civil society and the state, and for the nature of the development discourse that was emerging in India's districts and in the
regional press.

Development in 21st India century was no longer primarily the
province of the state machinery which ran local and state governments and controlled administrative budgets. The last quarter of the

20th century had seen the rise and enormous growth of civil society in India as agents of governance, campaigners, watchdogs. Their presence at the district and village level was visible, some categories of government funds were disbursed through them, and their role in deepening democracy and strengthening governance was constantly being assessed. The term civil society is used to encompass non-governmental organisations, members of panchayats, new social groups that have entered the political arena, activists who began to form broad-based social movements, trade unions, new political categories such as scheduled castes, women and environmentalists.

When newspapers began to localise one of the issues which emerged had to do with how this level of media served the agenda of development workers and social activists. And when three new states of the Indian Union were created out of Madhya Pradesh, Uttar Pradesh and Bihar, and there was a rush of media to the new state capitals, the question that arose was about the manner in which the new entrants might be able to serve the development agendas of the new state.

Civil society actors at the district level were not indifferent to newspaper localisation. Just as at the national level the non-governmental sector expects media support for its various struggles, so also local activists and social workers look for force multipliers while tackling intractable rural problems. In terms of increasing the volume of coverage, therefore, localisation was a godsend. Who would have expected the media to be present in strength at the district level? With competition growing there were in some places as many as three newspapers offering extremely localised coverage.

Their pages were accessible to village-level catalysts who said they now had plenty of space to highlight their issues (Figure 10.1).[2] Even if the local media discourse had severe limitations, issues were being raised and debated. For those working in a 'rights' mode, it helped to generate reaction and pressure. The 'come and give your news' policy of district editions with 90 per cent such news being printed made it possible for a variety of petitions and press releases to find their way into the newspaper. Several activists made the point that because many kinds of small news found their way into these local editions and circulated in the area, local newspapers began to serve as an important conduit of information for development agents at the village level.

FIGURE 10.1 *Vikas* (development), is the title of *Prabhat Khabar*'s 84-page special edition on Bihar, 11 July 2005—an exhaustive survey over seven sections of Bihar's backwardness and the development issues confronting the state

Said, Suresh Diwan of the Gramin Sevak Samiti in Hoshangabad 'The advantage for our organisation has been that we have been getting news about farmers, small and marginal farmers, women, *Adivasi*s, *panchayat*s, *sarpanch*s and *panch*s. We have also publicly raised issues regarding the above at the regional level, the state level and the all India level.'[3] For Rajendra Sail of the Indian Social Action Forum the benefit was that political, social and women-related news was documented thanks to these newspapers.[4] Another development worker said:

> We benefit. People like to read about social developments in their region. For example, when I was working in Sehore a few years ago, a woman sarpanch got a very big pond deepened in her village. Her endeavour was highlighted in a very positive manner by the media. Because of this, people in surrounding areas were inspired to follow her example.[5]

And at a round table at Seva Mandir in Udaipur the point was made that if you paid attention to the pattern emerging from scattered little items, it was here that you could spot the early indications of a drought building up.[6]

If the hospitable local pages were useful for civil society to find out what was going on, it was also useful for putting out information on what concerned them. Gopal Rati of Eklavya said that it had it had become a tradition that if you gave something in writing to these newspapers it appeared—sometimes word for word.[7] He and others like him said they preferred it that way because whenever a reporter or stringer came to do the reporting, it resulted in a distortion of news.

Also, aside from the documentation they provided, the considered view of village-level civil society was that while newspapers were anxious to be local and to be read, they had no sense of how to use their forum to provide purposeful coverage. If the big city press was obsessed with celebrities, the rural press was obsessed with crime, usually petty crime, which found an inordinate amount of space in the local pages. Your cause might get space, but not in a sufficiently sustained measure to exert pressure on the administration. 'In 2002, we organised a hunger strike to protest power cuts in the State. It made news only on the first day and after that newspapers forgot that we were still on fast.'[8]

But for those working in the training of panchayats in rural areas of Betul in Madhya Pradesh, and Bastar and Dhantewada in neighbouring Chhattisgarh, it was apparent that the change newspapers were bringing about was in the nature of politics.

They brought transparency in the dynamics of political parties, discussion on why parties follow a certain policy. In Chhattisgarh, it has been a trend for newspapers to carry interviews with Naxalites and analysis about them prior to elections. It has been felt that the Congress party has always assumed that the party's victory depended on fear that would be created by the Naxal activities. In its own way the *Highway Channel* boldly focused on this issue to bring to light several nexus that are at work behind these tactics.[9]

Local news, especially news about block politics, panchayat politics and politics of panchayat leaders, was read with great interest by people, and because of increased awareness village-level dynamics have changed. 'This is reflected in the interaction in the Gram Sabha too especially in the kind of questions that people have begun to ask. Also people who read and hear things from other people bring these up at the discussions and they often get frustrated when what they have heard is not realized at the Gram Sabha.'[10]

Though it was useful conduit for information, the local media did not seem very well equipped to report on social problems and the agenda of rural activism. Organisations or individuals working at the district level frequently differentiated between local and national media, and learned to recognise the limits of the effectiveness of each.

Aruna Roy's Right to Information (RTI) movement has been propelled forward in in no small measure by the media support it has received—local, regional and national. She was quick to acknowledge that the relationship has been both enriching and problematic.

It is not as if everything is rosy. But from the first public hearing we had in 1994 December, the press has come to us without much reluctance. We are very far away, nevertheless people have come. But we have also worked at communicating with the press at a level at which we have laid ourselves open to questions, answered questions, have been ready to discuss positions on which we do not agree, even argue sometimes. And accepted that the relationship with the press is important.[11]

And in some ways the relationship over the last few decades has become increasingly problematic. NGOs have grown in numbers and diversified, and a lot of polarisation has taken place. Government officers have taken to opening up NGOs in the manner of shops, just before retirement. As an older journalist in Jaipur said wryly, when a government official retires he becomes civil society. Rajendra Singh, a Magsaysay Award winner in Rajasthan observed:

Many voluntary organisations have become corporatised, hiring professionals and paying them decent salaries, whereas much of the media remains fossilised in its notion of what a voluntary agency should behave and look like. The sympathy that the media had for NGOs is fading. They have preconceived notions about NGOs. That we should be poorly clad, eat only once a day. We are expected to conform to those notions.[12]

The MKSS recognised that correspondents had their limitations and learned to work within those, interacting with a wide span of media. They developed a relationship with Ramprasad Kumawat who edited a daily newspaper called *Nirantar* in Beawar.

We have interacted with all the other local newspapers as well, but with him in particular because he edits and prints his own newspaper. And his differences, his support, his continuing interest in the issue has been quite remarkable. He's got a very good mind. And that mind has been able to critique us as well as report on us. He has been a part of raising pubic awareness about many issues in Beawar.[13]

This group also resisted the tendency of many activists to seek support only from those of their own ideological persuasion. They interacted with the local representative of the *Rajasthan Patrika* whose political affiliation was to the RSS. 'We've argued with him on our various political issues. Nevertheless he has reported on us. The thing is, you must enter into a debate ... a public debate with the

people with whom you do not agree.'[14] In Jaipur senior journalists
asserted that they supported Roy and the movement she leads because they saw her as intelligent, honest and committed. That was not
the case with every individual social worker or voluntary agency or
movement leader.[15] Local journalists would frequently cite reasons
why non-governmental organisations should be treated with at least
some of the scepticism usually reserved for government and politicians. At the field level this related to substantial grants given to
such bodies by government agencies and their visible utilisation.
Grants were made by the Government's Ministry of Environment to
NGOs to implement awareness-generation projects on environment.

> NGOs form *pariyavaran gosthi*s (environmental groups) at
> the community-level, but we see no impact of these. On World
> Environment Day, 365 such *gosthi*s (interactive sessions) were
> organized on the outskirts of Gorakhpur itself. But you talk to
> people about the environment and sustainable development,
> and you will find the same apathy.[16]

This journalist from *Jagran* had more examples to give. 'At least 56
NGOs received grants from a Delhi-based organisation to promote
communal harmony. On 2 March communal rioting broke out in
this city over something as silly as Pakistan's defeat in the Indo-Pak
cricket match. Where were these NGOs then?' He had a relatively
straightforward description of how he thought the press must function at the grassroots.

> Development reporting for us journalists includes analysing
> how development projects and welfare schemes contribute to
> progress of the people. Where we find loopholes we attempt
> to expose these so that concerned parties can perform their
> respective roles better. We are not here to demonstrate one-
> upmanship.[17]

To some within civil society the above was precisely the problem
with media representation of the non-governmental sector: the media
has no time or interest or categories by which they could look at
something more complex than success stories or disaster stories, or

individuals who they labelled as good or useless or corrupt. Even national newspapers like *The Hindu* had not learned to problematise sufficiently issues involved in discussing development initiatives or community organising. As long as it was led by Aruna Roy the assessment of the right to information movement she led was nonjudgemental. The instrument that the MKSS devised to crystallise the RTI movement was *jan sunvai*s (public hearings) and these got enormous media play. But how often did journalists go back to see how many people were utilising the right, and how much was continuing to change at the ground level? Did the movement acquire a momentum of its own separate from the leadership Roy and others provided?[18]

What it boiled down to, thought Ajay S. Mehta, executive director of the National Foundation for India which funded development initiatives, was a matter of the quality of media discourse. While at the local level it might reflect the limitations of the untrained stringers who did the reporting, at the national level too it remained stuck on facile assumptions: such as tribals as victim and governments as villains. What of one organisation's experience with tribal communities which showed that they prefered to encroach rather than be given forest land to manage? (Khetan 2004) There was a complexity in issues such as these unfolding in contemporary India which did not emerge in media discourses. The fourth estate had no recognition of the texture of many such problems. Journalists had not learned to figure out nuanced ways to evaluate the NGO sector, or the problems they were tackling. In the name of being critical they would trash. What was needed, though, was writing that was not pejorative, but served as a corrective.[19] This was the reflection of an observer at the grant-making level, removed from the practicalities of running a movement or a project. These who did so, even when they were perceptive individuals, often demanded a little more than publicity for their cause.

Developing journalist networks and using them to highlight problems was a skill social workers and activists everywhere were learning to acquire. In Udaipur an activist would profer clippings of the number of stories on the backward block of Kothda that he had helped engender. His local workers would ring him up if an atrocity concerning Advasis, or a starvation death occurred, and he would relay the news to a journalist who would then rush there.[20] Media, he said, was crucial to changing the status of a place like Kothda. At the same it became clear from his accounts of how the delivery system did not respond even after the district magistrate issued orders in response to a media report, that media exposes had their limitations.

Development Reporting in the New States

The media is always relevant in a democracy, but its role varies according to the circumstances in the region where it operates. When there is an agitation for the creation of a new state the media will play a role, the nature of that role will change substantially once a state is formed. The emergence of three new states in the Indian Union in November 2000 created a whole new dynamics for the media. Chhattisgarh was carved out of Madhya Pradesh, Jharkhand from Bihar and Uttaranchal from Uttar Pradesh. The press had played a role in the movements which preceded the birth of these states. There were specific emotive issues such as forest land ownership in Jharkhand, and environment, water and employment in Uttaranchal, which had shaped the public debate on the agitation for a new state. Once the states were formed, however, a media race began which was quickly overtaken by economic imperatives: the need to capitalise on the investment and expansion opportunities that emerged.

The new states came into existence with new budgets, the economy of the region got a boost, investors came flocking in, with advertising budgets to disburse. Newspapers were drawn to the new state capitals (Figure 10.2). Before the second anniversary of statehood dawned the number of newspapers publishing from Chhattisgarh had doubled from three to six. Two out of the three new ones were national dailies, *Hindustan Times* and *Jansatta*, and the third was *Hari Bhoomi*.[21] Where media owners were concerned all expansion was for a combination of clout , business reach and circulation revenue. The owners of *Jansatta* in Raipur were local businessmen who acquired the franchise to publish the paper from there. Like the owners of *Hari Bhoomi* (a Haryana newspaper owned by a political family) they were looking for a source of influence. In the new state of Chhattisgarh the owners

FIGURE 10.2 *Nava Bharat*'s special issue on the first anniversary of the creation of Chhattisgarh, 1 November 2001

of *Hari Bhoomi* owned land, coal washeries and a coal transportation business. It was an old principle of regional media expansion in India: when you have major economic interests to nurture or safeguard, having a newspaper helps.[22]

In commenting on the media boom in Chhattisgarh less than two years after the state came into existence, the then Chief Minister Ajit Jogi would say that the purpose of some of the new entrants such as *Hari Bhoomi* and the backers of the franchise edition of *Jansatta* was to earn respectability, after having earned money. 'If he was invited to a function earlier he would be seated at the rear, now he is in the first few rows. It is not so much to protect their business as to earn social status.'[23]

Once the new state capitals acquired state legislatures, they generated more political news than before. Where being a journalist in Raipur had meant being in the *mofussil* press, now newspapers were delighted to be publishing from the capital city. They also softened their coverage in the process. Though two years down the line he would become embroiled in controversy and be brought into disrepute by a national newspaper's sting, in 2002 Ajit Jogi had no complaints about the state's journalists. 'As I unfold my agenda they understand it,' he said expansively, adding that newspapers were playing a very positive role in building the new state's identity. Lalit Surjan, the editor of *Deshbandhu*, published from Raipur, was fulsome in his praise for the dynamism of the chief minister. The leader of the Opposition meanwhile was asserting that journalists were doing the state a disservice by not following up on issues raised by the Opposition in the state assembly.[24]

All three states saw rapid newspaper expansion through localisation. These were above-average states, in terms of literacy, and the increase in rural literacy made it possible to carve out a sustainable circulation base in the districts. Localisation quickly became the defining characteristic of the media in these new states.

Uttaranchal makes a good case study of how the media in the region conducted itself, before and after the state's formation, and to what extent it defined for itself what its role should be. It was created by carving out the hill regions of Uttar Pradesh into a separate state. Girish Ranjan Tiwari, the bureau chief of *Amar Ujala*, based in Nainital for the last 10 years, felt that the media in fact over-reached itself in hyping up the movement. 'In 1994, the movement for Uttarakhand was being run by the newspapers.'[25]

A senior bureaucrat contested the view that journalists were running the movement. The media had no role in it except to report it, he said.[26] But the first chief minister of Uttaranchal, Nityanand Swami, makes the point that the way they reported it was to give importance to every individual who took part in the agitation. 'One thing these two papers [*Dainik Jagran* and *Amar Ujala*] have done is taken care of agitations. Mention name of every lady and gent in the procession. Everybody's name they will write. Therefore these papers are popular.' Rajiv Lochan Sah, hotelier–journalist–activist, publisher of the fortnightly *Nainital Samachar*, took the point further by asserting that during the agitation for the new state the papers were mechanically covering rallies, making sure that the names of leaders appeared in print. But there was not enough attempt to highlight the issues for which the new state had become so necessary.[27]

Once the state was created, the media was no longer required to hype the demand for a separate state. It was required to pay a rather vital role in defining the agenda for the development of the state, highlighting long-neglected areas of activity, penetrating the rural hinterland and reporting tirelessly. But what it did instead was to seize commercial opportunity, expand editions to increase circulation, and make a pitch for the increased flow of advertising into the state. Subsequently this meant publishing 'given' news such as handouts from various parties with alacrity, looking for small scoops to provide excitement at the local level, keeping a hawk's eye on the new government, in a narrow rather than broad sense, and striving for conventional journalistic norms such as closing the edition late to accommodate the latest news. It deployed taxis to the furthest corners of the state to bring people newspapers at their doorstep. It was for instance, a point of pride with *Amar Ujala* that it was able to carry the news of the two major earthquakes that have occurred in this region, in the morning paper, though they occurred after midnight. And that the paper's copies reach pilgrims in Rishikesh and all along the pilgrim route before they start their trek at dawn.

Both *AmarUjala* and *Dainik Jagran* opened up employment opportunities in Uttaranchal by appointing a correspondent for every single district headquarter, and a stringer at the *tehsil* level. They had big networks and enough space to fill, but these tended to generate miscellaneous local news. *Dainik Jagran*, which used to have three pages for Kumaon increased them to nine. And much the same happened between *Prabhat Khabar* and *Hindustan* in Jharkhand, and between *Nava Bharat* and *Dainik Bhaskar* in Chhattisgarh. Competitiveness led to new editions opening up, penetrating the hinterland, and increasing circulation. *Jagran* doubled the number of staff it had in the region which became Uttaranchal; *Nava Bharat* similarly doubled the staff it had in Bastar.

The major allegations that civil society in Uttaranchal made about the role of the media after the state's formation was that it was clueless about how to be constructive: it did not sense major issues and then do grassroots as well as policy reporting on them. The head of the Rural Litigation Entitlement Kendra in Dehradun cited an example of what he considered gross incompetence on the part of the press in the state. Panchayat elections were due in 2001, at the end of the five-year term. When the five-year period was ending the new government brought an ordinance to extend the term of the panchayats by six months. Then it brought a second ordinance which amazingly, the press in the region never got to hear of and never reported. So nobody in the state knew it had been passed. Not a single journalist knew of the second ordinance, he said.

In both Jharkhand and Uttaranchal civil society groups and activists were discovering that between increased attention to political news emanating from the capital cities and small local news, issues that could focus on the region's development fall by the wayside. Civil society in Uttaranchal maintained that the role of the media after the state's formation fell far short of any purposeful agenda setting. It did not sense major issues, and then do grassroots or policy reporting on them. It was inclined to report the promises made by a political representative on tour, but not whether these were fulfilled.[28] It had no concept of reporting on human rights, or women's rights, or of seeing the latter in context. Environmental issues affect the quality of life for women in the hills but this was beyond the ken of the largely male force of stringers. Other women's issues in the hills such as violence against women, or the struggle for prohibition, eluded media understanding.[29]

There were many reasons why the media was not able to play a pivotal role. One was that news initiatives and priorities did not originate in the hills. Correspondents would remain correspondents all their lives, not graduate to writing edits or to positions of control in headquarters—in fact, they wouldn't want to, as they regard with horror the heat and dust of the plains. They would continue to report the statements of politicians with little discernment. The press was not fulfilling the challenge of playing a genuinely important role as catalyst, because its footsoldiers were extremely limited in their understanding of major issues.

A secretary in the state government, a bureaucrat respected for his integrity and commitment, explained with considerable exasperation why he had no use for local journalists in his state. 'They have only one mantra, to criticise, to be negative, to damn.' It was not their job, he said, to attempt to understand issues and project them, adding that a good example of this is how they function in the newly created states. 'The media will say, *naya state ban gaya, kuch nahi ho raha hai* [A new state has been formed, but nothing is happening]. So? Milk and honey will flow?' He thought that it was foolish to expect dramatic change without understanding the processes required. Did bureaucrats explain the issues sufficiently to journalists?

> If I am to spend time educating them I have to know that it is worth it. It isn't. They only want to write stories such as 'officers misusing air conditioners'. Not enough time is spent on a subject to understand it. Such local, itsy-bitsy reporting does not serve any purpose. I have media savvy colleagues but I prefer to stay away from the *Dainik Jagran* type of journalist.[30]

Another bureaucrat, the state's finance secretary, said that a realistic time frame in which change could be expected to be discernable in a newly created state was perhaps five years. 'It takes one year just to settle down. In one to one-and-a-half years [since the state's formation in November 2000] enough has been done. Five years is one plan period, that is a realistic period in which to judge performance.' A local journalist was unlikely to be moved by that reasoning. He was looking for 'here and now' stories to fill his local pages, to entertain and provoke his readers with. The allegation that the media is only there to be negative is borne out by a pithy statement that the seniormost journalist of *Amar Ujala* made in Dehradun about the tenor of reporting on governance: '*khinchai to karni hai*' (we have to find fault, after all), he said.[31]

Conclusion

Localisation affected the development discourse in the states of the Hindi belt. Because many kinds of small news found their way into these local editions and circulated in the area, local newspapers began to serve as an important conduit of information for development agents at the village level. Those working in the training of panchayats in rural areas sensed that the change newspapers were bringing about

was in the nature of politics. They brought transparency in the dynamics of political parties with the reporting they did. Moreover
developing journalist networks and using them to highlight problems
was a skill social workers and activists everywhere were learning to
acquire.

However, though the local pages created an expanded forum,
development workers felt that the media was clueless about how to
be constructive. It did not sense major issues and then do grassroots
as well as policy reporting on them. While at the local level the reporting might reflect the limitations of the untrained stringers who
did the reporting, at the national level too it remained stuck on facile
assumptions.

In the new states media outlets burgeoned, but an army of journalists looking for 'here and now' stories to fill its pages with, was not
always able to do justice to the development agenda emerging in each
of these states.

Notes

1. Convocation address, Asian College of Journalism, http://www.
   asianmedia.org/events/2003/convocation.asp, downloaded July 2006.
2. Sachin Jain, interviewed by Sushmita Malaviya, Bhopal, 17 March 2004.
3. Suresh Diwan, secretary, Gramin Sevak Samiti, interviewed by Sushmita
   Malaviya, Hoshangabad, 25 March 2004.
4. Rajendra Sail, organising secretary, Indian Social Action Forum,
   interviewed by Vasavi, Raipur, 18 February 2004.
5. Manish Mehra at Nitya, interviewed by Sushmita Malaviya,
   Hoshangabad, 25 March 2004.
6. Discussion at Seva Mandir, Rajasthan, 2 December 2004.
7. Gopal Rati, Eklavya, interviewed by Sushmita Malaviya, Pipariya,
   25 March 2004.
8. Ibid.
9. Amitabh Singh, Debate, interviewed by Sushmita Malaviya, Bhopal,
   31 January 2004.
10. Ibid.
11. Aruna Roy, MKSS, quoted in Sevanti Ninan, 'NGOs and the Local Press',
    www.thehoot.org, http://www.thehoot.org/story.asp?section=&lang=
    L1&storyid=w2khootL1k0613023&pn=1 (accessed 18 June 2005).

12. Rajendra Singh, quoted in Sevanti Ninan, 'NGOs and the Local Press', www.thehoot.org, http://www.thehoot.Org/story.asp?section=&lang= L1&storyid=w2khootL1k0613023&pn=1 (accessed 18 June 2005).
13. Aruna Roy, MKSS, quoted in Sevanti Ninan, 'NGOs and the Local Press', www.thehoot.org, http://www.thehoot.org/story.asp?section=&lang= L1&storyid=w2khootL1k0613023&pn=1 (accessed 18 June 2005).
14. Ibid.
15. Sevanti Ninan, 'NGOs and the Local Press', www.thehoot.org, http:// www.thehoot.org/story.asp?section=&lang=L1&storyid=w2khoot L1k0613023&pn=1 (accessed 18 June 2005).
16. Rohit Pandey, subeditor, Dainik Jagran, Gorakhpur, interviewed by Indrajit Roy, 23 June 2003.
17. Ibid.
18. Ajay S. Mehta, executive director, National Foundation of India, interviewed by author, Delhi, 17 June 2005.
19. Ajay S. Mehta, interviewed by author, Delhi, 17 June 2005.
20. Madan Mody, interviewed by author, Udaipur, 1 December 2004.
21. Sevanti Ninan, 'Statehood Good for Media?', The Hindu, 22 and 29 September 2002.
22. Sevanti Ninan, 'Media thrives in Chhattisgarh—or does it?', thehoot.org, posted 24 May 2002.
23. Ibid.
24. Ibid.
25. Manjula Lal and Sevanti Ninan, 'Media's Role in a New State', thehoot.org, http://www.thehoot.org/story.asp?storyid=hoothoot L1K089023&pn=1.
26. Ibid.
27. Ibid.
28. Ibid.
29. Ibid.
30. Ibid.
31. Ibid.

11

Reconfiguring the Public Sphere

'*We have divided society.*'

The pithiest summing up of what localisation of Hindi newspapers was achieving came in a one-line assessment from Kailash Vijayvargia, a minister in the Babulal Gour government in Madhya Pradesh, in February 2005. He said, '*issse kya hota hai, chote pathak ko badi news milti hai, bade pathak ko choti news milti hai*' (what this achieves is that the small reader gets big news, and the big reader gets small news). He went on to add that while the small reader may not have much use for major news, for the big (important) reader small news certainly held value.[1]

Implicit in this formulation was the integration of separate news universes that was being achieved when newspapers started delivering a daily paper which was simultaneously national and local. The main section of the paper brought what was happening in the nation and world to the family that lived in a village or a *kasba*. Elections, the presentation of a budget, the daily tumult of partisan politics in Parliament, all this entered the consciousness of those on the fringes of the political mainstream through the newspaper that arrived at the village doorstep first thing in the morning. If the family had television they sought more details of the previous day's headlines from the morning newspaper; if they did not, they were made conscious of events they did not know of. The most eagerly awaited 'big news' often related to cricket, as a circulation executive and a hawker both attested in Pipariya in Madhya Pradesh.[2] The hawker said that at the village level, orders for more copies were placed when a big match was being played.[3]

Conversely, the four-page district pull-out, full of items about local mishaps, small agricultural crises, cheating in board exams, local religious news and civic collapses such as water shortages or water logging, was reaching the people whose villages and localities figured in them, but when the news was dramatic enough it also figured in the one, two or three pages of district news reaching people in the state capital. Bureaucrats and politicians saw them and, if it was their job to do so, took note. Even at the local level, the news of what was happening in his backyard had begun to reach the district magistrate and his officers as it did members of the legislative assembly (MLAs). Earlier, they had no comparable channel of information as detailed and regular. If the MLAs were away in the state capital because the legislature was in session, their constituency staff was assigned the job of sending photocopies. Thus the 'big' or important reader was getting small news.

Though they were lapses and limitations, of which note was constantly taken, newspaper localisation was integrating national and local news universes to an extent not done earlier in northern India. Television had created an integrated viewing universe by bringing the same cricket match or a new prime minister's speech to nearly 100 million homes (more than half the total) in rural and urban India. But such communication was a one-way street: the news of what was happening at the smallest level of habitation did not travel up to those in power before this. Even if all that reached the state capital on most days was three-quarters of a page filled with reports drawn from a dozen or more district-level pull-outs, if you took these pages together, you were getting from two or three dozen regional pages appearing in different parts of the Hindi belt, feedback on the backyard of the nation.

In small town India, a print-enabled public sphere certainly existed before, served by a variety of small newspapers that were numerous enough to have an association of their own (The All India Association of Small and Medium Newspapers), and be counted as an advertising category for the Government of India. But it was reshaped and expanded as a result of the expansion drive described in this book. The number of pages through which local consciousness was generated and local identity reinforced multiplied, as did the number of citizen reporters reporting from around where they lived. They created an expanded forum, but expectations from this space, and local critiques of the way it was being shaped, grew. The political class found that the changing public sphere had implications for their functioning. So did rural and urban social activists, and civil society at large. The emergence of a number of local news universes within a state had implications for regional identity.

Once localisation began to take hold, it raised a myriad questions about the socio-political implications of the news being purveyed. How local should local news be? What kind of a public sphere was it creating? At which point did it become a counter-productive exercise? As the universe of local news became more and more circumscribed, persistent questions were raised from states across the Hindi belt about what it was doing to regional identity and regional consciousness.

One complaint was that, with localisation, regional had become zonal. Newspapers established editions as demand for copies grew. These got narrower in their coverage as their canvas shrank. By 2005, most multi-edition newspapers coming out of the state capitals in the Hindi-speaking states were releasing an edition every hour, starting from the evening, with pages finely tuned to cater to combined parts of different districts in some cases. In 2003, *Hindustan* was releasing 24 different editions a day from three centres to cover Bihar. By mid-2005 *Dainik Jagran* was putting the number of different editions from printing centres in Uttar Pradesh at 68. While the national and international news would remain the same in these editions, the front pages looked different because of the local stories chosen to go on them. And the inside pages changed to accommodate the changing focus on different circulation areas.

In 2004, all newspapers in Chhattisgarh were following the multiple district edition approach, but *Deshbandhu* carried news of all districts a little more than others. *Daink Bhaskar* had editions named Raipur, Bastar–Jagdalpur, Dhamtari, Mahasamund, Rajnandgaon, Durg Grameen, Bhilai Durg city, and Jagdalpur–Kanker. The Bilaspur centre was separate. There was a full-fledged edition there. *Nava Bharat* had seven district editions and its circulation manager Ramesh Tiwari attributed the necessity for so many local editions to the demand for local news which reflected grassroot problems.[4] Readers could not afford to pay for a 40-page newspaper, which is what would result if all the local news in the state was to be given in one any edition.

It was not financially feasible, hence the need for several editions. These inserted separate local sections into the day's newspaper, in different parts of the state.

Tiwari's counterpart in Madhya Pradesh who doubled as bureau chief and circulation in-charge of *Nava Bharat* in Itarsi, attributed the 25–30 per cent rise in circulation in his area over the last decade to the regional edition introduced for this region, called the Narmada edition.[5] Similarly, *Dainik Jagran* had introduced seven modem-facilitated editions in Madhya Pradesh, in Guna, Khargone, Jhabhua, Sagar, Harda, Khandwa, Shivpuri and Tikamgarh, and done door-to-door campaigning to tell people about their product. The paper claimed to have seen a 100 per cent increase in circulation in three years, mostly in the urban market.

The circulation gains came at a price. There was a print-mediated fragmentation of community identity that was all the more ironical because of its occurrence in an information society where Internet networking was making the coming together of different levels of community possible. Diasporic ethnic communities, for instance, were increasingly bound across continents by communication technologies, as were other communities of specific interests, described by Howard Rhiengold in his electronic book, *The Virtual Community*.[6] But here existing communities were being notionally divided.

The fragmentation had to do with the mappings that the new media proliferation was imposing over existing mappings. The segmentation of editions had its own logic, based on circulation and market feedback. It took into account contiguity of locations and methods of distribution. But in an editorial sense the overriding logic endorsed by marketing teams was one of catering to cultural aspirations and geographical affinities. Editions were devised accordingly, cutting across administrative divisions and parliamentary as well as legislative constituencies, which had their own basis for mapping.

As a result, there were administrative implications. *Dainik Bhaskar's* state editor for Rajasthan for instance, was acutely aware of what localisation was doing to regional identity. 'We have divided society', he said succinctly. His resident editor in Ajmer would point to other problems the segmented editions were creating, particularly for the district administration. In Rajasthan, for instance, Nagaur district was served by four different editions, because within a district, said the resident editor of *Dainik Bhaskar* in Ajmer, there were political, cultural and geographical differences. Nagaur proper was catered to by the Jodhpur edition. And the Sikar, Jaipur and Ajmer editions catered to other parts of the district. The entire district of Ajmer too was catered to by four different editions so that the inspector general of police had to get all four editions to know what was happening in the area under his jurisdiction.

The resident editor could also see that the newspaper's manner of segmentation was creating a problem for some of its readers.

> 'Readers have problem .... If you have a story on *rasta roko* (blocking traffic on the road as a method of protest) by irate citizens because of a civic problem, the sub-divisional magistrate will not see the story because he gets the city edition. The story has come in the Kishangarh edition. Sometimes, there are eight to ten such news items on one day, which do not reach the authorities who sit elsewhere.[7]

Further, with 32 districts in the state, the inspector-general of police for the state had no way of knowing what was happening in the whole of Rajasthan if he read the paper in Jaipur, because there was simply no space in the 'state' page to do justice to 32 districts. The Jaipur edition's pagination was such that in the 16-page main paper it gave seven pages of local news. The remaining nine had to take care of the front page, national news, sports, business, commerce, comment page and so on, leaving exactly one page for the rest of the state. The state police chief could of course turn it to his advantage and declare that law and order was fine in the state, because there was nothing in the paper to indicate otherwise!

In *Understanding Media* Marshall McLuhan cites the example of what the chief of police in Minneapolis said in 1962, when that city had been four months without a newspaper. He said, 'Sure, I miss the news, but so far as my job goes I hope the papers never come back. There is less crime around without a newspaper to pass around the ideas' (McLuhan 2003: 222). As the Ajmer resident editor of *Bhaskar*, Indu Shekhar Pancholi, put it:

> The administration is not bothered if the news does not come out; they will say, see there are no problems in the state.

The state government does not mind if statewide problems do not surface in Jaipur. But the readers are the losers in this.[8]

Dainik Bhaskar's rival *Rajasthan Patrika* also evolved its edition segmentation according to its understanding of which parts of the state had affinities with which others. For instance, it made sure that the Shekhawati and Bikaner regions were covered together. Another group of districts covered together included Jodhpur, Sirohi, Pali and Ajmer. But the paper found its own way of dealing with the difficulties the state and district administrations faced as a consequence. Nihar and Siddharth Kothari, the paper's third-generation owners, said they found that because of the kind of localisation they were doing, action was not being taken on the basis of reports featured in the paper. Obviously the reports were not reaching the bureaucrats who ran the administration in those areas. So they began to send district magistrates clippings of reports appearing in all the editions that dealt with the area under his jurisdiction. 'We send our clippings', they said, 'because we want our stories to have some effect'.

The political class was also affected and felt the detrimental effects of this news mapping quite keenly. 'From one zone to the other, news does not travel. So the reader remains deprived. In Bhopal we do not get Indore news', Vijaywargiya, an MLA from Indore would note. He was minister for public works in the state government, but as a minister he had also two districts assigned to his charge, Jhabua and Khandwa. When in Bhopal, he got news of neither, as the regional news pages in *Dainik Bhaskar* and *Navbharat* did not stretch to more than a page usually, or less if there were advertisements. He depended on government staff to fax relevant news items from these districts to him, on a daily basis.

In Bihar, Sushil Kumar Modi, the leader of the Opposition in the Bihar Assembly in 2003 when Lalu Prasad Yadav of the Rashtriya Janata Dal was chief minister, enunciated the problems for a politician as a result of this state of affairs: one, personal coverage of a politician did not reach all corners of the state, unless it was major news; two, local news found no regional resonance because there was no effort on the part of the newspaper to collate and organise local reports from across the state thematically.[9]

For instance, he said, the problems of litchi growers in Muzaffarpur and Vaishali made big headlines in the local editions but never made it into the state news pages that appeared in the capital. Such news then did not get seen by bureaucrats and politicians who mattered. Similarly in Madhya Pradesh, an activist would assert:

> The plight of *mahua* pickers is a state-level issue. However, the way I see it, it has been reduced to a regional issue. When we raise our voice at the grassroots level, our voice is heard only here and it never reaches the policy makers sitting in Bhopal.[10]

As for a political party wishing to draw attention to its stand on an issue of relevance to the state, Modi said his party would get five leaders to hold press conferences in five locations so that it was covered. In Chhattisgarh, the then Chief Minister Ajit Jogi[11]and the then Speaker of the Vidhan Sabha Prem Prakash Pandey[12] would in separate interviews reiterate one basic point: because all newspapers had different editions for different parts of the state, it was difficult to get news of the whole state in one place. A chief minister had to read several editions each morning to keep track of his state. Ajit Jogi said that a smaller newspaper from Chhattisgarh such as *Amrit Sandesh* was useful for him since it gave news of the whole state. In Bihar, the vice-president of *Hindustan Times* had a riposte to that criticism. 'Local newspapers are not only not custodians of state feeling', he said 'I am not here to do Ajit Jogi's job for him. Why does he want to keep track of a state through newspapers?'[13]

Part of the problem arose from the pattern of releasing editions early for publication so that they could be despatched to their areas of circulation. Politicians were learning to contend with the new limitations: if a statement was made in the assembly after 4 P.M. it did not get carried in editions meant for outlying areas, because they had an early printing deadline. But after 7 P.M. it could still be carried in the Patna edition. Much oratory went waste from the point of view of hopeful politicians: at a National Democratic Alliance rally in 2003, the leader from Delhi who had to catch a plane spoke first and departed before 4 P.M., and reporters duly filed their reports on his remarks, but to the chagrin of the top state leaders who addressed the rally subsequently, nothing they said made it to the next day's newspaper editions across the state, except in the city editions.[14]

In 2005 the *Hindustan*'s resident editor in UP said that this was more of an issue for politicians in Bihar than in UP. In states where the terrain was difficult the localisation was more; in central UP it was still not so much. 'When I was in Patna Lalu Prasad Yadav [husband of the then chief minister, and chief of the Rashtriya Janata Dal] would ring and say Joshiji, we have had a meeting, please see that it goes in all editions.'[15]

In Madhya Pradesh, another politician would raise the larger issue of how a rising politician would ever be able to build a statewide profile given the segmented nature of news coverage.[16] After expansion, he said, newspapers were so localised that even within a district there were different pages for different parts. 'What we do in one place by way of political activity does not reach others. If every leader is only a local leader, who will provide leadership at the state level?' The Bharatiya Janata Party's leader at that point, for instance, was scarcely known outside his own Bhopal constituency until he was made chief minister by his party. This, according to Suneelam, was directly related to the patterns of media coverage. However as television began to localise, a solution to this problem began to emerge. Local channels for Madhya Pradesh and Uttar Pradesh began to have regular bulletins covering political and other news from different parts of the state.

Localisation also fragmented the political space. A single Lok Sabha (Lower House in Parliament) constituency—Hoshangabad–Narsinghgarh (including Barelli *tehsil* and Raisen)—had been geographically divided by newspapers. So to read about one constituency, if you were a member of parliament, you had to track the local editions of all three or four regions. On political issues, said a social worker, we do not know what is happening outside our block. The flip side of this argument was that, earlier, you never got so much feedback anyway on what was happening within a constituency, fragmented or otherwise. And, as an MLA in Uttar Pradesh was discovering, nor did you get so much coverage before in different parts of the constituency.

Louise Khurshid was learning to take the negatives and positives of segmentation in her stride. Her constituency covered Farukhabad, Mainpuri and Kanauj in UP. One pull-out of *Dainik Jagran*'s Kanpur edition covered one segment of the constituency, another segment was covered by the paper's Agra editon. On the one hand, when the local correspondent demanded advertising in return for coverage, it became very expensive to advertise in different editions. 'When Diwali comes I have to give a lot of greetings to my people whether I want to greet them or not.' But on the other hand, she had been the beneficiary of a situation where, when she moved from one part of her constituency to another, attracting photographers in each place, she ended up getting five reports done on her in different local editions. And the advantage of very local editions was that, when she raised an issue covering that area in the legislature, it would become a very big headline locally. But, she said, she would not figure in the Lucknow press or the national press.[17]

Localisation worked to the advantage of local politicians in their own constituencies. With the coming of local editions, the copy desk in newspaper offices would send questions raised in the assembly by MLAs to those editions whose areas the questions pertained to. This was useful for the MLA concerned, his constituency would come to know that the question had been raised. But no other part of the state would get to know of the issue he had flagged. Local stringers were also generous with the coverage they gave local politicians on their own stamping ground. Earlier, in a single-edition newspaper, he could hardly had hoped for coverage, but now, with four pages to fill from a single district on a daily basis, even the most inconsequential political speeches got covered. As a Bihar politician put it, 'Now everywhere there is a battalion of journalists wherever you go. Very good for us.'[18]

Edition-wise segmentation, therefore, had both increased and decreased political space. The local arena expanded for the politician, but he dropped off the map when it came to the state. The excessive space given to the politics of one particular region reduced discursive space. It was reduced not because of commercialism, not because of excessive advertising, but because of representation. In a segmented news universe, the parameters of newsworthiness shrank to limit the newsmaker to the constituency he represented, and those parts of a district which fell within it.

In a reconfigured public sphere, therefore, there was a serious new problem for old players of the political game.

Anti-Mobilisation

As the edition approach began to segment regional coverage, social workers and development activists were also among those who began to discover its implications. In January–February 2002 in Jaipur both journalists and social activists talked of how excessive localisation worked against the mobilising of a mass movement.

This classification of editions is anti-people. A movement originating in Udaipur remains confined to Udaipur, you never get to hear of it in Ganganagar; it never will become a movement as a result. Earlier *Rajasthan Patrika* used to bring it all to the whole state, whatever was happening in any district. First you made people think of themselves as part of a state, then as part of a district, then division, you shrink his identity. Now I have become someone who only belongs to one town.[19]

This was a sentiment echoed in Raipur and Bhopal in February 2004, and in Udaipur in December 2004. Localisation's most worrisome drawback was one that many a fieldworker harped on, even as not a single newspaper executive thought of it as a negative issue. It was the fragmenting of regional identity thanks to a multiplicity of editions, so that news that might mobilise intervention across the state remained completely localised. It would get big play in the local edition, four columns, may be even a picture. But a wry activist described it as amounting to a peacock dancing in the forest. 'Nobody sees it.'[20] And certainly nobody in the state capital, from either the political or administrative class, would see it and therefore do something about it.

In 2002 *Nava Bharat* had seven editions in the state, all printed out of Raipur, but the news and even the pages came by fax from different centres. *Dainik Bhaskar* had seven editions printed out of Raipur and four out of Bilaspur. These local pages were crammed with small news items, often emanating from villages. Civil society in these states however quickly deduced here, as it did elsewhere, that excessive localisation had its drawbacks, because all the news being generated within a state would not reach all corners of the state. The resident editor of the *Nava Bharat* in Raipur felt this was logical:

the news published was so local that 90 per cent of it had no wider value. He also felt that the fact that every local edition of his paper carried a Rajdhani page with news emanating from the state capital had helped to bond people into a Chhattisgarhi identity, down to the villages.[21]

But other journalists dwelt on the negative aspect of localisation, stressing that if there was repression in one corner of the state, its reporting remained localised and a ripple did not get created. Activist groups working in the state echoed this concern. They felt that you could not build a statewide movement on any issue if the news of something that happened in one part of the state did not reach the other.

For development workers in Madhya Pradesh, Chhattisgarh and Rajasthan, the segregation in news was self-defeating.

> Regionalism is increasing because of this. The Raipur and Mahasamund papers will not have news of Bhilai. And local news is getting trivialised. The *mundan* [A Hindu ceremany of the first haircut] ceremony of somebody's child becomes news. Working people do not make news, sensational news is printed, development news gets little space, local papers love to print news about the 'lionesses' of the local Lion's Club.[22]

It was felt that debates at the local level were, are not being raised at the government's level as the district pages were not seen by people in Bhopal.[23]

BJP MLA Brij Mohan Agarwal, felt likewise that people were deprived of news from other parts of the state.[24] The chief minister's take on this was that he had to read at least five different editions of each local newspaper to know what was happening in the state he governed. 'If the chief minister makes a policy statement on Jagdalpur it does not go to Raigarh or Sarguja. There should be some way by which some things should be known to everybody.'[25] *Deshbandhu*, a paper which has a self-proclaimed focus on development news and had won 10 *Statesman* Rural Reporting awards in 20 years, was uncomfortable with the negative aspects of localisation. Having experimented with how much of the state news it made available to all parts of the state, it decided that it would carry news of people's movements in all editions of the newspaper.[26]

In Uttaranchal the communication revolution brought satellite editions of newspapers to the doorsteps of readers in Uttarkashi, Pithoragarh and Chamoli. Back in 1982, in remote villages, some of them 45 km from townships like Ranikhet, a newspaper posted from Bareilly would reach in a week. Now a subscriber could get a Hindi paper first thing in the morning, just like in the cities. It enlightened him on his immediate universe, and on the country and world. But it fell seriously short in making him a citizen of his state, and indeed did the newly created state a disservice by failing to build bridges between the two culturally distinct hill regions—Garhwal and Kumaon. What was true of excessive localisation of Hindi papers in other parts of the country was also true here: the edition which reached a particular region only carried news of that region, pandering to the egos of those who received coverage, but not carrying their news to other regions or vice versa.

There were those who felt the criticism was overdone. Every district level problem did not require a state level response. What was the percentage of problems arising, say in Betul district, which required policy intervention? Problems became policy issues if they recurred, if they seemed to be neglected by the local administration or if the frequency of occurrence pointed to a problem endemic to that area.[27] Otherwise they did not, and could be dealt with by local administrations. As for requiring statewide media coverage to convert local movements into statewide movements, it was becoming apparent that newspapers needed to have a way of coordinating and understanding what similar news from all the editions was adding up to. Zealous as they were about localisation, they also needed strong news desks to collate news from different areas and look for patterns. When that began to happen, it enriched the quality of feedback that actors in the public sphere got from the backyard of a nation.

Conclusion

When district editions began to appear in all these states a local-level public sphere began to be created, and the political class found that the changing public sphere had implications for their functioning. So did rural and urban social activists, and civil society at large.

There was a print-mediated fragmentation of community identity, all the more ironical because of its occurance in an information society where Internet networking was making the coming together of different levels of community possible.

The fragmentation had to do with the mappings that the new media proliferation was imposing over existing mappings. When editions were devised according to cultural aspirations and geographical affinities, they cut across administrative divisions and parliamentary as well as legislative constituencies, which had their own basis for mapping. Edition-wise segmentation then had both increased and decreased political space. The local arena expanded for the politician, but he dropped off the consciousness of the rest of the state.

The most serious charge against localisation was that it increased regionalism and made statewide mobilisation of a mass movement on the basis of issues more difficult. Movements remained confined to their place of origin, and papers shrank a citizen's identity by giving people less and less news of the state as a whole. In Uttaranchal, civil society felt that whereas the media could have bonded the two distinct regions of the state, Kumaon and Garhwal, it was actually playing a divisive role in building the new state's identity.

Notes

1. Kailash Vijaywargiya, interviewed by author, Bhopal, 17 February 2005.
2. 'For example after India won the Samsung Trophy against Pakistan, everybody wanted the minutest details. This holds true for even for people in rural areas who have keen watching the matches', Raghevendra Dubey, *Nava Bharat*, Itarsi, District Circulation executive for Hoshangabad and Harda, interviewed by Sushmita Malaviya, 25 March 2004.
3. Kamlesh, hawker, interviewed by Sushmita Malaviya, Pipariya, 26 March 2004.
4. Ramesh Tiwari, circulation manager, *Nava Bharat*, Raipur, interviewed by Vasavi, Raipur, 16 February 2004.
5. Raghevendra Dubey, *Nava Bharat*, Itarsi, district circulation executive for Hoshangabad and Harda, interviewed by Sushmita Malaviya, 25 March 2004.
6. http://www.well.com/~hlr/vcbook/vcbookintro.html.

7. Indu Shekhar Pancholi, resident editor, *Dainik Bhaskar*, interviewed by author, Ajmer, 15 September 2005.
8. Ibid.
9. Sushil Kumar Modi, interviewed by author, Patna, 4 June 2003.
10. Suresh Diwan, secretary, Gramin Sevak Samiti, Hoshangabad, interviewed by Sushmita Malaviya, 25 March 2004.
11. Ajit Jogi, interview with the author, Raipur, May 2002.
12. Prem Prakash Pandey, interview with Vasavi, Raipur, February 2004.
13. Y.C. Agarwal, vice president, *Hindustan Times*, interviewed by author, Patna, 3 June 2003.
14. Sushi Kumar Modi, interviewed by author, Patna, 4 June 2003.
15. Naveen Joshi, resident editor, *Hindustan*, interviewed by author, Lucknow, 1 June 2005.
16. Suneelam, Samajvadi Party MLA, interviewed by author, Bhopal, 19 February 2005.
17. Louise Khurshid, interviewed by author, Lucknow, 30 August 2005.
18. Sushil Kumar Modi, interviewed by author, Patna, 4 June 2003.
19. Narayen Bareth, BBC stringer, interviewed by author, Jaipur, February 2002.
20. Gopal Rati, Eklavya, interviewed by Sushmita Malaviya, Pipariya 25 March 2004.
21. A.P. Shukla, interviewed by author, Raipur, May 2002.
22. Rajendra Sail, organising secretary, Indian Social Action Forum, interviewed by Vasavi, Raipur, 18 February 2004.
23. Sachin Jain, media advocacy consultant, Bhopal, 17 March 2004.
24. Brij Mohan Agarwal, interviwed by author, Raipur, May 2002.
25. Ajit Jogi, interviewed by author, Raipur, May 2002.
26. Lalit Surjan, interviewed by author, Raipur, May 2002.
27. S.C. Behar, interviewed by author, Bhopal, 17 February 2005.

12

Change and Attrition

'Only the language press has saved democracy.'

By 2006 Hindi journalism as an institution was undergoing considerable change. There were many elements to this transformation. Its growth and size made it a serious commercial player. The changes it was manifesting had to do with the transformed media sphere in the country. Its financing was undergoing a shift. Its self-confidence in relation to the English press was growing. It was becoming more conscious of the quality and integrity of its journalism. But it was editorially less influential than before. It mattered commercially more than it did as a pillar in public life. Editors as assertive and independent entities were a rapidly fading species.

The other significant change in the universe of Hindi journalism was that smaller players were getting squeezed out of the market by the financial muscle and advertising dominance of the multi-edition players. Post-1991, India and the Indians who comprised its reading classes changed in many ways. It was only logical that the products meant for them to buy would cater to this transformation. And while the bigger Hindi newspapers, the national movement's gift to the country, had no problem repositioning themselves as products, the small ones struggled for relevance and survival. Their fragility in the face of multi-edition might was perhaps an early sign of the Indian media industry's impending consolidation.

Despite its warts and vulnerabilities, by 2006 Hindi journalism like the newer forces in heartland politics had acquired the self-confidence which comes with numbers. Both had succeeded in establishing that they mattered to the future of the rest of the country. Just as the Bahujan Samaj Party or Samajwadi Party could bring crucial numbers to central government coalitions with the fading of the two-party system, the Hindi press was offering numbers to the media industry, the advertiser, the market. It was read, it was acquiring the financial muscle to take on the English press, and it had influence. The highest valued media property on the Indian stock market was the Hindi satellite TV network, Zee. When *Dainik Bhaskar*'s owners and Zee got together in 2005 to storm the bastion of *The Times of India* in Mumbai with an English newspaper, it was above all an assertion of the confidence of Hindi media players.

In her essay 'English for the Elite, Hindi for the Power Elite,' Mrinal Pande offers the media practitioner's perspective on the emergence of regional languages as the foremost medium of political discourse.

> One day we found that almost all the chief ministers were talking in their regional languages, they wanted to talk in their own languages ... and English was irrelevant for them. We also found that even when it comes to Parliament, most members either talk in their regional languages or in Hindi and by and large, English is irrelevant for them as well. (Pande 2006)

She goes on to describe how the English satellite channel Star News had to cast around for someone to explain what Laloo Prasad Yadav, Chief Minister of Bihar was saying when his sound bites were used in the news bulletins. As political scientist Yogendra Yadav put it, Hindi in India had political significance, whereas English had economic significance.

Back in 1992 the late Surendra Pratap Singh was asserting that the establishment controlled by the 'minority elite group of this country' was afraid of Hindi journalism.

> This elite group that is controlling media and society is afraid because it is losing control over media. These people will be really scared if the Hindi press starts getting advertisements in proportion to their circulation figures. Slowly the elite group would lose hold over the levers of power.

The discussion at which this was said was an extraordinary one because it spoke of the growing influence of the Hindi press but at the same time lamented the absence of quality and integrity in some sections of it (*Vidura* Roundtable 1992).

By 2005, riding the crest of a growth wave in the regional media, Hindi proprietors were anxious to make the point that the quality and integrity of Hindi journalism were improving too. Sudhir Aggarwal of *Dainik Bhaskar* was asserting that great care was taken to see that election coverage in his newspaper was fair and honest. Guidelines were given, a complaints cell was set up, equal space was given to all parties, the local journalist doing the coverage was not allowed to decide who was winning.[1]

Mahendra Mohan Gupta, chairman of *Dainik Jagran* was also asserting vociferously that 'Hindi journalists and Hindi stringers are the most honest people on earth.' They did not allow their stringers to book advertising he said. Nor were his stringers blackmailers. And nor did his journalists live in government housing like the English journalists. 'It is the English journalists who are biggest blackmailers. By not printing the negative aspect you are also accepting a bribe.' The reference was to the fact that English journalists, according to him, never took on ruling politicians. But was not *Dainik Jagran* supportive of whichever government was in power? No, said Gupta, 'we are totally pro our readers'. Added his nephew Sanjay Gupta, editor of the paper, 'If *Jagran* was trying to destabilise government working for small petty matters, every one year we cannot keep destabilising government. Having elections is disturbing. Only the language press has saved democracy.'[2]

Besides, they said, it was not true that they never took on ruling politicians. M.M. Gupta had been jailed during the Emergency, they had been attacked by Mulayam Singh during his *Halla Bol*, and V.P. Singh never forgave them because their opposition to the implementation of the Mandal recommendations resulted in his losing his government. M.M. Gupta offered the clinching argument that the English newspaper reader was irrelevant to democracy because he never voted, never reacted, never came out on the street. 'The government changes only because of the readership of the language press.'

A Transformed National Media Sphere

With their newfound self-confidence the stalwarts of the Hindi press began to take their place in a transformed national media sphere.

Being a microcosm of India's flourishing media industry, Hindi news-paper publishing reflected, in the period under review, the editorial and business trends noticeable in the industry as a whole. While it was inconceivable at the end of the decade of 1970s that regional newspapers would see themselves as part of multimedia empires, this was a reality in several cases in 2005. A scion of the Ananda Bazar Group had become a majority owner in a TV news partnership with Rupert Murdoch. Ramoji Rao, owner of *Eenadu*, the newspaper that helped launch N.T. Rama Rao[3] was by 2005 proprietor of not just the largest multi-edition newspaper in the state but a vast multi-channel satellite TV network as well.

The owners of *Dainik Jagran* launched a television channel in early 2005 in which they later sold controlling equity and were going in for an initial public offering in January 2006 to finance a foray into outdoor media. They also acquired FM radio stations in UP in 2006. *The Times of India*, in the same month was set to launch a tele-vision news channel, following its earlier launch of an entertainment channel. Its parent company Bennett, Coleman & Co. also launched a book publishing division in 2005. In Tamil Nadu the Sun Network, owners of cable distribution and satellite TV channels, bought two newspapers. By mid-2006 they had also acquired FM stations across the country.

The Indian press grew in size and market valuation even as tele-vision appeared to overwhelm the Indian media landscape. After an advertising slump which lasted from 1999 to 2001, after seeing its share of the advertising pie shrink from 70 per cent to 50 per cent between 1995 and 2005, the sector recovered and recorded growth as television created a hunger for print and changes in policy and in the investment climate opened up new avenues of investment. What's more, as television became segmented advertisers began to return to the print medium whose circulation figures are more stable than a TV channel's television rating points. In 2004–05 the growth of print media advertising surpassed that of television. The expansion and growth has meant that in early 2005 the print media industry was getting 50 per cent of the total advertising expenditure on media, valued at Rs 120,000 million.[4]

As for individual growth, the most striking example will illus-trate the point. In 1988 Bennett, Coleman & Co. had a turnover of Rs 1,200 million for all its publications combined, which at that point included *The Times of India, Navbharat Times, Economic Times, The Illustrated Weekly, Filmfare, Femina* and so on. It made around Rs 50 million profit at that time. In 2005 it had a turnover of Rs 25,000 million and made Rs 5,000 million profit. Turnover has grown at 20 per cent a year, and profit at 12 per cent a year during this period. Others have also grown as the business grew and in the intervening years almost all viable newspapers introduced some colour. *The Times of India* was the first to do so at the beginning of the 1990s and in 2005 it went all colour, as did *Hindustan Times,* and *Hindustan* in Delhi.

Some regional newspapers began to go national. The *Rajasthan Patrika* expanded into Gujarat, Chennai, Kolkata and Siliguri, *Prabhat Khabar* of Jharkhand published from Bihar, Kolkata and Siliguri, the *Nava Bharat* of Maharashtra was present in Chhattisgarh and Madhya Pradesh, and the Telugu newspaper *Eenadu* expanded its presence to Orissa, Delhi, Karnataka, Tamil Nadu and Mumbai from its native Andhra Pradesh.[5] In 2006 *Rajasthan Patrika* announced plans to expand to Madhya Pradesh, and *Hindustan* set its sights on MP and Rajasthan. *Dainik Jagran* had already begun to reach much of the country—Punjab, Jammu and Himachal Pradesh, in addition to the Hindi belt states. *Dainik Bhaskar* was in Rajasthan, Madhya Pradesh, Haryana, Punjab and Gujarat, in addition to having launched an English newspaper called *DNA (Daily News and Analysis)* in Mumbai, in association with Zee TV.

Financing

The financing of the newspaper industry has undergone interesting shifts. The early proprietors laid a lot of store by real estate acquired often through political connections not just for their presses and offices, but also as insurance against the uncertainties of the industry. The most striking example of a newspaper baron who was both a missionary as well as a shrewd real estate player, was Ramnath Goenka. Starting from 1929 in Madras, he periodically 'bought prime real estate in major cities all over the country ... which time and again proved a hedge against political and commercial misfortune' (Verghese 2005). Other newspaper owners such as the proprietors of *Dainik Bhaskar*, *Nai Duniya* and *Rajasthan Patrika*, acquired substantial real estate, some of it through government allotments. When you had real estate, and had no money to pay salaries if the government chose to deprive you of advertising, you could depend on an income from rentals as Ramnath Goenka did from time to time in Delhi and Mumbai. His biography records how the sympathetic Indian head of the multinational IBM kept him going through the emergency with advance rentals (Verghese 2005).

But times changed and by the end of the 20th century his own paper the *Indian Express* was among those seeking more modern methods of financing. Even as they expanded, the more ambitious newspapers were already feeling the need for capital for greater investment and the campaign for a change in the status quo with regard to foreign direct investment in the media picked up from the early 1990s. Television had begun to establish itself and garner advertising and faced no restrictions on foreign direct investment. Lobbying had begun from some quarters of the English and language press for a change in the long established government norm that there should be no foreign investment at all in the print media in India.

In 1955 a cabinet committee headed by Jawaharlal Nehru, India's first prime minister, had debarred foreign investment in the print media. The decision was proposed by the external affairs ministry to subserve the Indian foreign policy of non-alignment.[6] The solitary exception allowed was *Reader's Digest*. The decision was to remain unquestioned for almost four decades. In 1994 the first ministerial review of the decision was undertaken by a Congress government, It did not lead to a lifting of the ban, but it did allow the incorporation of an exception: foreign investment in print media dealing with technological and scientific subjects was allowed from then on.[7]

Leading the charge in the lobbying for the lifting of the ban on foreign direct investment (FDI) in print was proprietor Narendra Mohan of *Dainik Jagran*. By early 1998 a Bharatiya Janata Party government had come to power, to be followed the next year by another government which was the BJP-headed National Democratic Alliance. Narendra Mohan who was to become a Rajya Sabha Member of Parliament for the ruling party in Uttar Pradesh, would lobby relentlessly along with publications like *India Today*, *Indian Express* and *Business Standard*, even as the permitting of FDI was strenuously opposed by established English language publications and some language ones. *The Times of India*, *Hindustan Times* and *The Hindu* were among those who opposed FDI in print.

In 1999 when the Indian Parliament cleared a bill called FEMA (Foreign Exchange Management Act) to replace the Foreign Exchange Regulation Act (FERA), foreign equity participation through portfolio investment became possible. However, when Mid Day Multimedia became listed in the stock market in 2001 and marketed its issue to both Indian and foreign investors, the government amended FEMA specifically prohibiting foreign portfolio investment in Indian print media. The *Business Standard* called it punishing Indian media, pointing out that competition in the Indian media market had become more intense. It was the age of convergence, media had become too big a business to be managed with the resources of family managements, and print companies faced competition from rival media with full access to international capital.

Finally, in June 2002 the government revised its policy and announced foreign investment up to 26 per cent would be allowed in the Indian print media. *Hindustan Times*, *Business Standard* and *Daink Jagran* went on to acquire foreign investment partners over the next three years. The visible growth in the newspaper business caught the attention of investors looking to widen their portfolios. Private equity firms put $1.1 billion into India in 2004 and the figure was expected to double in 2005 with potential investors targeting media as one of the key sectors.

Meanwhile, from 2000 onwards, starting with the *Mid Day* group of publications, newspapers and other publications were becoming listed on the stock market, and the print media became part of the valuation business. While the Living Media group which publishes *India Today* and owns television news channels, the *Hindustan Times*, *Deccan Chronicle* and the *Cyber Media* group of magazines came up with initial public offerings one by one, the Zee Bhaskar group's foray into the English newspaper market in Mumbai in 2005 was funded by a private placement of equity shares. *Daink Jagran* became the first media company in 2006 to offer an IPO.

Media stocks in India became very lucrative as the decade of 2000 wore on, and offered handsome valuations to media companies. The *Deccan Chronicle* which went public in December 2004 saw its stock appreciate by 80.77 per cent. *Hindustan Times* entered the market in August that year with a valuation of Rs 2,500 million, topping the valuation at that point of New Delhi Television (NDTV), a leading television software player. And stocks became encashable currency to be used in expansion. Both *Deccan Chronicle* and *Hindustan Times* were to sell blocks of share in 2005 to finance a move out of their traditional strongholds; the former entered *The Hindu*'s bastion in Chennai, the latter took on *The Times of India* in Mumbai.

In March 2005, ahead of the joint entry by two Hindi media stalwarts (Zee TV and *Dainik Bhaskar*) into the English newspaper market in Mumbai, *Business World* estimated that over Rs 10,000 million of capital had come into the newspaper publishing sector over the previous year or so. That included more that Rs 3,000 million of foreign direct investment into *Hindustan Times* and *Dainik Jagran* and a foray into the stock market by *Deccan Chronicle*. The 2004–05 period saw more newspapers moving out of their territories, even as television companies such as Sun TV and Zee TV were actively contemplating an entry into the print sector and NDTV was researching the option. The market for newspapers was expanding. In January 2006 both *Hindustan Times* and *Dainik Bhaskar* announced the launch of business dailies, the latter in Indore.

In December 2005, *Dainik Jagran* held its first Jagran Forum at a prominent Delhi hotel. Its owners and their new international partner, the owner of *The Independent* in Ireland, shared the dias with the Indian prime minister. Later sessions presented chief ministers, as well as economists from India, Singapore and the United Kingdom and one was chaired by the deputy chairman of India's Planning Commission. Unlike similar forums organised by *India Today* and *Hindustan Times*, there were no glamorous figures, but a number of contemporary heavyweights. This publishing group was signalling its arrival on a high profile public stage where only English newspapers and magazines had until then held sway.

This first foreign direct investment in the Hindi market took place with the chief executive of the investing group, Independent News & Media PLC, Sir Anthony O'Reilly being quoted in the *International Herald Tribune* as saying that the Indian market was now 'the new theatre of strategic investment'.[8] His company bought a 26 per cent stake in Jagran Prakashan Pvt Ltd, owners of *Dainik Jagran*, for 28 million euros. This was after tracking the Indian market for five years. Why *Jagran*? According to Sir Anthony O'Reilly:

> If we are location and language indifferent, we are good at procurement, printing, advertising, why should we confine ourselves to the English language? They are the biggest. They are very aggressive, but it is a very united aggression. They are focused. They wanted our capital and expertise so that they could expand. There has been a dialogue. We taught them certain things, they taught us certain things.

Shortly after Independent News and Media became a partner Jagran Prakashan announced that it was going for an initial public offering. Then it announced plans to use the money raised partly to finance a foray into outdoor media advertising, and event management, including mobile advertising targeted towards rural India.[9] The group was making a rapid transition from being a newspaper publisher to an aspiring media conglomorate.

Meanwhile, its new partner was waiting for government permission to bring *The Independent* to India. The Indian market for advertising was growing, in Europe it was shrinking. And with the level of literacy being what it was, the Hindi market was almost as big as the European market. Tying up with it could lead to synergies. Sir O'Reilly said,

> As a company we buy 300,000 tonnes of newsprint. There is the actual printing. We have a number of printing configurations around the world.... We have 12 major presses in 3 locations in Ireland.... We have a lot to teach people. All of that experience is intensely helpful in the long term it its potential for cost reduction and improvements.

Apart from the global integration of *Dainik Jagran*, the *Dainik Bhaskar* group in partnership with Zee, the TV broadcaster, moved into the English market in Mumbai. It was a move which took the media industry's breath away. The strategy was predicated on the realisation that the maximum advertising revenue was generated by the Mumbai and Delhi markets, and that it went primarily to the

English newspapers. The actual launch was preceded by the most expensive hoarding campaign ever undertaken by a publication. With its entry the paper also launched a price war, pricing itself at half the cover price of *The Times of India*. As the Hindi journalists in its stable watched, English newspaper journalists were hired for the new paper, *DNA*, at twice the salaries those journalists were getting. It was clear to the media world at large that Hindi publishing had become a stepping stone to bigger things.

Distribution

The competition arising from media expansion highlighted the importance of the distribution trade in the publishing industry. Hawkers have always had some clout in the Indian newspaper market: witness their influence on a newspaper's pricing as far back as in the 1970s when *Aj* came into *Dainik Jagran*'s bastion in Kanpur in 1975. The latter used to pay 30 per cent commission to the hawker, the former 20 per cent. When hawkers raised the demand for a higher percentage, the older of the two papers in that territory raised its price to accommodate the higher percentage. Later both newspapers joined hands to force the percentage back to 30 per cent.[10]

Varanasi from the mid-1990s, Jharkhand from 2001 onwards, Mumbai in 2005—any of these locations serves to illustrate the wooing of the hawker and distributor who became part of the newspaper industry in its rapidly changing competitive scenario. A.P. Singh, whose family has run Varanasi's newspaper distribution trade from 1947—each brother handling the distribution of a different paper in the city—has seen a media scene dominated by *Aj* at the time of independence grow to accommodate three other Hindi morning dailies and an eveninger, *Gandiv*. But the most spectacular wooing experienced by him was by *The Times of India* which is February 2005 was selling no more than 10,000 copies in Varanasi, 6,500 copies sourced directly from Delhi and 3,500 from Lucknow. He has preserved letters from *The Times* management hailing him as a member of *The Times of India* family, and could reel off the holiday destinations the group laid on for its distributors once a year, both in India and abroad.[11]

In Ranchi, in October 2003, young hawkers sorting newspapers on the pavement at the crack of dawn were enumerating the gifts they had received from competing publications: fridges, Hero Honda motorcycles, CD players and TV sets. The competition here was between the local *Prabhat Khabar* and the outsiders, *Dainik Jagran* and *Hindustan*.[12] And in March 2005 *Business World* was profiling Charudutt Dangat of the Dangat Newspaper Agency which supplied just under a third of the estimated 3.5 million copies of all newspapers sold in Mumbai and its suburbs every day. The largest of four major distributors in the city, his reach was across 70 distribution depots and 10,000 newspaper hawkers. He was being wooed as *DNA* from the Zee Bhaskar stable and *Hindustan Times* readied to enter the Mumbai market later that year. But he was yet to make up his mind on which paper to distribute.[13] The magazine was also describing the scene in Chennai in the south where *The Times of India*, about to enter the market to take on *The Hindu*, was working assiduously on a database which would help it woo the city's 2,000-odd newspaper hawkers on their birthdays and wedding anniversaries and issue them identity cards.[14]

Editorial Dynamics

And what of journalism? When the business is in transition it affects the profession. One fundamental shift which took place was the depoliticisation of the news. Reader interests became paramount in news judgement, particularly after localisation. New reporting beats blossomed. These had to do with fashion, food, society events, motoring, corporate launches and religion. A reflection of the new Indian who managed to be wordly and spiritual at the same time was to be found in the newspapers he read. On Mondays *Punjab Kesari* published a four-page supplement which reproduced sermons of popular Hindu preachers, with token space also given each week to Islam, Sikhism and Christianity. On Tuesdays it published an entertainment supplement taking care to scatter scantily clad women over its pages each week.

Dainik Jagran's Wednesday supplement was called *Josh* (zeal). In a smaller font below *Josh*, it said, *Aage Badne Ka* (to move ahead).

The call to upward mobility in the supplements of Hindi newspapers is overt. An advertisement in *Josh* was headlined in English: 'How about a career as a TV newsreader?' The details were in Hindi (*Josh*, 15 February 2006). On the first page of this supplement was an advertisment which guaranteed you good English. And other advertisements scattered through its pages assumed a bilingual reader for a range of careers on offer to the young Indian: from the IAS Academy, the Indian Navy, the Air Hostess Training Academy, the Indian Institute of Aircraft Engineering and so on. *Jagran* was also the first Hindi daily to start a travel supplement, which was called *Yatra*. *Punjab Kesari*'s matrimonial classifieds were entirely in English. When the *Hindustan* relaunched in December 2005 its new Saturday supplement was called *FEST*, in English, covering food, entertainment, shopping and travel. It had several full page colour advertisements. Its classified section was called 'Search Engine', written in Devanagari. All the leading newspapers had several supplements on offer in the course of the week, some of them every day. *Dainik Bhaskar* had launched a stand-alone monthly in 2004 called *Aha Zindagi* (Figure 12.1), but other than that Hindi magazines were an endangered category as the upward mobility index of daily newspapers climbed.

Tradition and modernity went hand in hand. On the same page of *Punjab Kesari* you would find a feature on the festival *Makar Sankranti*, followed by one on wine facials. And its religion supplement, *Dharm Sanskriti*, on Mondays contrasted with its cinema special on Thursdays called *Manoranjan*. On Fridays it had a column on new products.

Overall, print journalism grew softer, but flooded with glossy supplements the reader might not have noticed. The glamour of television meant that TV anchors became sought-after columnists in. daily newspapers. The country's second largest newspaper at this point, *Hindustan Times*, had three.

When the dynamics of the newspaper business began to change it was inevitable that it would have its repercussions on journalism: on the status of journalists, and more significantly, on the status of editors and their primacy in determining the editorial product. When the newspaper went from being a relatively high-minded vehicle for creating political awareness and fostering nationalism (Jeffrey 2000) to a colourful product intended for the entire family, competing with

प्रेम कैसे होता है
प्रेम की केमिस्ट्री
प्रेम की फिलॉसफी
प्रेम और ईर्ष्या
प्रेम का मनोविज्ञान
प्रेम और सेक्स
प्रेम कथाएं
अहा ! ताज

प्रेम अंक

FIGURE 12.1 *Dainik Bhaskar*'s monthly *Aha Zindagi* presents it *Prem Ankh*, its special issue on love, in February 2005

similar colourful products in the same market, who would call the shots while shaping it? Up to the 1980s editors were editorially pre-eminent. By the end of the century *The Times of India* was famous for having demonstrated that a commercially successful newspaper need not be headed by an editor. But in the 1950s when the Dalmia group published is annual brochure it published photographs of *The Times of India* assistant editors. In many family-owned newspapers the *lala*s, as the owners were known, were awed by their editors who pronounced from their offices on matters of state and rubbed shoulders with the rulers.

In 1974 *Hindustan Times* had a strong editor, a strong employees union, and a proprietor who like God was believed to exist but not visible to the mere mortals who worked there. Shortly thereafter, however, God made his presence felt, leaning on the editor B.G. Verghese for the editorial line he had taken on Indira Gandhi's annexation of Sikkim in 1974. The latter was sought to be dismissed and the editorial staff fought a court battle on his behalf. After the court gave a judgement in their favour he was replaced none the less. The editors who followed him learned to know their place. The Emergency was declared the following year, and while it lasted until February 1977, the government called the shots, and the paper acquiesced. Some editors stood up to Indira Gandhi's Emergency backed by their proprietors or, in the case of Rajendra Mathur at *Nai Duniya*, always a pro-Congress newspaper, regardless of them. Others buckled, prompting Opposition leader L.K. Advani to pronounce famously that when asked to bend Indian newspapers chose to crawl.

The editor–proprietor relationship developed along different tracks in the English and language media. In the former it went from newspapers having hired professional editors to having shareholders or proprietors move in as editors. In the latter which were commonly run by owner-editors, growth and expansion saw the hiring of professional editors to head different editions. A third development, only in the English newspapers, was that of professional editors taking over the publisher's function and acquiring a percentage of share equity.

From the 1980s onwards, in some English newspapers non-shareholding editors began to disappear, and shareholding family members began to replace editors. When they came into the business they also took over editorial roles, particularly in the English language press. M.J. Akbar was the founding editor of *The Telegraph*, but when he left proprietor Aveek Sarkar took over as editor. *The Statesman* of Kolkata used to have independent editors but C.R. Irani gradually took over the editorial role. In some cases it was because the second- and third-generation newspaper proprietor was different from the earlier generation in that many of them had studied at universities abroad and were not so overawed by editors. At *Indian Express* Ramnath Goenka's grandson Vivek Goenka made himself managing editor and at *Hindustan Times* Shobana Bharatiya became editorial director, even though both papers continued to be run on a day to day basis by professional editors. There were exceptions. At three southern newspapers, *The Hindu*, *Deccan Chronicle* and *Malayala Manorama*, top editorial posts had always been held by members of the publisher's family. At *India Today* too, the founder was from the beginning both proprietor and editor.

At *The Times of India* the entry of the second generation into the family business injected dynamism and innovation. Samir Jain, son of *The Times* proprietor Ashok Jain, came into the family business in 1986 and revolutionised for his own company as well as for the industry, the perception of a newspaper. Jain set in motion changes in newspaper marketing which influenced other major players in the business. Working on both the product mix and the marketing of it, he brought people from the fast moving consumer goods industry to maximise the returns of each brand in the publishing stable and shut down several magazines which were not money spinners. In Delhi Jain started a price war with *Hindustan Times* and introduced the idea of different pricing on different days, both of which would be copied across the trade. *Times of India* and *Economic Times* expanded to other cities and used the price war approach to carve out markets in each of these. Within those cities they sought to develop local supplements for the city and the suburbs, the first hint of localisation.

Samir Jain rubbished the notion that editorial space was sacrosanct, and that journalists were to be treated deferentially. Senior journalists were put on contracts, and editors were cut to size. The wall between advertising and editorial was dismantled: advertisements popped up in intrusive positions in the news space, and in some cities *The Times of India* did away with an editorial page altogether.

Other proprietors began to share some of these views. 'We think editors are not reader friendly,' Ramesh Chandra Agarwal proprietor and chief editor of *Dainik Bhaskar* would say, adding that in a changed media universe the editor needed to have the knowledge and capacity to visualise the total product, instead of just wielding a good pen. His newspaper, for instance, employed a huge number of journalists, and had several different sections. 'You need five editors for all of them. You need to manage 1,500 journalists. You need to understand the pulse of the people.' The editor according to him was an elevated creature, not friendly to the public, and unlikely to be approachable to the common reader.[15]

Earlier regional language publications were run by owner editors who did most things themselves: covering press conferences, writing on sports, and managing the small staff that was there. There was no system of professional editor in old times because resources were limited. Between 1960 and 1965 *Dainik Bhaskar* had only five to 10 people on its editorial staff. The paper's economy did not permit it to have a separate editor, according to its owner. But all that changed over the decades with the arrival of a new generation of Agarwals to assist their father in the management of the newspaper. As the paper became multi-edition, appointing professional editors to head editions became necessary and the owners only aspired to retain overall control, both business and editorial. At the *Jagran* group however there was still reluctance to give resident editors of editions print lines. The only exception was Vinod Shukla in Kanpur who was also on the board of directors of Jagran Prakashan. And the editorship of the newspaper was retained by a Gupta family scion, Sanjay Gupta.

A concomitant of the increasing reliance on reader opinion was a decreasing reliance on editors to shape the newspaper. Increasingly, proprietors were impatient with the traditional role of an editor, asserting as Ramesh Agarwal did above, that the job description had changed.

At *Aj* the third-generation proprietor Shardul Vikram Gupta was asserting that no paper had flourished under the leadership of an editor. 'They cannot run newspapers.'[16] The perception of the trade too was that editors were no longer pre-eminent in shaping the product. Varanasi's leading distributor would observe, 'Earlier the editor used to sell the paper. Now marketing sells the paper.'[17] *Dainik Bhaskar*'s state editor in Jaipur would add wryly that the change that had come over proprietors in the language press was that their journalistic ambitions were on the decline. 'On *Dainik Bhaskar*'s print line my name is there, Ramesh Agarwal's is not there. He recognises that he is more powerful as a proprietor.'[18]

Even as the Hindi editor was being editorially marginalised he was being materially upgraded. Said Ramesh Agarwal, 'Hindi editors used to ride two-wheelers. I can say we are the only people in the country who were the first to give Esteem cars to editors.' Journalist salaries touched six figure levels once television began to poach on the same talent. Wage boards declined in relevance and in the bigger newspapers contract employment became fairly common. Upmarket Hindi newspapers hiked pay packets, but for the generals, not the foot soldiers. They also began to look for reporters who spoke English well. As A.S. Raghunath, brand manager at *Dainik Jagran* put it, 'You need reporters with a socioeconomic category A background to send to launch of a Mercedes car.'[19] *Dainik Bhaskar* meanwhile was giving classes in English to its reporters.[20]

Attrition

Expansion in the Hindi press by newspapers such as *Dainik Bhaskar*, *Dainik Jagran*, *Amar Ujala*, *Rajasthan Patrika* and *Hindustan* over a period of 10 years from 1995 to 2005, saw each of these newspaper create multi-edition chains. As they added pages and colour, invested in machines and marketing networks and initiated price wars, local stand-alone newspapers were squeezed. They could not invest as much in production or distribution as the competition. They could not compete effectively for advertising without pan-Indian numbers to offer. Some died, others put up a fight, still others became a pale shadow of their former selves.

Some like *Aryavartha, Indian Nation, Pataliputra Times*, all in Bihar, had died even before this multi-edition domination began. The newspapers that once gave Hindi journalism renown—*Aj* and *Nai Duniya* to name the best known—fell on hard times and struggled to compete. The Indian Readership Survey Round 1 of 2001 (IRS R1 01) recorded some telling cases of falling readership. At one level these included *Nai Duniya* and *Jansatta*, both papers with national reputations. At another level the list covered smaller papers like *Nav Jyoti, Choutha Sansar, Rashtriya Sahara, Deshbandhu, Ranchi Express* and *Sanmarg*.[21]

Nai Duniya, based in Indore, had been a pioneer in bringing rotary offset to India; the paper got it and started printing on it in 1967. Its journalism under the editorship of Rajendra Mathur won it renown. As its proprietor tells it, from the early 1980s till the mid-1990s the paper was adjusting to rapid technological transition: from hand composing to photo offset in 1981–82, to laser composing in 1985 and networking within the newspaper in the early to mid-1990s. All through this period the ownership of the newspaper was also in transition. Founded by three partners in 1952, all three original owners died between 1981 and 1993–94. According to its current proprietor Abhay Chajlani, during this period, while *Nai Duniya* was self-absorbed with internal changes, newspapers in northern India were taking off as multi-edition entities. 'By the time we thought of multiplying newspapers became capital intensive.'[22] In other words, the paper missed the bus and did not have the resources to catch up until its competition had moved too far ahead.

Though *Nai Duniya* it had been the undisputed market leader in the city for the previous four decades, *Dainik Bhaskar* overtook it in the mid-1990s. By 2001 its readership in Indore (0.13 million) was roughly a third of its leading competition (*Bhaskar*, at 0.36 million) and it was also number three in Madhya Pradesh after *Dainik Bhaskar* and *Nava Bharat*.[23] By 2005 *Nai Duniya* in Madhya Pradesh had become a pale shadow of its former self even though in that year it added its first new printing site, at Gwalior.

IRS 01 R1 was also showing that *Jansatta* from the *Indian Express* group which had established itself rapidly in the 1980s, had lost as much as 45 per cent of its readership in less than a year. It experimented with a franchise edition in Chhattisgarh but the experiment failed. Other than that it never did venture out for numbers in the Hindi heartland. Starved of resources by the parent group, it was conspicuous by its lack of colour and gloss at a time when newspapers were smartening up.

There were also others in Rajasthan, Chhattisgarh and Uttar Pradesh that felt the heat of competition. One newspaper in Ranchi, *Prabhat Khabar*, fought back with persistence, innovation and the power of its journalism. But till the time of the writing of this book, the going remained tough. Outsider localisation pushed to the wall the truly local media of the region. That was its biggest irony.

At *Aj*, the UP newspaper whose founder was so wealthy that he was reputed to have underwritten the expenses of the Congress party in the region extending from Delhi to Bengal during the struggle for independence, the year 2005 saw a situation where most employees did not get salaries with any regularity. The paper according to the region's leading distributor had fallen to fourth place in Varanasi, after *Dainik Jagran, Hindustan,* and *Amar Ujala,* after having been the indisputable market leader in Uttar Pradesh for much of the 20th century. The current owner, great-grandson of the founder Shiv Prasad Gupta, would say that people worked without salaries because they wanted to be associated with the newspaper. 'How will they ask for a salary when they are free birds?' His explanation was that people could save themselves from local mafia and political victimisation by being associated with *Aj.* As for why his paper had fallen on hard times, he would say that his stars were bad, and that the competition resorted to unethical means to make their profits. His, however, was not a commercial organisation, it was a voluntary organisation.[24] In Bihar *Aj* managed to retain a semblance of circulation by being substantially cheaper than its major competition, at Rs 2 per copy to Rs 3.5 for *Hindustan.*[25] But underpricing only served to make its finances even more parlous.

In southern Rajasthan, Suresh Goyal, the proprietor of *Pratah Kal* would say that the fact that his newspaper was still alive was a major achievement. He founded his paper in 1979; *Rajasthan Patrika* started its Udaipur edition in 1980. When the paper started it was a single page, then it went up to four pages, then eight. 'As long as there was only *Rajasthan Patrika* we used to give them competition. Then *Bhaskar* came. They took our staff. When they see someone doing stories they buy the chap. I create correspondents. They take them.' In small places like Kothda, however, the same man was stringer for both these newspapers. Until *Dainik Bhaskar* came, he said, *Pratah Kal* got obituary advertising. But when it became the third in the market they ceased to give it to this paper. Only the leading two could expect to get most advertising. Government advertising also began to go to the leading newspapers, he claimed. The competition could afford colour photographs on glossy paper. It affected his circulation and advertising. He then had to go colour in 2004, which increased his costs.[26]

How does an indigenous newspaper survive in the face of formidable competition? Goyal started a Mumbai edition of his newspaper aimed at the Marwari community there. It began to get advertising which, its proprietor said, went a long way in helping to sustain the newspaper in its three centres—Udaipur, Mumbai and Jaipur.

He was also constrained to cut costs. If you wanted to compete in the outlying areas you had to maintain the same delivery time as the competition, which meant that you had to deploy taxis whereas earlier you could have used state transport buses to deliver the newspapers to villages and *kasbas* along the way. But then it became unaffordable. 'Our taxis used to go to seven places, then six, then five. It is not economical for us.'

Elsewhere in Rajasthan it was a similar story. The newspaper called *Nirantar*, published from the small industrial town of Beawar close to Ajmer, began in 1980 as a monthly magazine, then became a weekly, then a daily (Figure 12.2). Viability was a problem from day one, its owner Ramprasad Kumawat quit his day job as a lecturer and started a printing press so the job work would compensate for the losses incurred by the newspaper. Its focus was truly local, he had only district and local news, no state or national news, and the first lead every day was by convention, always Beawar-based. When he started there was no *Rajasthan Patrika* or *Dainik Bhaskar*, and *Patrika* did not even publish from Ajmer at that point. The paper had a part-time editor who spent more time on his cement agency than on the newspaper, two reporters, one photographer and no marketing person, because the owner could not afford one. He had offset printing on second-hand newsprint bought as scrap.[27]

Local as Kumawat was, it took competition for him to realise that he could not afford to be truly local. In 2005 while both *Patrika* and *Bhaskar* started village stringers, in the panchayats of Jawaja and Masuda, he could not afford them. His circulation which had climbed to 5,500 by 2000 had begun to drop thanks to competition, and in 2005 stood at around 3,000 copies. When his four-page paper was priced at Rs 1.5, on second-hand newsprint, *Bhaskar* arrived as competition, giving its readers 16 pages, weekend supplements and colour. 'For six months I tried to stick to my price. After that I began to take an annual subscription for the paper, annually Rs 300. No issue on Sunday.' As for future plans, he could not even think of expansion.

If we cover villages we cannot afford correspondents. Modem, fax costs also and we cannot afford, or to ply taxis to distribute

FIGURE 12.2 Mastheads of newspapers in Rajasthan, UP, Jharkhand and Chhattisgarh whose viability was imperilled by the multi-edition localisers

papers in rural areas. My problem is my paper may print by 4.15 [A.M.] instead of 4 [A.M.], the hawkers wil not wait for my paper. If *Patrika* comes and *Bhaskar* does not come, they will wait for *Bhaskar*. But not for *Nirantar*. When my price is Re 1, the hawker's commission will be less. My circulation is also less, their copies are more, the hawker gains more.

His circulation could not expand, because he could not afford to cover villages. It was a vicious circle.

Small newspapers are losing the battle on printing and technical quality. Newspapers like *Pratah Kal* and *Nirantar* like to point out that their journalism has more sterling qualities than that of *Dainik Bhaskar* and *Rajasthan Patrika*. But the reader wants gloss and up-beat features, and the economics is driving them out of business. Both are critical of the compromises the big papers make. Goyal said, 'They don't expose corruption, we do. We raise local problems.' And Kumawat said that in his industrial town his big competitors cover what should not be covered, but do not raise issues that should be raised.

They will not raise issues of cement production and industrial pollution because of advertising. They won't go against the advertiser. We raise such issues. The *bhoomi* (land) mafia in Beawar bought *goshalla* (grazing) land. I raised it, then others picked it up. They do one news item, and I keep it as a campaign.

Not far from Beawar, in the bigger city of Ajmer, the *Dainik Nav Jyoti*, one of the oldest newspapers in Rajasthan (1936), is a multi-edition paper, native to this city. It began as a weekly with editions in Barmer, Jaisalmer, Jalor, Sirohi and Pali. Competition has made it difficult to hold on to staff: they get wooed away by either *Bhaskar* or *Patrika* at twice the salaries they can offer. And since they cannot afford printing centres all over Rajashthan they are losing circulation at editions fed from Ajmer. This printing centre covers Nagaur, Bikaner, Bhilwara, Chittorgarh, Rajsamund, Udaipur, Banswara and Dungarpur. To reach papers to some of these distant towns means a very early closing deadline, Banswara is 500 km away, the paper that has to be sent there closes at 10 P.M. That makes them unable to compete with *Dainik Bhaskar* and *Rajasthan Patrika*. Both these are now printing in Banswara. The circulation of the paper dropped to half after *Bhaskar* came, and then stabilised at 200,000. The advertising the *Dainik Nav Jyoti* gets is because of old associations. The management is not inclined to confront the competition.[28] Some have lost the battle and closed down. *Dhanudhar*, begun in 1962, began to lose advertising in the 1990s and closed down in the year 2000. It could not keep up with the technology, said the owner's son, who then went on to work for *Pratah Kal*. In Jaipur, Rajasthan's first daily, *Rashtradoot*, limps along, with its proprietor dreaming of a recovery.[29] This was the paper that Kapoor Chand Kuleesh worked at before he went on to found the *Rajasthan Patrika*. Today it has lost most of its circulation and lacks the financial capacity to fight the competition in the city.

The symptoms of attrition are visible in local newspapers every-where: losing or stagnant circulation, falling advertising revenues, poor production values, a non-existent marketing set up. In Uttar Pradesh in Faizabad district, home to the Ayodhya controversy, a newspaper called *Jan Morcha* which began publishing in 1958 as a co-operative newspaper has been facing stagnation for the last seven years be-cause it is unable to compete. *Rashtriya Sahara*, *Hindustan* and *Dainik Jagran* have entered its territory over the years, offering far more pages than this paper could possibly afford. They are 16-page news-papers to *Jan Morcha*'s eight. The latter's newsprint is the cheapest, and therefore an unattractive grey. Is editor asks, 'When 10 news-papers lined up before you which one will you pick—the one with the best newsprint and colour, no?' For 10 years *Jan Morcha* has seen no circulation gain, its advertising revenue fell from around Rs 7.5 mil-lion in 1994–95 to 3.5–4 million in 2005. The paper cannot cut back on taxis or it will lose circulation, but it struggles to survive.[30]

South of Faizabad on the Madhya Pradesh border in Banda district of Uttar Pradesh another newspaper, 30 years old, was also facing a bleak future. *Nav Karmyug Prakashan*'s premises in the town's in-dustrial estate bore tell-tale signs of an enterprise fallen on hard times. Bought out in 1987 from its original owner by Rameshwar Prasad Gupta, a working journalist, it did well enough until *Jagran* began to swamp this part of the state with its localised edition with pages for

Banda and Chitrakoot districts. That was in the mid-1990s. Ten years down the line, in 2006, Gupta's son would recall how the advertisements slowly disappeared:

> Earlier the advertising agencies would give us advertising. Then they started saying you don't have colour, you are not multi-edition, we won't give you the ads. Government advertising also goes to big multi-edition papers. They have people in Lucknow to chase up advertising. I don't.

'We survive', the owner said, adding that it was too late in the day to try any other form of livelihood.[31]

The day he was interviewed was better than most others: the paper had several columns of advertising put in by local government agencies because a minister from the state government was visiting and being duly feted. All the papers in Banda on that day were festooned with greetings for Shiv Pal Singh Yadav.[32]

His fellow local proprietor Chandra Mohan Sahu, owner-editor of *Sri India*, was feeling more upbeat. A short, expensively-dressed man with a ring on every finger, Sahu was disarmingly frank: he was a businessman who decided to acquire a newspaper after experiencing what he described as major harassment by the government. 'As a businessman I could see how much importance government people give to the press. And for the politician media is like a *mandir*. I had no flair for politics, so I decided media was the next best thing.' After investing Rs 7 million over seven years the paper was still losing money. 'For so much money, I could have bought a lot of journalists', he joked. But he was hopeful that once he got a new machine, and added pages and colour, he would turn the corner. The business had now got into his blood, he was reluctant to give it up. Unlike other small newspaper owners he had money to invest. He had been in the *gutka* (chewing tobacco) business so his paper was named after the brand of gutka he sold: Sri Gutka. Now he was no longer in *gutka* but in hoteliering and tea packaging. Evidently though he still thought it prudent to retain a media entity for his protection.[33]

By 2005 yet another Madhya Pradesh newspaper, *Deshbandhu*, was finding it difficult to pay salaries and suffered a crippling strike. Its proprietor would say that if a paper like his had to rely on cover price and advertising it would find it difficult to survive. Having a high cover price was not viable when the competition was indulging in price wars and handing out plastic chairs as incentives to subscribe. And the advertising available was not enough to go round when the number of players in the market were multiplying.

> Advertising for newspapers [is] becoming a self-defeating proposition. You have to offer unrealistic rate structures because advertising rates have gone down. My advertisement manager got into a barter deal with a soft drink company. They said they will pay in concentrate. We have to hawk the concentrate and recover the money.[34]

Deshbandhu was a newspaper which had consciously resisted excessive localisation because it believed that a regional rather than excessively local outlook was more constructive. It also tried to make giving news about local movements and grassroots initiatives its USP. Historically it was a newspaper whose founder Mayaram Surjan had done some memorable reporting on hunger and rural oppression. For a while, after the formation of Chhattisgarh, it wore its pro-Congress affiliation on its sleeve. But overall, by 2006 it was in financial trouble.

Another local paper which had to face formidable competition from the outsider localisers was *Prabhat Khabar* of Ranchi. But it fought back. It had become accustomed to fighting: after it worked on a series of investigative stories to break the fodder scam in Bihar the state government sought every means it could to harass the newspaper. It was also accustomed to taking on its fellow newspapers, for their communal reporting, or for extracting favours from the government of the day. It complained to the Press Council when it found that one newspaper was monopolising invitations to accompany the prime minister or president on visits abroad.[35]

The editor of *Prabhat Khabar* says he realised early on that to survive you had to expand. First a franchise approach to more editions was experimented with, but that did not work. Then he decided to expand using old machines, bought from others. 'For 3 lakh rupees [Rs 300,000] I bought a third hand machine which had earlier been used by the *Indian Express* in Chennai.' Then he tied up with the *Telegraph* of Kolkata to print an edition for them and the association helped *Prabhat Kahbar* negotiate a bank loan. Later he would buy another old machine from *Eenadu* to start an edition in Devgarh. The competition, meanwhile, came into Jharkhand with enviable resources at its command. In February 2000 *Hindustan* started with a new machine with 20-page paper printing capacity. They could give readers five supplements, *Prabhat Khabar* only three. In February 2002 *Jagran* arrived, willing to take back full unsolds from the hawker. They offered four pages of colour in Jamshedpur; the older paper could afford to offer only two, and had to keep control on unsolds. On such nitty-gritty issues are survival battles fought.[36]

If times have changed and reader interest has become pre-eminent, you have to go along. And tailor your initiatives to your resources. *Prabhat Khabar* used 'young boys' instead of a survey agency to obtain reader feedback, and found that readers wanted, for instance, more colour in their pages. It also found that though newspapers continue to be obsessed with issues of communalism and secularism most readers are not. It learnt to find the resources to give agents and hawkers gifts, just as the competition did. And it sought other ways of dealing with advertiser demands.

Advertisers tell us you must have A+ families among your readers. There are two ways you can do it. You can put pictures of them. I don't do too much of that. I give business coverage that they cannot do without. If the state's industrial policy changes we give details of that. When the Mittals signed a 9 billion doller MOU with the state government there were mass protests movements against giving them land. We gave full details of that so these industrial houses were forced to read our paper.[37]

And as the wealthier newspapers bought over *Prabhat Kabhar*'s journalists (*Hindustan*, 20 at one go), the paper started a journalism training institute so that getting replacements became easier. While all these measures helped to keep the competition at bay for a while, it could not help for long. The paper's edition in Bihar was losing the battle because there were no resources to spare for it. And even in Jharkhand by 2005 *Hindustan* had overtaken *Prabhat Khabar* in readership. By 2006 the newspaper turned to the banks to get the resources to shore up its presence in Bihar and expand to Siliguri. Of all the independent newspapers pushed to wall by a relentless process of media consolidation, *Prabhat Khabar* was the most dogged in crafting its comeback strategies. By June 2006 it was announcing triumphantly that its circulation lead in Jharkhand, over the competition, was intact.

Finally, its emergence as a successful multi-edition localiser tends to obscure the fact that an early and prominent victim of expansion in the Hindi belt was in fact *Rajasthan Patrika*. Caught unawares initially when *Dainik Bhaskar* invaded its territory at the end of 1996 it lost no time in copying its aggressor's strategies and fighting back. Once it dropped its own price, its circulation grew, though *Bhaskar* pulled ahead and maintained a lead for some years. By 2005–06 when it regained a circulation lead over *Bhaskar*, readers and even journalists within *Dainik Bhaskar* attributed this to the fact that *Patrika*'s journalism had greater credibility (Table 12.1).

TABLE 12.1 Resurgence in Rajasthan

Audit Period, July–December 2002	
Dainik Bhaskar, Rajasthan Total circulation, 5 editions 647,338	*Rajasthan Patrika* Total circulation, 9 editions 598,822
Audit Period, July–December 2005	
Dainik Bhaskar, Rajasthan Total circulation, 8 editions 845,438	*Rajasthan Patrika* Total circulation, 10 editions 963,168

Source: Based on totals of Audit Bureau of Circulations figures for editions in Rajasthan.

The third generation here was also learning to innovate and strategise. And to make common cause with other newspapers facing an invasion from *Dainik Bhaskar*. Nihar Kothari would admit that he had shared his experience in fighting the *Bhaskar* group with the *Gujarat Samachar* owners in Ahmedabad who faced an onslaught from *Dainik Bhaskar*'s Gujarati publication, *Divya Bhaskar*. And when *Bhaskar* and Zee launched in Mumbai, the Kothari family was there too, to offer solidarity to the owners of *The Times of India* and keenly observe the launch.

Conclusion

For Hindi journalism the decade and a half from 1991 to 2006 was a period of enormous transition. Hindi readership numbers grew exponentially, and as Hindi emerged as the foremost medium of political discourse its journalism acquired self-confidence and its political and commercial importance grew. The most dramatic assertion of growing self-confidence was the decision of the *Daink Bhaskar* group (in partnership with the owner of Zee TV) to take on *The Times of India* in the Mumbai market with a new daily offering in English. Meanwhile Hindi newspaper proprietors were making the point that the quality and integrity of Hindi journalism were improving too.

The relationship between press and politicians in this region was calibrated by the needs of both. Some strong regional newspapers had identifiable political affiliations which they did not bother to deny. New entrants into the ranks of media owners were spurred by the advantages the status of media baron offered to a businessman with interests to protect.

Nationally, this period was one of striking change and growth. The financing of newspapers underwent a transition, In 2004–05 the growth of print media advertising surpassed that of television. Hindi newspapers increased their dependence on advertising and changes in government policy saw at least one of them acquire a foreign equity partner. The same paper also listed on the stock market in 2006. While it was inconceivable at the end of the decade of 1970s that regional newspapers would see themselves as part of multimedia empires, this was a reality in several cases in 2005.

One fundamental shift which took place was the depoliticisation of the news. A concomitant of greater dependence on reader opinion was a decrease of reliance on editors to shape the newspaper.

The newspapers that once gave Hindi journalism renown—*Aj* and *Nai Duniya* to name the best known—fell on hard times and struggled to compete. Small local papers realised after competition arrived that they could not afford to be truly local because they could not afford as many village stringers as the big localisers. They also realised that they big ones would not do the stories the smaller papers sometimes did such as exposing corruption, or pollution by an industry which was also an advertiser. *Prabhat Khabar*, the only paper that energetically crafted strategies to stay ahead of more powerful competition, managed to maintain its circulation lead in Jharkhand over the others.

Notes

1. Sudhir Agarwal, interviewed by author, Mumbai, 27 January 2005.
2. M.M. Gupta and Sanjay Gupta, interviewed by author, Noida, 2 September 2005.
3. Chief Minister of Andhra Pradesh, 1982–89.
4. 'Print media outpaces TV in advertising', Adex study, *Hindu Business Line*, 5 January 2005. http://www.blonnet.com/2005/01/05/stories/2005010502010400.htm.
5. Sevanti Ninan, 'Regional Ouslaught,' *The Hindu*, 29 February 2004.
6. 'Punishing Indian Media', *Business Standard* editorial, 21 February 2001.
7. Rajesh Gajra, 'Business of Words', *Outlook*, 5 March 2001.
8. Sir Anthony O'Reilly, interviewed by author, New Delhi, 8 December 2005.
9. 'Jagran IPO Likely to Hit the Market by March-end Next Year', exchange4media News Service, 5 December 2005.
10. Vinod Shukla, interviewed by author, Lucknow, 25 August 2005.
11. A.P. Singh, A.P. Singh and Co., interviewed by author, Varanasi, 18 March 2005.
12. Sevanti Ninan, 'Wooing Hawkers,' *Media Matters*, *The Hindu*, 26 October 2003.
13. 'Breaking News!', *Business World*, pp. 40–52, 28 March 2005.
14. Ibid.
15. Ramesh Agarwal, Mumbai, interviewed by author, 27 January 2005.
16. Shardul Vikram Gupta, interviewed by author, Varanasi, 16 March 2005.
17. A.P. Singh, A.P. Singh and Co., interviewed by author, 18 March 2005.
18. N.K. Singh, interviewed by author, Jaipur, 16 September 2005.
19. A.S. Raghunath, interviewed by author, Jaipur, 16 September 2005.
20. Babulal Sharma, editor, *Dainik Bhaskar*, interviewed by author, Bhopal, 19 February 2005.
21. 'Big fish–small fish syndrome among Hindi dailies?', exchange4media analysis of IRS 01 R1 readership survey data, 4 July 2001, exchange4media.com.
22. Abhay Chajlani, interviewed by author, Indore, 15 February 2005.
23. See note 21.

24. Shardul Vikram Gupta, proprietor, *Aj*, interviewed by author, 16 March 2005.
25. In 2003.
26. Suresh Goyal, editor-proprietor, *Pratah Kal*, interviewed by author, Udaipur, 29 November 2004.
27. Ramprasad Kumawat, editor, *Nirantar*, interviewed by author, Beawar, 15 September 2005.
28. Rajendra Gunjail, *Dainik Navjyoti*, interviewed by author, Ajmer, 15 September 2005.
29. Rakesh Sharma, editor-proprietor, *Rashtradoot*, interviewed by author, 17 September 2005.
30. Sheetla Singh, editor, *Jan Morcha*, interviewed by author, Faizabad, 27 August 2005.
31. Ramchandra Pathak, interviewed by author, Banda, 11 July 2006.
32. UP cabinet minister visting Banda that day. Author's personal observation, Banda, 11 July 2006.
33. Chandra Mohan Sahu, interviewed in Banda, 11 July 2006.
34. Lalit Surjan, interviewed by author, Delhi, 21 March 2005.
35. Cited in unpublished seminar paper by Harivansh, *Freedom of Press in the Era of liberalization*.
36. Harivansh, editor, *Prabhat Khabar*, interviewed by author, New Delhi, 27 October 2005.
37. Ibid.

Epilogue—Habermas Revisited

In the region of Bundelkhand which straddles both Uttar Pradesh (UP) and Madhya Pradesh (MP), in district Chitrakoot, is a village called Markundi which comes alive every day at around 8 a.m. That is when the local passenger train pulls in if it is on time, and unleashes a frenzy of activity. Women who have been sitting with headloads of wood gathered from rapidly depleting forests scramble on, with children. They will ride ticketless into Madhya Pradesh, sell the wood at Satna which is three or four stations down the line, buy provisions with the money and catch the evening train back. It is a daily routine, and one that is followed by other women who will shove their headloads onto the same train from Tikaria, Itwa, Majgaon and Chitara. The men don't go because, unlike the women, they will be harassed by the train guard for travelling without a ticket.

There is little other means of livelihood in these parts, it is a hilly area where rainfall is scarce and ground water not accessible because of the topography. The steady deforestation has the makings of an impending ecological crisis. The compulsions of the women and the plight of the forests are both covered in a page one lead story in the 1–15 May 2006 issues of *Khabar Lahariya*, the eight-page fortnightly in the Bundeli dialect that is brought out by Dalit women from these parts. It is a clear-eyed, non-judgemental account. Markundi and the surrounding Manikpur block figure in other ways in other issues of this paper as well: It.has a hospital without a doctor, and a 20-year-old school building in need of repairs. Right after the morning passenger train pulls out there is a fair presence of locals and visitors at the tea shop close to the tracks. Its owner keeps a copy of both the daily newspapers that reach these parts, *Dainik Jagran* as well as the latest issue of *Khabar Lahariya*, because the women have badgered him to buy a copy. Its dialect also makes it popular in this region.

Tea shops throughout the Hindi belt subscribe to at least one daily newspaper, and if they are price-conscious they buy *Aj*, which at

Rs 2 is priced the lowest. There are thousands of tea shops in these parts just as there were some 3,000 coffee houses in early 18th century London (Calhoun 1993: 12). While they are far removed from the coffee houses which helped Habermas formulate his early theory of the public sphere, they bear out in a different locale, a different era and in a very different economic sphere his theory of a 'diffuse public' which emerges in the course of the commercialisation of cultural production (Habermas 1989: 38). The coffee houses were the early manifestation of a public sphere, the penny press came much later. He idealised the rational–critical debate which he ascribed to the former (ibid.: 182–85) and assumed a degeneration of the public sphere as the media passed into capitalist hands and became a mass product. He predicted the control of media organs by the state and corporations and termed this a refeudalisation of the public sphere. At the same time he theorised that to be truly 'public' the public sphere needed more participants (Calhoun 1993: 3).

Comparisons

If one were to apply Habermas's formulations to the changes that were transforming the public sphere at the turn of 21st century in the Hindi belt, both the parallels and divergences are compelling. The journals that were part of the bourgeois public sphere in 18th century London were small ones, not widely circulated mass publications. Similarly the early public sphere in the Hindi belt had consisted of small literary and political journals discussing a variety of issues and had begun to focus by the 1920s on the movement for freedom from British rule that was gathering force. Post-independence many regional newspapers, big and small, came into existence and helped create a local public sphere in the states of the Hindi heartland.

The refeudalisation of this public sphere in Habermasian terms took place when some of these regional newspapers began to expand in order to compete, adopted a commercial policy of localisation to add to their circulation and moved out of their traditional circulation areas into new ones in order to offer bigger numbers to advertisers. The catalysts of the shrinking of an existing local public sphere and its reinvention were the second and third generations in the leading newspaper owning families, and their appetite for grasping the challenge of the market. In its reinvented state the public sphere in these parts became more local and drew in larger numbers, becoming 'truly public' in the process. The village tea shops were helping to bring in these participants, but because their clientile was hardly drawn from highly educated gentry, Habermas might have judged them incapable of elevated political debate.

But in fact when commercially-driven newspaper barons pushed their products into small towns and villages with the help of price incentives, the effect was not entirely one of degenerating the public sphere. These newspapers democratised debate so that an impoverished head-loader could figure in it, as much as a chief minister. True, local editions stocked by tea shops were avidly read for local crime and gossip, but they also raised public expectation that the state would respond to the needs and grievances of ordinary people, aired in these newspapers. In a literal sense if you listened in, the debate was both rational and critical though perhaps not as intellectually lofty as in Habermas' bourgeois public sphere. On this morning (11 July 2006) the local denizens drinking tea in Markundi described the paradoxes of modern development in their village.

Mobile phones had come to Chitrakoot the year before, and a public sector telephone provider was planning to offer mobile services this village. Equipment to set up a mobile tower had arrived a few months ago but had been languishing there since, rotting in the open in sun and rain. Nobody had come to set up the tower and activate the service. Meanwhile the electronic telephone exchange in this block which served land line telephones for the entire block had been lying dead since February. Many complaints had been lodged. Apart from *Khabar Lahariya*'s female correspondent who visited at least once a fortnight to check what was new with this part of the district, there was an *Amar Ujala* correspondent in the village who had written on it more than once and even carried a picture in his newspaper of the defunct exchange with padlock on its door. To no avail. A pensioner in the village said succinctly in English, 'The pen has got no power nowadays.'

Shabir Hussain, a tailor at his sewing machine a few shops further down from the tea shop in the main alley of Markundi, offered a comparison on the mainline press represented by *Jagran* and *Amar Ujala* and the community press represented by *Khabar Lahariya*. The big papers looked at small crime but they did not give sufficient importance to small things which loomed large in the life of the village he said, such as black marketing of rations at the local ration shop. The *Khabar Lahariya* women did, what's more they did not just report, they got to the bottom of it. '*Bhanda phod karte hai.*' *Bhanda phod* is the colloquial Hindi term for an exposé.[1]

To return to the dead telephone exchange, what of the political representative from this area? Was he not able to persuade an errant telephone department to set this exchange right? This time somebody else replied in Hindi that he was from the Bahujan Samaj Party, but a 'gunpoint *ka* candidate'. Meaning, he had been elected by getting his henchmen to intimidate voters at gunpoint. (Chitrakoot is known for the bandits who hold sway here.) He was consequently disinclined to put himself at the service of his constituents in the villages.

To the extent that a public sphere reflects broad political consciousness, its constituents in Markundi were conscious of the mockery of political representation, the complete and fearless indifference of the servants of the state, and the impotence of the mainstream press. The village was reported on by both kinds of media. By the small, independent press represented by *Khabar Lahariya* (sustained by grant funding), which was committed to foregrounding news of Dalits and those at the bottom of the power structure. And it also had a representative of the local edition of a very big multi-edition newspaper, replete with advertising and commercial intent, but even so not as devoid of public conscience as Habermas made out in his chapter on 'The Transformation of the Public Sphere's Political Function' (Habermas 1989: 181). The local correspondent was not entirely focused on becoming 'the gate through which privileged private interests invaded the public sphere' (ibid.: 185). He strove to represent the pressing problems of the village community as a whole. But neither the big nor small media vehicle was able to be always effective against the brazen indifference of the state and the political class.

Publicity, Good and Bad

At the same time, there could be other circumstances in which at the most local level, at the level of the village, elected people's representatives were leveraging the national–regional–local media to achieve publicity, a concept Habermas defines in various ways. He links publicity with public opinion, and distinguishes between manipulative publicity and critical publicity (Habermas 1989: 247–48). In the district of Banda in Uttar Pradesh adjoining Chitrakoot, a *pradhan* (the term used in Uttar Pradesh for a *sarpanch*) of a Dalit village had learnt to use the good offices of the Brahmin local correspondent of *Aj* to publicise the work he did in his village. Munna Lal Varma of Barsana Khurd said that in his area a pulse polio programme was in progress and he had achieved 100 per cent coverage of the children in his village. He wrote up the news, he said, and gave it to the correspondent who published it. Was this manipulative publicity? Or did it have demonstration value that could put it in the category of critical publicity? Indeed much of the coverage of local events, gentry and panchayat and block activities had a public relations patina to it, yet it helped to promote a sense of community and inclusiveness, creating a participatory public sphere. To Habermas' older categories of elevated and not-so-elevated discourse and public opinion, were being added more nuanced uses of communication that an advertising-driven mass media was making possible.

For instance once the local correspondent or stringer became know as being accessible, rural folk learn to make the most of his presence. With a fine sense of what might be called critical publicity, a village readership only lately acquainted with the usefulness of newspapers had learned to turn local correspondents eager for village news to their own advantage. Varma described how panchayat *karamchari*s (functionaries) were kept on their toes in his area because village people had taken to rushing to newspaper correspondents with their grievance, every time they had a problem with a *karamachari*.[2] Whereas the bureaucratic machinery might ignore bad publicity as seen in the case of Markundi above, a mere functionary who felt vulnerable might be more easily brought to heel by such judicious planting of complaints. Accountability was thus becoming an element of the public sphere.

Identity in the Hindi Public Sphere

A reinvention of the public sphere implies some degree of reshaping of public perceptions. The relationship between media consumption and the sense of belonging that a citizen acquires has been frequently explored. With the advent of cyberspace comparisons are now made between how newspapers have traditionally fostered a sense of community (through acts of community spirit boosterism such as those described in Chapter 4) and how the Internet atomises identity by enabling a user to create his own individual news product.[3]

How media shapes a community's sense of belonging is perhaps better understood by applying Benedict Anderson's theory of 'Imagined Communities' to the way in which local communities were beginning to perceive their own identities in the Hindi speaking states. Anderson defined a nation as an imagined political community—imagined as both inherently limited and sovereign. 'Finally, it is imagined as a community, because, regardless of the actual inequality and exploitation that may prevail in each, the nation is always conceived as a deep, horizontal comradeship' (Anderson 1991: introduction). He also asserted that the practice of print-capitalism facilitated the imagining of the nation: '... made it possible for rapidly growing numbers of people to think about themselves, and to relate to others, in profoundly new ways' (quoted in Jeffrey 2000).

In India's Hindi heartland the notion of how linguistic, cultural and political entities imagine themselves is still evolving. Yogendra Yadav points out that the creation of states along linguistic lines in the Indian Union has resulted, in time, in a stateisation of both politics and the press.[4] In the 1950s and 1960s neighbouring areas artificially divided by political boundaries tended to behave in the same way. They had a cultural contiguity, and the politics of neighbouring regions would have been the same politics. But over time there has been a federalisation of Indian politics with identifiable state politics emerging within state boundaries.

Now on both sides of an artificial political boundary such as Buldelkhand in UP and MP you will find they are politically different. There's no Samajwadi Party on the MP side. At one time it seemed there was a little bit of influence of BSP but not much.

Similarly, Yadav adds, Haryana and western UP have different politics though they are geographically contiguous. There is political divergence from one state to another, but homogenisation within a state. 'In other ways eastern UP and western UP are totally different, but not in politics. Their politics was not so similar before.'

Regional newspapers, says Yadav, fit in perfectly with that trend. Their coverage reinforces the notion of each state as an entity with its own language and politics, and state capitals as mini capitals within the country. Over 50 years since the division of states, the press and politicians have been alive to the creation of a state identity, which is periodically reinforced by state elections. The imagining therefore of the citizen voter was on two planes—as belonging to a state, within the larger identity of belonging to India. The primary identity being based on language and ethnicity, of belonging to Mithila in Bihar, or Mewar or Marwar in Rajasthan, was subsumed. The early regional papers that had statewide readership tended to nurture a state identity, whether it was *Rajasthan Patrika* in Rajasthan or *Nai Duniya* in Indore, rather than pander to regional entities within a state, perhaps because they were consciously nurturing federalism within a still-young India.

Towards the end of the 20th century when cultural divergences grew into divisive movements with perceived grievances, as with the movement for Jharkhand in Bihar, or for Chhattisgarh in Madhya Pradesh, or for Uttaranchal in Uttar Pradesh, regional newspapers in the disaffected regions tended to support these movements. You go with the sentiment of the market.

And by the 21st century, the wheel of identity turned full circle as market forces began to respond to the sheer scale of the country by creating cultural niches. As Yadav puts it, 'All the processes we identify with modernity have this dual effect, they create homogenisation and through that also carve out zones.'

As newspapers developed national–local strategies, reviving elements of dialect to incorporate into local editions became part of the strategy, appealing as it were to latent cultural identities. Hence the attempts by different newspapers to revive dialects such as *Angika* in Bhagalpur, *Maithili* in Bihar, *Wagri* in Rajathan's Banswara district and *Bundeli* in Chitrakoot. It was an element in the conscious reinvention of the public sphere that was taking place, an attempt to create diverse homogenities. It had both a geographical and cultural dimension. It was nurtured both by dialect and by celebrating in the newspaper local religious festivals and fairs. Now, more than before, readers were encouraged to imagine themselves as part of a local culture that would reinforce the nurturing of a local market.

The worrisome question that I raised in Chapter 11 was whether this circumscribed public sphere would begin to weaken the 'deep horizontal comradeship' that used to bind different corners of the same state—a poser from the Hindi heartland for both Habermas and Anderson, that newspapers sensitive to public opinion were beginning to grapple with, in the year 2006.

Notes

1. Shabir Hussain, interviewed by author, Markundi, Chitrakoot, 12 July 2006.
2. Munna Lal Varma, interviewed by author, Banda district, 11 July 2006.
3. Michael Zielenziger, 'Newspapers in Retreat', http://www.alumni.berkeley.edu/calmag/200603/newspapers2.asp, downloaded July 2006.
4. Yogendra Yadav, interviewed by author, New Delhi, 5 July 2006.

References

Anderson, Benedict. 1991. *Imagined Communities* (Rev. Edn). London: Verso Books.

Bhatnagar, Ramratan. 2003. *The Rise and Growth of Hindi Journalism 1826–1945*. Varanasi: Vishwavidyalay Prakashan.

Calhoun, Craig. 1993. 'Introduction', in Craig Calhoun, ed., *Habermas and the Public Sphere*. Cambridge, MA: MIT Press.

Canning, John (ed.). 2001. *100 Great Modern Lives* (Twelfth Impression). Delhi: Rupa & Co.

Census of India. 2001. 'Provisional Population Totals: India', Paper I.

Desai, M.V. and Sevanti Ninan (eds). 1996. *Beyond Those Headlines*. New Delhi: Allied Publishers.

Chaturvedi, Jagdish Prasad. 2004. *Hindi Patrakarita ka Itihas*. Delhi: Prabhat Prakashan.

Dwivedi, Hazariprasad. 1999. *Hindi Sahitya—Udbhav aur Vikas*. New Delhi and Patna: Rajkamal Prakashan.

Franklin, Bob and David Murphy. 1998. *Making the Local News*. London and New York: Routledge.

Fraser, Nancy. 1992. 'Rethinking the Public Sphere: A Contribution to the Critique of Actually Existing Democracy', in Craig Calhoun, ed., *Habermas and the Public Sphere*. Cambridge, MA: MIT Press.

Gates-Reed, G.H. (ed.). 1956. *The Indian Press Year Book*. Madras and London: The India Press Publications.

Green, Lelia. 2001. *Communication, Technology and Society*. London: Sage Publications.

Habermas, Jurgen. 1989. *Structural Transformation of the Public Sphere*. Cambridge, MA: MIT Press.

Halberstram, David. 1979. *The Powers That Be*. New York: Alfred A. Knopf.

Hasan, Zoya. 1998. *Quest for Power*. New Delhi: Oxford University Press.

Hill, C.P. 1985. *British Economic and Social History 1700–1982* (Fifth Edn). London: Edwin Arnold Publishers Ltd.

Jeffrey, R. 1997. 'Hindi: "Taking to the Punjab Kesari Line",' *Economic and Political Weekly*, 18 January, pp. 77–83.

———. 2000. *India's Newspaper Revolution: Capitalism, Politics and the Indian-Language Press, 1977–99*. New Delhi: Oxford University Press.

Jeffrey, R. (with Peter Friedlander and Sanjay Seth). 2001. '"Subliminal Charge": How Hindi-language Newspaper Expansion Affects India', @*Media International Australia*, 100: 147–66.

————. 2004. 'The Three Stages of Print' conference paper, 15th Biennial Conference of the Asian Studies Association of Australia in Canberra 29 June–2 July 2004. http://coombs.anu.edu.au/ASAA/conference/proceedings/Jeffrey-R-ASAA2004.pdf (accessed 8 June 2005).

Jharkhand Development Report 2006, published by *Prabhat Khabar*.

Khetan, Neelima. 2004. 'Enigmas of Development Action', *A Common Cause*. New Delhi: National Foundation for India.

Kulish, K.C. 1996. 'The Rajasthan Patrika Story,' in Sevanti Ninan and M.V. Desai, eds, *Beyond Those Headlines*. New Delhi: Allied Publishers.

Kumar, N. 1971. *Journalism in Bihar* (Supplement to the *Bihar State Gazetteer*, Government of Bihar), Patna: Gazetteers Branch, Revenue Department.

Mathew, George. 1999. *The Panchayat Raj Factor*. New Delhi: Institute of Social Sciences.

McLuhan, Marshall. 2003. *Understanding Media*. Corte Madera, CA: Gingko Press.

National Human Development Report. 2001, 2002. Government of India. Planning Commission, Government of India.

Orsini, Fransesca. 2002. *The Hindi Public Sphere 1920–1940, Language and Literature in the Age of Nationalism*. New Delhi: Oxford University Press.

Pande, Mrinal. 2006. 'English for the Elite, Hindi for the Power Elite', in Uday Sahay, ed., *Making News: A Handbook of Media in Contemporary India*. New Delhi: Oxford University Press.

Parikh, S. Kirit and R. Radhakrishna (eds). 2002. *India Development Report*. New Delhi: Oxford University Press.

Rai, Alok. 2000. *Hindi Nationalism*. New Delhi: Orient Longman.

Rai, Amrit, 1984. *A House Divided*. New Delhi: Oxford University Press.

Rajagopal, Arvind. 2001. *Politics after Television*. UK: Cambridge University Press.

Report of the Second Press Commission. 1982. Government of India.

Schudson, Michael. 1993. 'Was There Ever a Public Sphere? If So, When? Reflections on the American Case', in Craig Calhoun, ed., *Habermas and the Public Sphere*. Cambridge, MA: MIT Press.

Singh, Bachchan. 2003. *Adhunik Hindi Sahitya ka Itihaas* (Revised Edn). Allahabad: Lok Bharti Prakashan.

Sridhar, Vijaydutt. 1999. *Shabd Satta*. Bhopal: Mahavrao Sapre Smriti Samachar Patra Sangralay.

Stahlberg, Per. 2002. *Lucknow Daily*. Stockholm Studies in Social Anthropology. Stockholm: Stockholm University.

Third Human Development Report. 2002. Madhya Pradesh: Government of Madhya Pradesh.

Vaidik, Ved Pratap (ed.). 2002. *Hindi Patrakarita: Vividh Ayaam.* New Delhi: Hindi Book Centre.

Verghese, B.G. 2005. *Warrior of the Fourth Estate: Ramnath Goenka of the Express.* New Delhi: Viking.

Vidura Roundtable. 1992. 'Who is Afraid of Hindi Journalism', *Vidura*, Vol. 29/No. 2, June.

Vyas, Lakshmishankar. 1960. *Pararkarji aur Patrikarita.* Kashi: Bharatiya Gyanpeeth.

Vyas, Yashwant. 1999. *Apne Gireban Mein.* Delhi: Radhakrishna Prakashan.

Yadav, Yogendra. 2004. 'The Elusive Mandate of 2004', *Economic and Political Weekly*, 18 December.

Index

Abhudaya, 41
Abhyuday, 41
access, democratisation of, 31
advertisements, dependence on, 190; educational, 195; political, 195; sampling of, 147
advertising, 22, 23; in Bihar, 97
advertising potential, 82
Agarwal, Dwarka Prasad, 46
Agarwal, Girish, 74, 105, 187, 190
Agarwal, Ramesh Chandra, 61
Agarwal, Sudhir, 101
Agarwal, Y.C., 20, 106
agricultural distress, reports on, 176
agriculture, reports on, 178
Aha Zindagi, 272
Ahmed, Faiyaz, 148
Aj, 41, 47, 52, 277; expansion of, 92; history of, 27; Kanpur, 58; launch of, 51
Akhbar Gwalior, 37
Amar Ujala, 17, 45, 47; Chandigarh, 107; Dharamsala, 108; Jalandhar, 107
Amrit Bazar Patrika, 39
Anandbazar Patrika, 16
Anderson, Benedict, 295
Ansari, Mohammed Karim, 130
Arya Darpan, 39
Aryavartha, 44, 218
audience, transition of, 27
Audit Bureau of Circulation, 16
awareness creation by electronic media, 84

Ayodhya issue, 223–24

Bal Bhaskar, 200
Balachand, K., 219
Bandhua Mukti Morcha, 122
Bangbasi, 39
Bangdoot, 36
Benares Akhbar, 37
Bennett, Coleman & Co., growth of, 263
Bhaiyya, Raja, arrest of, 220
Bharat Gyan Vigyan Samiti, 72
Bharat Mitra, 38, 50
Bharat Varsha, 39
Bhatt, Pandit Balakrishna, 38, 40
Bhumihar Bharman Patrika, 43
Bible in Indian languages, propagation of, 34
Bihar Bandhu, 38
Bihar, advertising in, 97; consumer goods market in, 97
Boosterism, 103
Brahman, 39, 40
brand-building, 200

Cable TV, advertising in, 96
calculated communalism, 224
Calcutta Samachar, 41
caste in the media, 217
Chattisgarh Mitra, 38
Chaturvedi, Tejpal, 129
cheating, stories on, 170
Chincholkar, Pandit Ramrao, 38
Choupal, 20
circulation schemes, 187, 188

citizen-journalists, 116
civic awareness, creation of, 24
civil society, 231
come-and-give-your-news prin-
    ciple, 119
communication infrastructure, 78
communication revolution in
    Uttaranchal, 257
community spirit boosterism, 99
competition, growth of, 189
Consumer goods market in Bihar,
    97
consumer goods, penetration of, 98
cricket fever, 181
critical publicity, 294
cultural divergence of states, 296

Daily Thanthi, 16
Dainik Bhaskar, 14, 20, 43, 46,
    47, 74, 93, 105, 120, 136, 137,
    248; Banswara, 151; boost-
    erism in, 101; Chandigarh, 105;
    changes in management of, 275;
    Chhattisgarh, 105; Haryana,
    105; Indore, 194; partnership
    with Zee, 268; quality improve-
    ment in, 137; Rajasthan, 117;
    report on panther, 144
Dainik Jagran, 14, 16, 17, 20, 44,
    47, 55–57, 93, 100, 101, 104,
    227, 248, 249; and Dainik
    Bhaskar, 94; circulation of, 99;
    Dharamsala, 108; expansion of,
    92, 106; Ludhiana, 107; Palamu,
    107; Siliguri, 107; use of the
    Ayodhya issue, 224
Darbhanga, Maharaja of, 44
Delhi Times, 197
delivery networks, 115
Deoskar, Sakaram Ganesh, 50
Deshbandhu, 73, 74, 168, 248,
    283, 284
development and poverty, reporting
    on, 174

development and social activity,
    media's role in, 231
development reporting, 238
Devraj, Lala, 46
Dhanudhar, 282
Divya Himachal, 108
Diwan, Suresh, 233
Doordarshan, contests in, 187
dot-com boom, 13
Dubey, Shashi Bhushan, 124
Dwija Patrika, 43
Dwivedi, Mahabir Prasad, 40

economic liberalisation, policy of,
    13
edition-wise segmentation, conse-
    quences of, 254
editorial localisation, 103
editor–proprietor relationship, 273
education and health, reports of,
    168
educational advertisements, 195
Eenadu, 16; expansion of, 104
emergency, imposition of, 58
expansion and localisation of Hindi
    press, 20

farm incomes, rising of, 15
FEMA (Foreign Exchange Manage-
    ment Act), promulgation of, 266
foeticide, reports on, 180
foreign direct investment, in Hindi
    market, 267
foreign investment ban, in print
    media, 265; lobbying for lifting
    of, 265
foreign investment in Indian media,
    266
foreign portfolio investment in
    Indian media, prohibition of,
    266

Gaur Kayastha, 39

gift schemes for hawkers, 189, 270
government's advertisement budget,
    208
Gramin Sevak Samiti, 233
Gulab Kothari, 226
Gupta, Mahendra Mohan, 17
Gupta, Purnachand, 53, 55, 56
Gupta, Sanjay, 79, 262, 275
Gupta, Shardul Vikram, 92, 275
Gupta, Shivprasad, 47, 48
Gupta, Yogendra Mohan, 53
Gurgaon, news in, 155
Gyanoday, 43

Habermas' formulations, 291
Hari Bhoomi, 44
Harishchandra Chandrika, 38
Harishchandra Magazine, 38
Harishchandra, Bharatendu Babu, 37
Harivansh, 101, 104, 160–61, 225
health-related news items, 171
Hind Samachar, 47
Hindi newspapers, language in, 59
Hindi Bangvasi, 50
Hindi Bihari, 41
Hindi journalism, changes in, 260;
    development of, 44; evolution
    and growth of, 33–64; evolution
    of, 35; history of, 34; in Bengal,
    34; language of, 62; Paradkar's
    contribution to, 53; phases in
    the history of, 37; shaping of,
    47; transition of, 287
Hindi journalists, self-confidence
    of, 260
Hindi language, expansion of, 20;
    localisation of, 20
Hindi Milap, 44
Hindi newspaper revolution, 17
Hindi newspapers, expanding the
    market for, 186; importance of
    crime in, 163; localisation of,
    246, 247; supplements of, 271

Hindi Pradeep, 38, 40
Hindi press, expansion and local-
    isation, consequences of, 20; ex-
    pansion of, 91; localisation of,
    91; second phase of the growth
    of, 38
Hindi publishing, development of,
    34; growth of, 91
Hindi Sahitya Sammelan, 52
Hindi Sampraday, 53
Hindi vocabulary, evolution of, 52
Hindi, shift in the use of, 60, 61;
    status of, 62
Hindustan, 14, 20, 39, 44, 47, 96,
    106, 163, 166, 248; Bhagalpur,
    136, 151; Bihar, 160, 161; news
    monitoring in, 161; Palamu,
    107; Patna, 96; Santhal Pargana,
    159; Sitamarhi, 158; total circu-
    lation of, 98
Hindustan Times, 20, 96, 101, 148
Hindustan's lifestyle supplement, 19
Hindustani, 39
Hitvadi, 50
Hitvarti, 50
hunger, reports on, 176

illiteracy, decadal decline in, 15
Imagined Communities, theory of,
    295
Impact Features, 23
incomes in rural India, 80
Independent News & Media PLC,
    267
Indian Express, financing of, 265
Indian Nation, 44
Indian National Social Action
    Forum, 72
Indian newspaper, evolution of, 18
Indian press, growth of, 263
Indian Readership Survey 2002, 86
Indian Social Action Forum, 233
India–Pakistan cricket match, re-
    ports on, 181

Indore Samachar, 44
insurgency, reports on, 166
irrigation, importance of, 177

Jagran Forum, 267
Jain Prakash, 43
Jain Prakash Hindustan, 43
Jain, Ramesh Chandra, 120
Jain, Samir, 274
Jan Morcha, 282
Jansatta, 14, 277; launch of, 61
Jayaji Pratap, 41
Jayaprakash Narayan movement,
the, 60
Jayaswal, R.N., 121
Jharkhand, survey conducted in, 170
Joshi, Naveen, 135
Joshi, Prabhash, 14, 61
Journalism, and communal pol-
itics, 223–27; development of,
13; fundamental shift in, 270
journalist networks, development
of, 237
journalists, favours given to, 207
journalists' support to Aruna Roy,
236
Junior Jagran, 200

Kanshi Ram, 219
Kasauti, 101
Katri Hitashi, 43
Kaushal, Avdesh, 208
Kavi Vachan Sudha, 37
Kayastha Conference Samachar, 39
Kayastha Kaumudi, 43
Kayastha Patrika, 39
Kayastha Samachar, 39
Kesari, 39, 50
Khabar Lahariya, 31, 146, 293;
Bundelkhand, 145
Khabar Lahariya's coverage of,
plight of forests, 290; women's
plight, 290
Khadilkar, R.R., 52

Khan, Shamshed, 129
Khari Boli Hindi, emergence of, 33
Khichri Samachar, 39
Kishore, Surendra, 218
Kshatriya Patrika, 43
Kshatriya Samachar, 43
Kshitij, Sanjeev, 133
Kulsia, Jagdish Chandra, 53
Kumawat, Ramprasad, 279

literacy growth in, Bihar, 71;
Chhattisgarh, 71; Jharkhand, 71;
Kerala, 68; Madhya Pradesh,
71, 73; Rajasthan, 68, 73; Uttar
Pradesh, 68
literacy movement, 72
literacy, increase of, 68
local advertising, 192, 193
local media, advertising in, 95
local news collection, professional-
isation of, 139
local news judgement, 150
local news networks, growth of,
116
local news, sampling of, 147
local newspapers, attrition of, 282
local stand-alone newspapers, di-
minishing of, 276
local supplements, creation of, 20;
mastheads of, 21, localisation of
news content, 95, 113
localisation, advantages of, 254;
consequences of, 113, 139; contribution of, 61; detrimental
effects of, 251–53, 255; evolution of, 106, 139; impetus of
115; meaning of, 105; of coverage, consequences of, 26; of
Hindi press, consequences
of, 20

Madhya Deshiya Vanik Patrika, 43
Madhya Pradesh, revitalisation of
panchayati raj in, 18

Mahakoshal, 44
Malaviya, Madan Mohan, 41
Malayala Manorama, 16
Malayalam, newspaper penetration of, 66
Malwa Akhbar, 37
manipulative publicity, 294
market survey approach, 196
marketers' revolution, 196
marketing, 22
marketing schemes, 187
Markundi village, 290, 292, 293
Maryada, 41
Mathur, Rajendra, 44
Mayawati, 17, 218, 220; birthday celebrations of, 221
media access, democratisation of, 118, 139
media expansion, competition from, 269; stages of, 23
media intensity in UP and India, 83
media relations with caste politics, 218, 222
media representation of the non-governmental sector, 236
media, caste composition of, 220; employments by, 241; seizing commercial opportunities by, 241; failure to play a pivotal role, 242
Media's role, during communal unrest, 223; in a democracy, 238
Mhuri Mayanka, 43
Misra, Pratapnarain, 40
multi-edition newspapers, consequences of, 25

Nagarjun, Sukant, 218
Nai Duniya, 43–46, 94, 276, 277
Narain, Lala Jagat, 47
Narendra Mohan, 226
nation, definition of, 295
National Council of Applied Economic Research data, 80

National Sample Survey Organisation data, 81
national–local strategies, development of, 296
Nav Karmayug Prakashan, 282
Nava Bharat, 43, 44, 73, 94, 119, 239, 248, 249
Navbharat Times, 44, 45
Navjeevan, 45, 56
Navjyoti, 46
new reporting beats, development of, 270
news judgement, comparison on, 154
news mapping, detrimental effects of, 251–53
news universes, integration of, 246
news, commodification of, 30
news-gathering, democratisation of, 114
newspaper audience, evolution of, 19
newspaper circulation and literacy, relationship between, 73
newspaper editions, administrative implications of, 249
newspaper expansion, 113
Newspaper industry, financing of, 264
newspaper localisation, 113; political fallout of, 25
newspaper management, changes in, 199
newspaper penetration, 67; in the Hindi belt, 15; into villages, 76
newspaper readership, growth in, 91
newspaper revolution in North India, 65
newspaper, financing of, 185
newspaper-related gift schemes, 185, 186, 188
newspapers, in the new states, 238; benefits from government to, 207; changes in, 234; changes

made by, 24; establishing editions by, 248; industrial interests of, 204; readership of, 16; role of, 240
news-you-can-use, 87
NGOs (non-governmental organisations), growth of, 235; grants received by, 236
Nirantar, 279

Ojha, Rajiv, 123
Oodunta Martand, 35–37
O'Reilly, Sir Anthony, 267–68
Outlook, 22
outside world, reports on, 181

Page 3 journalism, 197
Panchal Pandita, 46
panchayat elections, 156, 195
panchayati raj, revitalisation of, 75
Panchayika, 85
Pande, Mrinal, 88, 261
Pandey, Ram Murthy, 122
Paradkar, Baburao Vishnu, 42, 49–52; contribution to Hindi journalism, 53
Pataliputra Times, 218
Patel, Dipak, 132
Pioneer, 222
political advertisements, 195
political awareness, creation of, 24; growth of, 75
political consciousness, increase of, 30
political divergence of states, 296
political power, shift in the social basis of, 216
political public sphere, participation in, 29
political space, fragmentation of, 253
politicisation of people, 218
politics, news value of, 156
Prabhat Khabar, 104, 166, 277,

284, 285; news monitoring in, 161; Palamu, 107; Palamu report in, 143; *Ranchi*, 101; Siliguri, 107; *Prabhat Khabar's* report on naxal actions, 167
Pradeep, 44, 45
Pradhan, Sharad, 221
Prakash, 42
Prasad, Baldev, 43
Prasad, Chandra Mohan, 130
Pratah Kal, 278
Pratap, 41, 53
press and government, confrontation between, 211
press propaganda, age of, 38
press, transition of, 28
price incentives, 189
print media advertising, growth of, 263
Projamitra, 36
public sphere, 26, 27, 293; evolution of, 29; expansion of, 31; refeudalisation of, 291; reinvention of, 295; resistance to British rule, 30; publications in stock market, listing of, 266
Punjab Kesari, 44, 46, 47; Dharamsala, 108

Quality of news, 121

Rai, Alok, 60
Rai, Amrit, 34
Raj Express, 22
Rajasthan Patrika, 20, 46, 93, 102, 120, 137, 226; edition segmentation of, 251; Jaipur, 96; Kolkata, 107; Siliguri, 107
Rajasthan, increased literacy in, 14
Ram, Kanshi, 219
Ramjanmabhoomi campaign, 224
Ranchi Express, Palamu, 107; report on terrorism, 144
Rashtradoot, 45, 46, 282
Rashtriya Navin Mail, 107

Rauniar Hitaishi, 43
Rauniyar Vaishya, 43
readership of newspapers in,
68; Bihar, 67; Chhattisgarh,
67; Himachal Pradesh, 67;
Jharkhand, 67; Madhya Pradesh,
67; Rajasthan, 67; Uttar Pradesh,
67; Uttaranchal, 67
readership surveys, 66
regional newspapers, 263; political
affiliations of, 210
relations with the government, 206
religious news, 152
right to information movement,
234, 237
Robin Jeffrey's study of India's
newspaper revolution, 65
Roy, Aruna, 230, 234
Rozgar aur Nirman, 85
rural indebtedness, reports on, 177
rural India, incomes in, 80
rural market, 81; presence of, 83
rural readership, increase in, 66

saffronising of news rooms, 226
Sail, Rajendra, 72, 233
Samachar Darpan, 36
Samachar Sudhavarshan, 37
Samyadand Martand, 37
Sapre, Pandit Madhavrao, 38
Saraswati, 40, 41
School Bhaskar, 200
Searchlight, 43
Second Press Commission, report
of, 65
self-censorship of Uttar Pradesh
press, 213
Sharma, Babulal, 61
Sharma, Hazarilal, 45
Shourie, Deepak, 22
Shri Venkateshwar Samachar, 41
Shrivastava, Mahesh, 22
Shukla, Chandra Shekhar, 127
Shukla, Jugal Kishore, 35, 37

Shukla, Vinod, 57, 104
Singh, Anil Kumar, 132
Singh, N.K., 150
Singh, Shiv Kedar, 126
Singh, Siddhanath, 125, 126
Singh, Surendra Pratap, 61
social development issues, 172
spiritual matters, regular column
on, 153
sponsored coverages, 197, 199
Sri India, 283
Srivastav, Santosh, 128
stringers in Mirzapur, 125
stringers, importance of, 117; net-
works of, 42, 117
Surjan, Lalit, 74
survey conducted in Jharkhand,
170
Swarup, Anil, 149
Swatantra, 54
Swatantra Bharat, 45, 56

telecommunication links, 78
telecommunications, expansion of,
15
television audience, evolution of,
19
television, crime reporting in, 164;
penetration of, 15, 88
Teli Samachar, 43
The Dainik Nav Jyoti, 281
The Hindu, 39
The Indian Nation, 217
The Indian Sun, 36
The Times of India, 16, 20, 45, 95,
197, 274
Tiwari, Amrendra Kumar, 136
Tiwari, Gyaneshwar, 126
Tripathi, Shashank Shekhar, 134

Ujala Jhadi, 146
UK, Forster's Education Act of
1870, 28; state-promoted literacy in, 28

Upadhyay, Ajay, 219
Uttar Pradesh, political transition of, 18
Uttaranchal, communication revolution in, 257; media in, 240; role of the media in, 241

Vidyarthi, Ganesh Shankar, 53, 54
Vikas, 232

village-level elections, 23
Vir Pratap, 44

weekly supplements, 198
women, reports on, 179

Yadav, Lalu Prasad, 17, 218
youth segment, coverage of, 200
Yadav, Yogendra, 211, 216, 295–96

About the Author

Sevanti Ninan is a media analyst and newspaper columnist based in New Delhi. The founding editor of *TheHoot.org*, she writes for *The Hindu* and *Hindustan*. She has been with the *Indian Express* (1982–90) and the *Hindustan Times* (1974–78). A media critic and researcher, she has authored *Through the Magic Window: Television and Change in India* (1995) and has contributed a chapter titled 'History of Indian Broadcasting Reform' to *Broadcasting Reform in India: Media Law from a Global Perspective* (1998) edited by Monroe E. Price and Stefaan G. Verhulst.